CONCEPTIONS OF THE HUMAN MIND

Essays in Honor of George A. Miller

CONCEPTIONS OF THE HUMAN MIND

Essays in Honor of George A. Miller

Edited by

Gilbert Harman
Princeton University

LEA
1993

LAWRENCE ERLBAUM ASSOCIATES, PUBLISHERS
Hillsdale, New Jersey   Hove and London

Lawrence Erlbaum Associates, Inc., Publishers
365 Broadway
Hillsdale, New Jersey 07642

Library of Congress Cataloging-in-Publication Data

Conceptions of the human mind : essays in honor of George A. Miller /
 edited by Gilbert Harman.
   p. cm.
 Includes bibliographical references and index.
 ISBN 0-8058-1234-2 (alk. paper)
 1. Philosophy of mind. I. Miller, George A. (George Armitage),
 1920–   . II. Harman, Gilbert.
 BD418.3.C63 1993
 128′.2 – dc20   93-2407
                                                                CIP

Books published by Lawrence Erlbaum Associates are printed on acid-free paper,
and their bindings are chosen for strength and durability.

Printed in the United States of America
10 9 8 7 6 5 4 3 2 1

Contents

Preface

Conceptions of the Human Mind: A Conference to Honor George A. Miller was held at Princeton University, October 2–4, 1991. This conference brought together a distinguished panel of speakers from various disciplines, including psychology, philosophy, neuroscience, and artificial intelligence, to respond to George's query:

> What has happened to cognition? In other words, what have the past 30 years contributed to our understanding of the mind? Do we really know anything that wasn't already clear to William James?
>
> The question is thrown out as a challenge, and I would be disappointed if the answer were obvious to anyone—it surely isn't to me. Each person will, I hope, contribute his or her own perspective, and maybe we can combine our individual views of this elephant into something more than any one of us could manage alone.

The 16 speakers represented a variety of approaches. Each tried to stand back a little from his or her most recent work and to address the general question from his or her particular standpoint. The chapters in this volume derive from that occasion. (The conference organizer, Philip Johnson-Laird, did not give a talk on that occasion, but has been prevailed upon to contribute a chapter.) Two speakers, Willem Levelt and Ned Block, are not represented in this volume because their talks were already committed for publication elsewhere. Thomas Bever's talk could not be included, but his toast to George is included.

Michael Gazzaniga begins the discussion with a persuasive demonstration that the differences between humans and other animals is not just that humans have proportionally larger brains. Human brains also function differently. Gazzaniga discusses particular specialized neuronal circuits and ends up with the suggestion that consciousness is a special feeling about the specialized capacities one has.

William Hirst then describes features of amnesia that require the postulation of deep processes of memory, processes that are surprising from the perspective of normal experience and that go beyond such relatively surface distinctions as that between long- and short-term memory or that between explicit and implicit memory.

Jill Fain Lehman, Allen Newell, Thad Polk, and Richard L. Lewis discuss ways in which language influences thought. Using the SOAR model, they distinguish language as a mere transducer between outer language and inner thought from a system of inner moves using linguistic principles. They see the need for the latter sort of moves in the way humans do syllogistic reasoning, even if such reasoning makes use of nonlinguistic mental models.

Steven Pinker presents evidence that distinguishes aspects of the linguistic system that depend on associationist or connectionist principles and aspects that are rule governed. He sees the need for both connectionist associations and strict rules.

Edward Jones discusses ways in which social psychology is cognitive, by concentrating on how a situation is experienced or perceived, even when the perception is in some sense below the level of consciousness, and even though social psychology tends not to invoke models that appeal to the deeper sorts of processing characteristic of cognitive science.

Richard Nisbett describes evidence that people can be taught to make general use of very general abstract principles of statistical and economic reasoning, for example, the principle of sunk costs that allows someone to leave a boring play in the middle even though the tickets were very expensive.

Gilbert Harman discusses aspects of the mind that resist objective description. Some things about others can be understood only by translating them into experiences of one's own.

Jerome Bruner sees more than one way in which the mind works and contrasts Newton's mind with Jonathan Edwards', Newton's explanation of color with Edwards' interpretation of Newton's explanation.

Susan Carey discusses experiments establishing that even very young children have a notion of physical object that is distinct from the notion of a physical substance, like sand. Infants distinguish between one, two, or three objects at a very young age, even before the age at which they expect a chair to remain a chair and not become a toy elephant.

Wendell R. Garner describes the mind as function aimed at knowledge, as a creative flexible critical realist, and as arising from evolution. Garner's almost Hegelian mediations contrast with Philip Johnson-Laird's account of thinking as a form of computation. Johnson-Laird explains what computation means in this connection and presents computational accounts of reasoning and of creative thinking.

Roger Shepard reports on investigations into color perception with particular attention to the experienced quality of color. He shows that various aspects of color quality have a physical explanation, but also concludes that there is still an elusive aspect of color experience that escapes such an account.

Finally, Michael Cole describes ways in which a conception of the future arising from memory of the past can influence the present from the perspective of a cultural psychology. Children are treated differently depending on their perceived sex, and children in the United States are perceived and treated quite differently in the United States and in Japan.

— Gilbert Harman

Toast for G. A. Miller

Thomas Bever

If you are smart, ambitious, and live in the south during the first part of the 20th century, you have two strong interests: gold, and the creative writing of novels. It may be unfortunate for the literary world that George did not become a novelist, that is, a published novelist. It is certainly fortunate for us that he chose to use science to subjugate language. He mastered phonemes, syntactic rules, semantic features, and now words . . . one by one.

The word for today is "emeritus": we are celebrating George's elevation to that august state. Unlike George, I don't create dictionaries, so I had to look up emeritus, to see exactly what it is that we are celebrating. The English definition is somewhat inappropriate to describe George's elevation, because it has the "R" word in it, "Retirement"; that is incorrect, so I refer to the meaning of the Latin root of emeritus, emerire: "to earn through service." If that is true of anyone, it is true of George.

When the organizer(s) of this event asked me to toast George, I felt it might be better if one of his contemporaries did that. After all, while I now count myself a friend, I started very much as his student, aged 19 years, when he was very much my teacher. I thought that one of his older friends who did not have that history could give us a collateral perspective, rather than one from the bottom looking up. But then I realized that we are all looking up to George, he is the teacher of us all, regardless of our era.

So, I am no less qualified than the rest of us to speak about George. I have two sets of observations; one about him as a public figure, a scientist and writer; the other, more personal, what we, his students, learned from him.

Three kinds of contributions are salient in George as a scientist. First, as has been frequently implied at the conference, no single person in the 20th century has done as much to legitimize and expand the scientific and experimental study of the mind. He started doing it in the midst of the behaviorist hegemony, which relegated the study of mind to the philosophers. He reaches out to other areas of science, learns them well, and then brings them back to psychology, applying them to the investigation of mental life. In doing that, he shows psychologists that cognition is a real science; he shows us by example how to make more cognitive science from what he has started.

The second contribution resides in the many specific facts about the mind that George has discovered. I won't list them, but only point out, following Pim Levelt's conception, that they are so deeply embedded as established important facts about the mind, that the next generation will probably not even know who discovered and proved them.

George's third contribution as a public man is to urge us and to show us "how to give philosophy away": how to make it useful for society; how to take the best in our science and make it work for the common good.

Now I turn to what I learned from George my teacher, particularly three things I learned about how to be a professor and scientist. First, is to treat students with open curiosity and intellectual honesty. Phillip Johnson-Laird introduced my talk with George's recollection of me at age 19. According to George, I spent much of my time in his office, arguing. That is correct, but what I also remember is that George was a rare professor because he argued back. Other Harvard professors either staved me off via obdurate secretaries, or listened to me sullenly and waited for me to leave. But George listened, engaged me, and led me to think much more deeply about scientific problems than I had wanted to: I just wanted to argue. Now, I am a professor, and I have my own students to listen to. Now I realize how much tolerance and wisdom it took for George to put up with my naive thoughts, expressed with total self-assurance: Even I am embarrassed when I recall these discussions.

The second quality I emulate in George is generosity with ideas. He always urges others to take his ideas and make themselves famous with them if they can. I have realized how wise this policy is. If you get someone else to work out an idea then you don't have to do the work yourself. Even more important, you don't have to think about the idea anymore, so you are free to move on to something else. I think this is part of the key to George's prodigous ability to learn new fields, which he can then bring back to cognitive psychology.

The third professorial attribute George teaches does not need much elaboration: loyalty—to the field, to institutions, to colleagues, to students.

These are my thoughts about George as we celebrate his emeritification; truly an honor he earns through service — service to the field, to society, and to many, many individuals.

I close with an elaboration of an analogy Dick Nisbett used to illustrate the "Bad Old Days" of associationist behaviorism. Dick described the situation as one in which, on a beach the big S–R bully kicked sand in the face of the 90-pound weenie who wanted to study "the mind." I recall that image as part of a short ad that appeared in comic strips of my youth. The next panel showed the bully walking off with an alluring girl in a bathing suit. The next panel was given to a muscular body builder, Charles Atlas, who proposed to sell you exercise equipment you could use to get in shape; the final panel showed the former weenie, now muscular, walking off with the girl, to the chagrin of the bully. The relevant moral in this is that Charles Atlas did not come to the aid of the weenie; rather, he provided what was needed so the weenie could take care of himself. That is what George does for us: He gives us the tools we need to strengthen and deepen our science.

I now propose we toast George Armitage Miller, the Charles Atlas of the Cognitive Sciences.

1

The Implication of Specialized Neuronal Circuits Versus Neuronal Number for Concepts Concerning the Nature of Human Conscious Experience

Michael S. Gazzaniga
University of California, Davis

Sitting on top of the evolutionary process is the human brain. Its vast complexity, its capacity for complex problem solving, for inventiveness, for everything we know and appreciate about human cognition represents the finest achievement of the wondrous blind processes of selection that have gone on for millions of years. Many scientists have approached trying to gain clues to the understanding of the human brain's special mechanisms of action by studying other species. Fair game for this enterprise includes comparisons between bugs and beasts of all types and kinds. Everything from our genetic mechanisms to the capacity to sleep, to feel, to remember, to transmit retinal information to visual cortex and a myriad of other processes have all been enlightened by careful animal experimentation over the years. Some have even seen in these studies so many similarities in neural structures that proposals are commonly put forward that animals have perceptual and cognitive process much like our own—indeed, a consciousness much like our own. Such views are usually qualified by the assertion that whatever differences do exist in conscious processes between species can be easily explained by the greater size of the human brain. Somehow having more neural cells is thought to produce a greater computational capacity that in turn yields that special quality of human conscious experience.

In fact, it is well known that the human brain is inordinately large after

1

being corrected for body weight. Allometric considerations find the human brain falling off the correlation line assessing body size and brain size. This gigantic biologic organ weighing between 1,100 and 1,300 grams sits magnificently on top of a small body, guiding its sensations, actions, and desire for reproduction. These elements of human activity are indeed quite similar to those seen in both near and distant evolutionary relatives sharing many common brain mechanisms. Even basic dimensions of mental life, such as memory, attention, and visual perception, seem to share mechanisms and brain structures in common, certainly with other primates. As a consequence, the extra cortex in humans is viewed as critical for the higher cognitive functions we enjoy.

Yet, there is this puzzle. We humans do not seem to need great quantities of our huge cerebral cortex in order to carry out our intellectual activities. A cardinal feature of split-brain research, for example, is that following disconnection of the human cerebral hemispheres, the verbal IQ of the left hemisphere remains largely intact (Nass & Gazzaniga, 1987). Indeed, the problem-solving capacity of the left hemisphere remains unchanged (Le-Doux, Risse, Springer, Wilson, & Gazzaniga, 1977). Although there can be deficits in recall capacity (Phelps, Hirst, & Gazzaniga, 1992), by some performance measures the overall capacity to carry out problem solving seems unaffected. In other words, isolating essentially half of the cortex from the dominant left hemisphere causes no major change in intellectual function of the left hemisphere. This finding represents strong evidence that absolute cortical cell numbers have, at best, only a loose relation with human intelligence.

Related to the notion of special circuitry is the fact that disconnected right hemispheres are seriously impoverished in their ability to carry out a variety of computational tasks that the left would find easy to complete. In studies done some years ago in a small group of split-brain patients identified as having language capacities in each disconnected hemisphere, we carefully examined the problem-solving ability of the disconnected right and left hemispheres. Most commissurotomy patients do not have such abilities in their right hemisphere; correlated with that absence is an inability to carry out even the simplest perceptual and cognitive tasks. The small group we examined with language-capable right hemispheres were unable to make verbal inferences, solve spatial problems (Gazzaniga & Smylie, 1984), or generate indirect antonyms (Gazzaniga & Miller, 1989), to name a few of the tasks examined.

Although the right hemisphere remains superior for some activities such as the recognition of upright faces (Gazzaniga, 1989), some attentional skills (Mangun et al., 1992), and perhaps also emotional processes (Nass & Gazzaniga, 1987), it appears to be lacking in its overall cognitive capacity. In fact, it appears to be inferior to the mental capacities of a chimp.

The idea of the importance of specialized circuits is central to the field of human neuropsychology. Untold numbers of disease states have been reported that suggest there are specific disorders following focal lesions or long fiber-tract disconnections (Nass & Gazzaniga, 1987). Human brains seem to house a constellation of special-purpose networks that are given over to rather specific tasks. When that fact is considered in light of evolutionary processes, it is hard to imagine it could be any other way. Why would evolution leave to chance the building up of networks needed for each human to survive from scratch with each birth? Surely it is advantageous to be delivered into this world with as much original equipment as possible. Millions of years of evolution would allow for exactly this kind of thing; it seems more and more apparent that this is what has occurred (Gazzaniga, 1992).

This evolutionary perspective on brain organization and cognition suggests a number of important issues for cognitive neuroscientists (Gazzaniga, 1992). First, the implication is hard on everyday and classical ideas about learning, with the underlying assumption that any neural network can learn anything once inputs and outputs are specified. The evolutionary viewpoint would argue for not only the critical implications of the importance of specialized circuits but also the view that the human brain has a unique structural organization supporting these specialized circuits. I review data from my laboratory that is consistent with this view.

Second, the evolutionary view suggests that there should be some things humans are poor at learning. If humans have specialized circuits committed to performing particular traits, exposure to environmental stimuli to which they had not adapted might require cognitive processes they do not possess. There are many examples of such phenomena in the fields of language learning and perceptual psychology (Gazzaniga, 1992). For present purposes, these kind of data provide further evidence of the probability of identifiable capacities the human cognitive system possesses that other animals do not possess. Furthermore, because these data reflect the presence of specialized circuits, they should be found in one hemisphere or the other. There are many such examples; I relate observations from studies on the human capacity to make voluntary facial expressions (Gazzaniga & Smylie, 1990).

SPECIALIZED CIRCUITS FOR HUMAN CAPACITIES

Accepting the view that the human brain has special circuits for carrying out its various mental functions, one can consider the various levels of organization within the nervous system where this might appear. In what follows, the argument is made that the cerebral cortex is the custodian of new circuits critical for human cognitive processes. In this light, it is commonly observed that the overall plan of the mammalian brain seems quite similar among species. This is particularly true when comparing the primate and human brain. One of the reasons comparative studies are carried out is the belief that homologous brain structures may carry out common functions in the primate and human. Yet, there are important exceptions to this overall view. The human brain, quite simply, is different from the monkey brain. There are any number of similar structures carrying out different functions in the two species. Let me review work comparing two structures that we have studied directly and indirectly in our labora- tory—the anterior commissure and the superior colliculus—and relate observations that emphasize the importance of studying the human brain per se.

The animal literature clearly shows that the anterior commissure transfers visual information. Although only the callosum was found to subserve interocular transfer in cats, the anterior commissure was found to be involved in visual transfer in chimpanzees (Black & Myers, 1964) and rhesus monkeys (Gazzaniga, 1966; Sullivan & Hamilton, 1973). Taken together, this kind of evidence provides strong reasons to believe the same might be true for humans.

Prior to the development of magnetic resonance (MR) imaging, we examined some patients who, by surgical description, had their anterior commissure intact and their callosum fully sectioned. Many of these patients transferred visual information. In an effort to account for this, we proposed that the remaining anterior commissure could vary in the kinds of information it could and could not transfer. We have now had the opportunity to scan many of those supposedly split-brain patients. In fact, the MR scans show the splenium had been spared in those cases where transfer of visual information was possible, thus explaining the transfer of information. In another series of patients, similar results were noted (Gates, Leppik, Yap, & Gumnit, 1984). Every time there is evidence of transfer of visual information that requires exact matching of stimulus features following supposedly full commissurotomy, there has been sparing of the splenium. This suggests that the anterior commissure, a structure that is clearly able to transfer visual information in the monkey and chimp, does not do so in the human.

The difference seen with fiber-tract systems is also apparent in more nuclear structures such as the superior colliculus. In this case, there is clear evidence from the monkey that this structure is crucially involved in the control of eye movements. Wurtz and colleagues (Mohler & Wurtz, 1977), for example, were able to demonstrate some years ago that primates with lesions of primary visual cortex were able to detect and direct their eyes in response to visual stimuli presented in the scotoma. They suggested that the superior colliculus, working either alone or in complementary fashion with visual cortex, could carry out these functions within the scotoma. Others have claimed that even higher order functions are possible following such occipital lesions (Pasik & Pasik, 1971; Weiskrantz, Cowey, & Passingham, 1977). Although similar claims have been made for the human (Weiskrantz, 1990), we have not succeeded in demonstrating residual function following lesions to primary visual cortex (Holtzman, 1984). More recently, we have been able to carry out microperimetry of patients with occipital lesions using an image stabilizer (Fendrich, Wessinger, & Gazzaniga, 1992; Wessinger, Fendrich, & Gazzaniga, 1991).

These studies have clearly shown that patients with so-called homonomous hemianopsia can have small islands of spared vision. In these islands, there is visual function. In most of the scotoma, however, there is no visual function, confirming the earlier work of Holtzman. In short, when visual function is possible there seems to be spared visual cortex. This observation was confirmed with MR brainprinting that revealed some intact primary visual cortex. Overall, it suggests that the spared superior colliculus in the human contributes in a different way to oculomotor functions.

The clear difference in function seen between monkey and human brains, combined with possible new anatomical correlates supporting these differences, suggests a cautious note when attempting to compare the function of similar brain structures across species. It suggests the arguments against such cross-species comparisons are as crucial today as they were when originally argued years ago.

With it established that the human brain has its own unique organization, it would be interesting to see how much of this organization might be due to genetic processes. For the past few years, we have been examining this issue by studying the brains of monozygotic twins. Our initial findings regarding the corpus callosum showed that this enormous fiber-tract system was more similar in area and shape in monozygotic twins than in unrelated twins (Oppenheim, Skerry, Tramo, & Gazzaniga, 1989). Using a new method of assessing the cortical surface areas of the human brain (Jouandet et al., 1989; Loftus, 1992), we have now studied the cortical surface of both male and female monozygotic twins (Green et al., 1991; Tramo, Loftus, Newton, & Gazzaniga, 1990; Tramo, Loftus, Thomas, Green, & Gazzaniga, in prep.). Such twins look alike, talk alike, behave similarly, think similarly, and so on. Are their brains alike? Normally there is great variation in the gross morphology of the brain. Although all brains have a similar overall plan, they vary tremendously in the details. Some brains have bigger frontal lobes than others. The pattern in the visual appearance of the cortex is called the gyral/sucal pattern. It varies, and that variation presumably reflects differences in underlying brain organization. Could it be that monozygotic twins had brains that were more similar than not? The fact that their overall cognitive skills are more alike would suggest a physical basis for their more similar cognition.

Until recently, no one has had information on this crucial point. Our laboratory has been working on quantifying MR images in a way that would allow one to examine various regions in each half brain and to assess their similarity in surface area. In this technique, MR imaging is used to form some 50 image slices of the brain, which are then reconstructed to make maps of the human cerebrum. With the maps made, it is easy to measure the cortical areas of the various major lobes of the brain, allowing us to estimate surface area from the three-dimensional reconstruction of the cortical surface itself. We have discovered that 15 regions in the left and 4 regions in the right hemispheres of females showed less variance in the twins as compared to unrelated controls. For male twins, there were fewer areas in the left and about the same number in the right hemisphere. Overall, we can conclude that twin brains are more alike than unrelated brains. These data also indicate that the development of left-hemisphere structures is under considerably more genetic control for women than for men.

THE CASE FOR UNIQUE
HUMAN SYSTEM FUNCTIONING

If the human brain has unique organizational features and appears to have many of its major cortical surface areas specified by genetic mechanisms, then it might also seem likely that there would be capacities humans could engage in that other primates could not. The multitudinous new circuits in the much larger human cerebrum carry out activities other species simply do not possess. One such example of a human specialization is the capacity to make voluntary facial expressions. This is a very palpable trait of humans and easily accessible for study. It is not found in other primates including the chimpanzee (Premack, personal communication).

There is a variety of beliefs about how the brain is organized to perceive and produce facial expressions. In the perceptual domain, it appears that the right hemisphere has special processes devoted to the efficient detection of upright faces (Gazzaniga, 1989). Although the left hemisphere can also perceive and recognize faces and can reveal superior capacities when the faces are familiar, the right hemisphere appears specialized for unfamiliar facial stimuli (Gazzaniga & Smylie, 1983). Interestingly, this pattern of asymmetry for perceptual processes has also been shown for the rhesus monkey (Hamilton & Vermiere, 1988).

We recently examined the brain mechanisms involved in carrying out facial expressions in split-brain human patients. Disconnecting the two cerebral hemispheres allows the role the corpus callosum plays in controlling voluntary and involuntary expression to be assessed. It also allows examination of the ability of each hemisphere to initiate facial expressions. To understand the pattern of observed results, it is important to review the known neural mechanism active in controlling both voluntary and involuntary facial expressions.

The pattern of innervation for the upper half of the face is different from that of the lower half of the face, and the differences involve both central and peripheral systems. The neural mechanisms involved in voluntary facial postures are controlled by the cortical pyramidal system, whereas the control of spontaneous postures is managed by the extrapyramidal system. This diversity of innervation is reported to be responsible for the preservation of symmetrical spontaneous facial postures in the presence of unilateral damage to motor cortex. Patients with this lesion will evidence a contralateral facial droop that will resolve when smiling spontaneously. In this instance, although the pyramidal input to the facial nucleus is destroyed, the extrapyramidal input is not. It is also commonly reported that patients with extrapyramidal disease such as Parkinson's disease will display a masked face when at rest and then look more normal when smiling to command.

In our study, we examined the capacity of each cerebral hemisphere to initiate voluntary facial postures. Additional observations were made on spontaneous expressions. The results reveal marked differences in the capacities of each hemisphere to carry out commands, indicating that the corpus callosum plays a critical role in the normal production of voluntary symmetrical facial expressions. Examination of asymmetries in smiling to command revealed that when the command to smile was lateralized to the left hemisphere, the right side of the mouth dramatically commenced retraction as much as 180 milliseconds before the left side responded. When the command to "smile" was presented to the right hemisphere, none of the patients were able to carry out the response. In another series of tests on Cases JW and DR a lateralized drawing of a "happy face" or a "sad face" found the right hemisphere performing at chance. On trials in which an incorrect response had been made, say frowning to a happy face, JW was nonetheless able to draw out a picture of the happy face stimulus with his left hand. Additionally, no consistent asymmetries were noted on trials in which the left hemisphere responded correctly to the command to "frown." Although there were occasional indications that the lower right half face showed some earlier posturing, the overall bilateral response of the upper half face masked any consistent pattern.

In previous studies we have demonstrated that the right hemisphere is capable of producing involuntary or spontaneous responses such as smiling and laughing (Gazzaniga, 1970). In the present study spontaneous episodes were video recorded and analyzed with the optical disc method. No asymmetries in the facial response pattern were observed. It therefore appears that either hemisphere can generate spontaneous emotional events and that, because there are no apparent asymmetries in the facial response, different neural mechanisms are active for these expressions.

Most disconnected right hemispheres in split-brain patients are unable to carry out verbal commands (Gazzaniga, 1970). In the present study the right hemisphere failed not only when the command was printed out but also when the command was a graphic that depicted either a "happy" or "sad" face. Yet, many right hemispheres, including all three of the present cases, have the capacity to carry out some kinds of commands. It can respond to requests to move individual digits as well as make hand postures of all sorts (Gazzaniga, Boger, & Sperry, 1967; Volpe et al., 1982). It can control the upper facial muscles. Why, then, can it not respond to the command to smile or frown?

As already reviewed, mental operations ranging from making simple inferences to solving simple problems are all outside the cognitive range of the right hemisphere. These kinds of observations emphasize the superiority of the left hemisphere in interpreting events and its dominant role in organizing responses to those events. In the present context, high-level evaluative processes must be invoked to override a potentially spontaneous facial expression such as smiling. Such processes appear to be possible only in the left hemisphere; hence, that hemisphere appear to control voluntary expression. This sort of "voluntary" control appears different and involves more complex processes than those associated with making voluntary hand or foot postures in response to a cue. Therefore, where evaluations involve more psychological aspects of a person's expressions, the left hemisphere appears dominant. Specialized circuits carry out specialized functions.

SPECIALIZED CIRCUITS
AND HUMAN CONSCIOUS EXPERIENCE

The human brain enables human conscious experience, and a working brain scientist always strives for insights into the nature of human conscious experience. Some might view the human with all of its domain-specific capacities, which have accumulated over millions of years of evolution, as a denigrated view of who we are and what we accomplish. The human brain's unique organization—its unique capacities for problem solving, for language, for making voluntary facial expressions, for deception, and for belief formation—empower a viewpoint of specific systems in the brain for enablement of these capacities. They can be lost through specific brain damage or can be isolated by disconnection procedures. The capacities must reflect the actions of specific circuitry within the human brain.

Still, many other scientists believe the sensations we experience as human conscious agents are the product of the vast computational power our huge cerebral cortex must allow — with each person starting from scratch and building up his or her own story over a lifetime. This mix of ideas generates a difficult-to-state and fairly vague view that human conscious experience is a "thing" that emerges from the human being's information-processing capacity. This view finds solace in the idea that neural networks can be trained to do almost anything and that, given the right circumstance, good cognition will follow.

My own view is that there is another way of looking at these issues. An idea that builds on the realization that human consciousness, at its core, is a feeling — a feeling about special capacities humans possess.

The modern human brain is a bundle of special-purpose systems allowing people to communicate, evaluate facial expressions, make inferences, interpret feelings, moods, and behaviors, and all the rest. Studying patients with brain damage reveals how specific these capacities can be. One capacity can go without the other. Each of these activities is managed by neurons in ways that find scientists fundamentally ignorant. Millions of neurons are churning away to produce these human talents. Yet, to define that as consciousness is somehow missing the point. Consciousness is a feeling about these specific capacities that are managed by specialized circuits. My guess is that we are looking in the wrong wood pile for the answer to the problem of human consciousness.

There are some obvious aspects of human consciousness that we always lose sight of. First, one does not learn to be conscious! When the brain starts to function, up it comes, just like steam out of a turbine. There is no getting rid of it. The feeling of consciousness is not unlike other seemingly unfathomable feelings like the feeling to survive. It is there. Oddly, philosophers and biologists have not tortured themselves about understanding such feelings. Yet, it is surely no simpler to understand and know the mechanisms about those feelings than to understand human consciousness itself.

Second, the feeling of being conscious never changes in life. Let me illustrate this with an anecdote. A few years ago, my 76-year-old father, a physician of enormous intelligence and savvy, sat in his easy chair contemplating something or another doing so after years of strokes that were slowly consuming his cerebral cortex. Mercifully, the strokes did not impair his language and thought processes. He knew of my profession and the kinds of issues that interested me. I asked him how he felt, to which he replied, quite simply, "Mike, I feel 12. I always have and I always will." For him, his consciousness was the same. The computational skills were vanishing just like they are for all aging brains, but the feeling of being conscious never seems to go.

To put some neural hardware on this idea, modern brain science knows that subcortical structures are heavily involved in the management of feeling—of felt states. These systems change very little with aging. They stay more insulate from the ravages of the cell death accompanying aging, and it is these same brain areas that generate the feelings associated with the specialized perceptual and cognitive capacities humans have accumulated over millions of years. Consciousness is a feeling—a feeling about domain-specific capacities that have accumulated over millions of years of evolution.

ACKNOWLEDGMENTS

Preparation of this chapter was aided by the Office of Naval Research N00014-89-J-3035, the Airforce Office of Scientific Research AFOSR-89-0437, NIH Grants NINDS 5 R01 NS22626-06 and NINDS 5 PO1 NS17778-09, and the James S. McDonnell Foundation.

REFERENCES

Black, P., & Myers, R. E. (1964). Visual functions of the forebrain commissures in the chimpanzee. *Science, 146,* 799–800.

Fendrich, R., Wessinger, C. M., & Gazzaniga, M. S. (1992). Residue vision in a scotoma: Implication for blindsight. *Science, 258,* 1489–1491.

Gates, J. R., Leppir, I. E., Yap, J. C., & Gumnit, R. J. (1984). Corpus callosotomy: Clinical and electroencephalographic effects. *Epilepsia, 25*(3), 308–316.

Gazzaniga, M. S. (1966). Interhemispheric communication of visual learning. *Neuropsychologia, 4,* 183–189.

Gazzaniga, M. S. (1989). Organization of the human brain. *Science, 245,* 947–952.

Gazzaniga, M. S. (1992). *Nature's mind.* New York: Basic Books.

Gazzaniga, M. S., Bogers, J. E., & Sperry R. W. (1967). Dyspraxia following division of the cerebral hemispheres. *Archives of Neurology, 16,* 606–612.

Gazzaniga, M. S., & Miller, G. A. (1989). The recognition of antonym by a language-enriched right hemisphere. *Journal of Cognitive Neuroscience, 1*(2), 187–193.

Gazzaniga, M. S., & Smylie, C. S. (1983). Facial recognition and brain asymmetries: Clues to underlying mechanisms. *Annals of Neurology, 13,* 536–540.

Gazzaniga, M. S., & Smylie, C. S. (1984). Dissociation of language and cognition: A psychological profile of two disconnected right hemispheres. *Brain, 107,* 145–153.

Gazzaniga, M. S., & Smylie, C. S. (1990). Hemispheric mechanisms controlling voluntary and spontaneous facial expressions. *Journal of Cognitive Neuroscience, 2*(3), 239–245.

Green, R. L., Tramo, M. J., Loftus, W. C., Thomas, C. E., Brown, P. J., Weaver, J. B., & Gazzaniga, M. S. (1991). Regional cortical surface area measurements in monozygotic twins discordant for schizophrenia suggest a left hemisphere basis for the disease. *Society for Neuroscience Abstract, 17,* 1455.

Hamilton, C. R., & Vermiere, B. A. (1988). Complementary lateralization in monkeys. *Science, 242,* 206–220.

Holtzman, J. D. (1984). Interactions between cortical and subcortical visual areas: Evidence from human commissurotomy patients. *Vision Research, 24,* 801–813.

Jouandet, M. L. Tramo, M. J., Herron, D. M., Hermann, A., Loftus, W. C., Bazell, S., & Gazzaniga, M. S. (1989). Brainprints: Computer-generated two-dimensional maps of the human cerebral cortex *in vivo. Journal of Cognitive Neuroscience, 1,* 88–117.

LeDoux, J. E., Risse, G., Springer, S., Wilson, D. H., & Gazzaniga, M. S. (1977). Cognition and commissurotomy. *Brain, 100,* 87–104.

Loftus, W. C. (1992). *Three dimensional minimal surface area reconstructions from planar contours using dynamic programming* (Tech. Rep. No. 100.2). Hanover, NH: Dartmouth Medical School, Program in Cognitive Neuroscience.

Mangun, G. R., Gazzaniga, M. S., Plager, R., Loftus, W., Hillyard, S., Luck, S. J., & Clark, V. (1992). *Monitoring the visual world: Hemispheric asymmetries and subcortical processes in attention.* Manuscript submitted for publication.

Mohler, C. W., & Wurtz, R. H. (1977). Role of striate cortex and superior colliculus in visual guidance of saccadic eye movements in monkeys. *Journal of Neurophysiology, 40,* 74–94.

Nass, R., & Gazzaniga, M. S. (1987). Lateralization and specialization of the human central nervous system. In F. Plum. (Ed.), *Handbook of physiology* (pp. 701–761). Bethesda, MD: The American Physiological Society.

Oppenheim, J. S., Skerry, J. E., Tramo, M. J., & Gazzaniga, M. S. (1989). Magnetic resonance imaging morphology of the corpus callosum in monozygotic twins. *Annals of Neurology, 26,* 100–104.

Pasik, T., & Pasik, P. (1971). The visual world of monkeys deprived of striate cortex: Effective stimulus parameters and the importance of the accessory optic system. In T. Shipley, & J. E. Dowling, (Eds.), *Visual processes in vertebrates* (Vision Research Supplement No. 3, pp. 419–435). Oxford: Pergamon Press.

Phelps, E. A., Hirst, A., & Gazzaniga, M. S. (1992). Deficits in recall following partial and complete commissurotomy. *Cerebral Cortex, 1,* 492–498.

Sullivan, M. U., & Hamilton, C. R. (1973). Interocular transfer and reversed and non-reversed discrimination via the anterior commissure in monkeys. *Physiological Behavior, 10,* 355–359.

Thomas, C. E., Tramo, M. J., Loftus, W. C., Newton, C. H., & Gazzaniga, M. S. (1990). Gross morphometry of frontal, parietal, and temporal cortex in monozygotic twins. *Society for Neuroscience Abstract, 16,* 1151.

Tramo, M. J., Loftus, W. C., Thomas, C. E., Green, R. L., & Gazzaniga, M. S. (in prep). *Monozygotic human brains are more similar for regional cortical surface area, forebrain volume, and callosal size.*

Volpe, B. T., Sidtis, J. J., Holtzman, J. D., Wilson, D. H., & Gazzaniga, M. S. (1982). Cortical mechanisms involved in praxis: Observations following partial and complete section of the corpus callosum in man. *Neurology, 32,* 645–650.

Weiskrantz, L. (1990). The Ferrier lecture, 1989. Outlooks for blindsight: Explicit methodologies for implicit processes. *Proceedings of the Royal Society of London, Series B, 239,* 247–278.

Weiskrantz, L., Cowey, A., & Passingham, C. (1977). Spatial responses to brief stimuli by monkeys with striate cortex ablations. *Brain, 100,* 655–670.

Wessinger, C. M., Fendrich, R., & Gazzaniga, M. S. (1991). Stabilized retinal perimetry with a hemianopic patient: Implications for blindsight. *Society for Neuroscience, 17,* 846.

2 On the Nature of Systems?

William Hirst
New School for Social Research

In inspiring this volume, George Miller asked a simple, yet overwhelmimg question: "What have we pychologists learned about the mind?" It is a daunting question, not only because of what it asks, but who asked it. I feel somewhat abashed at the prospect of telling George what we have learned about the mind, because I am sure he knows more than I could possibly convey. George is a deep—the deepest—well I know of when it comes to psychological insight, but for George, I will try to tell him what lies in my shallow pond.

COMPONENTS OF THE MIND

Single Versus Multiple Systems

If we have learned anything in the last few years, it is that the mind is organized into distinct systems, modules, or component processes. I discuss the various articulations of the differentiation of the mind later. For the present, however, I merely want to emphasize that the mind does not work as a whole. The workings of the mind cannot be reduced to a few fundamental principles. Early learning theorists tried to do just this, emulating physics, but as any historian of psychology will attest, they failed. No simple list of principles could be established. There had to be different principles for different kinds of learning (Neisser, 1978).

There have always been, of course, psychologists and philosophers who divided the mind into components. For instance, in the 18th century, the

Scottish school divided the mind into distinct faculties. Reid (1969) listed a half-dozen intellectual powers such as perception, judgement, memory, conception, and moral taste. Faculty psychology continued in a way with phrenologists. In modern guise, it is pervasive in cognitive science. Fodor (1983) brilliantly articulated the modern modular approach to mind in his appropriately titled book *Modularity*.

Transparent and Deep Systems

I suggest that when discovering the components of the mind, the distinctions that people make vary along at least two dimensions. The first dimension ranges from transparent to deep. As I use the term, *transparent* distinctions possess a folk psychological flavor and reflect the quality of our phenomenological experience. Reid's list has this folk psychological, intuitive quality. When people introspect they can feel, if you like, that a certain mental act involves memory or conceptualization, or perception. You could ask someone whether a certain mental act engages memory or perception, and they could, based on the content of their consciousness, answer this question.

One corollary of the assumption of transparent modules of the mind is that the mind's organization reflects the demands the world has placed on it. McGoon, Ratcliff, and Dell (1986) must have had such a proposition in mind when objecting to the distinction between episodic and semantic memories. They argued that the distinction was probably not valid, in part because one never uses purely semantic memory or purely episodic memory in the real world. Rather, every instance of memorizing and remembering appears to involve both semantic and episodic memories. When one attempts to remember a list of words, a proponent of the episodic/semantic memory distinction probably would say that the words are stored in an episodic memory but are organized by relying on semantic memory. Moreover, the activation in semantic memory as well as a search through episodic memory appears to govern remembering. For McGoon et al. (1986), it is not transparent when one looks at any particular task whether it is purely semantically or purely episodically. One uses a little of both.

I do not mean here to defend the distinction between episodic and semantic memory, but I do want to underline my concern with arguments such as that of McGoon et al. However the structure of the mind came to be, it did not evolve from scratch as it tried to meet the world's demands. Rather, it probably built on existing components to meet the new demands of a new ecological niche. From this perspective, the mind might have a Rube Goldberg quality rather than the elegance of a freshly designed machine.

It is not surprising, then, that a task cannot be devised to tap one and only one component of the mind. When faced with a task, especially those of human devising, people will naturally use all the resources they have available to them. It is not surprising when memorizing and remembering a list of words, people appear to rely not on one, but on many different systems. Nor can this hodge-podge characteristic be used as an argument against the division of memory into subsystems. The simultaneous use of different systems is as one might expect.

As these considerations suggest, the mind need not be divided into transparent components. Rather, it may be organized along nonintuitive, nonfolk psychological lines — an organization deeply buried beneath the surface of our behavior. In arguing against folk psychology, Churchland (1986) clearly adopted this approach. She contends that the structures of the mind may only be understood by careful experimentation designed to uncover the buried structures. I have much more to say about this position as the chapter continues, so I refrain from giving any examples now.

Structural and Process Systems

Besides the transparent–deep dimension, the mind can be divided into what I call *structural systems* or *distinct processing*. This structure-process dimension, of course, has figured in many diverse psychological musings. An analogy to a computer will help clarify the meaning of structural system. Computers usually have multiple memory systems — ROM, RAM, floppy disks, hard disks. Each of these memories are distinct structural systems. They have specifiable hardware, function independently of each other, and manifest different properties, for example, storage on hard disks is fast; on floppy disks it is slow. Sherry and Schacter (1987) adopted this definition of system when they defined a memory system as "an interaction among acquisition, retention, and retrieval mechanisms . . . [that] is a functionally autonomous unit in which the component processes interact exclusively with one another and operate independently of other such units" (p. 440). Thus, from their perspective, if information is encoded in System A, then it must be retrieved through processes in System A. Or, to put it another way, information in System A must be accessed through A. Hard disks, floppy disks, RAM, and ROM clearly have this property. Information that one stores on a hard disk is retrieved from the hard disk. Literally, the hard disk has its own encoding and retrieval mechanisms. These mechanisms are distinct from those of the floppy disk, RAM, and ROM.

Alternatively, the mind could consist of distinct processes. These processes are not bundled together to form encapsulated systems. They interact and exchange information as individuals rather than collectives. In terms of memory, the computer would not have four separate retrieval processes associated respectively with the structural systems: hard disk, floppy disk,

RAM, and ROM. Nor would each of these retrieval processes be paired inextricably with four distinct encoding processes. There may be one, two, four, or many encoding and retrieval processes. None are structurally paired with any other. Each work independently and are utilized according to the nature of the task.

These distinct, independent processes may be thought of as systems. There is even a way that encoding and retrieval can be linked. For instance, there may not be separate systems for the encoding and retrieval of spatial information; nevertheless, a failure to encode spatial location information would impact on the retrieval processes a rememberer could successfully employ inasmuch as the encoding of spatial location is intimately associated with the retrieval of spatial location. Although this close relation may create a package of related encoding and retrieval processes, the processes need not be *structurally* linked. This difference—between a structural tie among encoding and retrieval processes and a merely conceptual link—rests at the heart of the structure-process dimension.

Discovering Systems and Independent Processes

There are, of course, many different ways to discover the structures of the mind. For years cognitive psychologists have looked at behavioral dissociations. Cognitive neuroscientists have used a host of techniques—PET scans, single unit recordings, animal lesion work, and neuropsychology of the brain-damaged humans—to uncover mental structures. I am chiefly concerned here with the use of cognitive neuroscientific methodology to reveal mental structure. In undertaking this discussion, I assume that the brain has something to do with the mind. There was a time in the history of psychology when it was thought that there was no reason brain organization should parallel mental organization (Block, 1980). The logic of the software of a computer holds true, despite the machine the program runs on. Hardware and software are independent. Similarly, it was argued, the mental processing of an individual is independent of the specifics of the hardware. One need not assume that the structure found in the brain paralleled mental structure. Inasmuch as there was no logical reason to make this assumption, one would not be compelled to abandon a mental model simply because neuroscientific studies contradicted it. Similarly, if one would not reject a mental theory because of neuroscientific evidence, then one should not be compelled to adopt a mental theory because of neuroscientific evidence.

The intellectual environment has changed in the last 20 years, and these arguments for computational-representational functionalism no longer seem compelling. I do not want to survey all the arguments against them (see Hirst, 1992, for a review). Briefly, people no longer feel that even in computers, software and hardware are independent. Moreover, many scholars cannot grasp why people must wear theoretical blinders. Clearly, a neurologically informed mental model is better than one not constrained by neurology. For these and many other reasons, the use of neuroscientific evidence to both constrain and engender mental modeling has become widely accepted. This endeavor is known as *cognitive neuroscience*.

What can we learn about how the mind works by studying neuroscience? I want to concentrate mainly on what we can learn about the mind by examining people with brain damage. As already noted, there is much more to neuroscience than simply the study of the neurologically impaired. (I occasionally refer to this other evidence.) However, in this chapter I focus on the brain damaged. The assumption is that the breakdown in cognition observed in brain-damaged patients reflects the organization of not only the brain, but also the mind. Thus, by carefully characterizing the disrupted and preserved behavior found in the neurologically impaired, one can articulate the divisions that exist in the mind.

PERCEPTUAL SYSTEMS

Almost everyone I know who meets a brain-damaged patient comes away struck by the bizzareness of the patient's behavior. The folk psychological, transparent categories that they use for classifying and explaining behavior in general do not provide ready accounts of the patient's behavior. Consider, for example, patients with apperceptive visual agnosia and the related Balint's syndrome. One patient, described by Tyler (1968, p. 162), for example, "reported seeing bits and fragments" instead of a complete picture. When shown a picture of a flag, she said, "I see a lot of lines, now I see some stars." (p. 163) When shown a $1 bill, she said that first she saw a picture of George Washington. Moments later, when shown a picture of a cup, she said that she saw a cup with a picture of George Washington on it. When shown a cartoon series, another patient described by Adler (1944), said the boat feature in two drawings was different because of the different color. The second boat was "blue," he said, as he pointed to the water the boat was sailing in. Sacks (1985) made this disorder famous when he wrote a book entitled, *The Man Who Mistook His Wife for a Hat*.

Clearly, it is not enough to say that the perceptual mechanism is deficient: It is not that the person sees the world fuzzily or is blind. Nor can the phenomenon be easily tied directly to a deficit with memory or attention. The standard folk psychological, transparent mental categories simply do not provide a ready explanation for the phenomenon. This lack of a ready explanation is presumably why people find the phenomenon of mistaking your wife for a hat bizarre enough to capture their interest. An explanation of what structure of the mind is disrupted in these neurologically impaired patients requires deep analysis.

There is a variety of psychological and neuroscientific observations that provide some means of understanding the phenomenon. Consider Triesman and Gelade's (1980) work on illusory conjunctions. In their experiments, normal subjects were briefly shown a trigram of differently colored letters – a blue T, a yellow X, and a green R. Subjects spread their attention across the trigram during the presentation and reported what they saw. Subjects often got the conjunction of color and letter confused. For the presented trigram, they might say "blue R." Treisman and Gelade claimed that people process color and form separately and later, with the benefit of attention, conjoin them into a single percept. Thus, although people usually see phenomenonologically a green R, their perceptual system has two separate components – a color processor and a form processor. This observation, arrived at only through careful experimentation, makes the bizarre behavior of Adler's subjects less mysterious. Like Triesman and Gelade's normal subjects, Adler's patient erroneously conjoined one feature – the color of the water – with another – the form of a boat – and, as a consequence, saw a blue boat.

The systems of perception, then, are not transparent inasmuch as perception involves a multitude of different discrete and independent subsystems whose products are conjoined in later processing to produce phenomenological awareness. There is no way one could tell simply from introspection what these subsystems might be. As Treisman and Gelade's work showed, careful psychological experimentation can offer some insight. Neuroscientific analysis can also unearth the hidden components of perception. Consider electrophysiological work and lesion work with monkeys. Besides separate color and form perceptual systems, this work uncovered two more distinct tracks of perceptual processing: (a) one devoted to the perception of form, stretching from the occipital lobe to the temporal lobe, and (b) another devoted to the perception of spatial location, stretching from the occipital lobe to the parietal lobe (Ungerleider & Mishkin, 1982). Again, people do not perceive form separately from spatial location – indeed, objects always occupy space perceptually. Yet, these two components appear to underlie perception.

At this point, it is worth going back to McGoon et al.'s (1986) objection to the semantic–episodic memory distinction – that no act of memory is purely semantic or purely episodic. It is also the case that in everyday circumstances, no act of perception involves the perception of form without also the perception of spatial location or the perception of color. It is not conclusive, however, that there could not be separate systems for processing form, spatial location, and color. The evidence is overwhelming that there are. For perception, at least, the underlying processing systems are not transparent, but are deeply hidden beneath behavior. They require careful experimentation to bring them to the surface. For perception, if asked whether the systems of the mind were transparent, that is, accessible to conscious introspection, or deep, that is, masked by behavior, one could opt for the latter. It is not clear why McGoon and Ratcliff believe that a similar option cannot apply to memory.

LINGUISTIC SYSTEMS

The presence of a nontransparent processing system is found in domains other than perception. Consider language. The more known about the underlying mental structure of language, the more obvious how nontransparent the structure of the mind is. It has been understood since the time of Broca that damage to different areas of the brain — Broca's and Wernicke's areas — can yield different deficits. Damage to Broca's area produces halting speech, yet seemingly intact comprehension, but damage to Wernicke's area results in fluent, yet empty, speech and poor comprehension. Early models of language posited two different systems: one responsible for production, the other for comprehension (Geschwind, 1965). This division was transparent.

Further analysis, however, indicated that the original characterization was not subtle enough. Broca's aphasics — or at least a subset of Broca's aphasics known as agrammatics — have a comprehension deficit (Zurif & Blumstein, 1978). They cannot tell the difference between active and passive sentences. For instance, they cannot correctly point to pictures corresponding to the sentences, "The boy followed the girl" and "The boy was followed by the car." Moreover, a closer look at the speech of agrammatics revealed that they tend to leave out function words when speaking — just those words that mark the grammatical structure of a sentence. The commonality between agrammatic's comprehension and production deficits suggested that one system may mediate the grammatical functioning of both comprehension and production. The disrupted system in agrammatics could embody grammatical knowledge (Zurif & Blumstein, 1978). Such a system clearly involves functions deeper than those of either the proposed production or comprehension system.

The aphasia story does not stop here. Whatever the nature of the system disrupted in agrammatics, it cannot be characterized simply in terms of syntactic knowledge. Whereas agrammatics may be unable to use grammatical information to guide comprehension, they can tell whether a sentence is grammatical (Linebarger, Schwartz, & Saffran, 1983). Accurate grammatical intuitions would be impossible if the disrupted system simply represented grammatical knowledge. I do not attempt to outline the various characterizations proposed in the last decade of the system disrupted in agrammatics. Briefly, they do not have the transparent quality the original comprehension versus production distinction had. Sophisticated use of linguistic theory, such as the use of linguistic notion of empty categories, figures in some computational models (Grodzinsky, 1984). The point is clear: Just as with perception, whatever the structure of the mental system of language, it is not transparent.

MNEMONIC SYSTEMS

Persevered Memory Functioning in Amnesics and the Content of Memory

One of the most compelling means of exploring the systems of memory has involved the careful characterization of the anterograde amnesia following brain damage, specifically damage to the hippocampus or dorsal medial nucleus of the thalamus (Squire, 1992). Research on amnesia began in earnest with a series of studies of Patient HM (Milner, 1962), who had a radical bilateral hippocampoctomy in the hope of correcting severe epilepsy. Following surgery, his ability to consolidate new memories seemed severely disrupted. He could not remember people even minutes after meeting them, did not know anything about current events, and could not report the events of his day even in a general way. He could, however, remember the events of his life before the onset of his amnesia and could remember without rehearsal new material for a brief period — around 15 seconds, and for longer periods of time with rehearsal.

Researchers interpreted HM's memory deficit in terms of the then-current model of memory (Atkinson & Shiffrin, 1968). This model posited two distinct memory systems: (a) a short-term memory, lasting around 15 seconds, and (b) a long-term memory. HM's difficulty seemed to be in transferring information from short-term to long-term memory.

This characterization of memory as consisting of two distinct components — a short term and a long term — was insufficient to account for the memory deficit following amnesia (see Hirst, 1982, for a review). Apparently, the long-term memory disruption was selective. Specifically, amnesics appeared to be able to learn, at normal rates, some perceptual-motor skills, such as mirror reading. In an experiment by Cohen and Squire (1980), amnesics were shown the mirror image of three words and asked to read them. Their reading speed improved with practice. Interestingly, sometimes words were repeated; in other instances, the words were new. Amnesics only showed normal rates of learning for new words. They did not improve at normal rates for the repeated words.

Cohen and Squire (1980) argued that amnesics could learn to know how to read a mirror image of a word, but could not learn to know that a word had appeared previously. They suggested that long-term memory consisted of two subsystems: (a) a procedural memory, and (b) a declarative memory. Amnesia left procedural memory intact while disrupting declarative memory.

In addition to showing normal learning for perceptual-motor skills, amnesics also demonstrate normal levels of repetition priming (see Schacter, 1987, for a review). In a typical experiment involving stem completion, amensics studied a list of words including, for example, GARAGE. They were later asked to undertake an unrelated task. In this task, they were shown three letters, for example, GAR, and asked to say the first word that came to mind that began with these letters. The frequency with which they completed the trigram with a previously studied word was compared with the frequency with which they completed a trigram with a prespecified, but not previously exposed, word. Any increase in frequency due to prior exposure is referred to as *priming*.

Amnesics' normal priming can be contrasted with their depressed cued recall (Graf, Squire, & Mandler, 1984). Stem completion and cued recall are similar in structure, but important differences exist. In stem completion, subjects are shown the first three letters of a previously studied word and then complete the stem with the first word that comes to mind; in cued recall, subjects are shown the three letters of a previously studied word and then complete the stem with a word from the studied list. The two tasks clearly place different demands on the subject. In the cued recall task, subjects must explicitly remember a previously studied word. That is, the word they generate must be accompanied by the belief that the word had occurred in a specific event in the rememberer's personal past, the event of studying a list of words. In the stem completion task, subjects must only remember the word implicitly. No memory belief must accompany the generated word. To be sure, for priming to occur, the past event must affect present behavior, but such an effect differs from the conscious awareness of remembering (see Hirst, 1988; Hirst & Manier, in press, for a discussion of memory beliefs and implicit and explicit memory).

Schacter (1987) interpreted the normal priming and depressed cued recall of amnesics as reflecting a division of long-term memory that differs from that of Cohen and Squire. Specifically, they divided long-term memory into *implicit memory* and *explicit memory*. Explicit memory grants the generated word the consciousness that it had occurred in the personal past; whereas implicit memory does not have this consciousness-granting capacity.

Several things are worth noting about these dichotomies. Both the implicit/explicit memory distinction and the procedural/declarative memory distinction classify memories according to their content; that is, the distinctions are transparent. A memory is explicit if a memory belief accompanies it; it is implicit if it does not. A memory is procedural if it has the characteristics of a skill; it is declarative if it has the characteristics of a fact or autobiographical episode. Thus, the classificatory features are there in the memory itself. To make the appropriate classification, one does not have to delve deeply into the processes that elicited the memory or uncover some nontransparent feature of the memory. Whether a memory is a skill or a fact — implicit or explicit — lies in the surface features of the memory.

To be sure, there has been some controversy concerning how to classify some tasks. When it appeared that amnesics could increase their speed at arriving at a solution for the Tower of Hanoi at the same rate as normals, solving the Tower of Hanoi was classified as a skill (Cohen, Eichenbaum, Decadeo, & Corkin, 1985). However, when this finding seemed less robust than originally thought, solving the Tower of Hanoi suddenly engaged declarative memory (Butters, Wolfe, Martone, Granholm, & Cermak, 1985). Clearly, psychologists have yet to determine the defining features of a skill.

I should note that whatever the ambiguity in classifying skills, there is little controversy in determining whether a memory is explicit or implicit. For this distinction, the determining factor clearly rests on the surface characteristics of the memory — in the existence of the conscious belief that the memory occurred in the rememberer's personal past.

Relatively Preserved Recognition

It would appear, then, that memory may be an exception. Unlike perceptual and linguistic systems, the divisions of memory may be transparent, based on the phenomenological content of the memory itself. This conclusion, however, may be premature. It is known that not all so-called explicit or declarative memory tasks are disrupted uniformly with amnesia. Consider recognition, a task generally accepted as probing explicit or declarative memory. Amnesics' recognition is relatively preserved when compared to their recall (Hirst et al., 1986; Hirst, Johnson, Phelps, & Volpe, 1988). Several investigators showed that amnesic recognition can be surprisingly good. For instance, using pictures as stimuli, Freed, Corkin, and Cohen (1984) provided HM 20 seconds of study time (two exposures of 10 seconds each) and normals 1 second of study time. Under these conditions, both HM's yes–no and forced-choice recognition was equated to the performance of normals. Importantly, this similar level of performance was found not only after 10 minutes of delay, but also after a retention interval of 1 week. Similar results were found for retention intervals of 1 minute and 2 hours for a mixed group of nonalcoholic amnesics and also for a group of alcoholic Korsakoffs (Hirst et al., 1986, 1988).

Of course, amnesics' recognition, although good, may be at exactly the level of performance expected given the normal relationship between recall and recognition; that is, recognition is vastly superior to recall. Amnesic declarative or explicit memory may be structurally intact, but uniformly depressed. To put it in other terms, the system may remain intact with damage, but the "voltage" that drives the system may be turned down dramatically. As a consequence, the system will function in a manner that preserves the normal relationship between memory probes of declarative or explicit memory, such as recall and recognition. As with a lightbulb that does not get enough voltage, it will function as the memory system usually does, but it will be dim. From this perspective, both recall and recognition would be depressed in amnesics, but recognition would remain superior to recall.

However, amnesic recognition is better than one might expect from their severely depressed recall. Following Huppert and Piercy's (1977) lead, Hirst et al. (1986) succeeded in equating amnesic and normal forced-choice recognition by extending amnesic study time to 8 seconds for amnesics, while giving normals only .5 seconds. Whereas this manipulation equated recognition, it did not raise amnesic recall to normal levels. When amnesic and normal recognition were equated, amnesic recall was 200% to 1200% worse than normal recall.

These results are not a function of the relative sensitivity of recall and recognition. Amnesics were given two exposures of 5 seconds each for each studied word, while normals continued to see each word once for .5 seconds. Yes–no recognition followed after 2 minutes of distraction. At this time, amnesic recognition was actually greater than normal recognition but, despite this superior recognition, amnesic recall continued to be significantly worse than normal recall (see Figure 2.1).

These findings appear to apply to all forms of amnesia. We examined a group of amnesics with mixed etiology and a group of alcoholic Korsakoffs and found similar patterns of results. Freed et al.'s report that HM's recognition can be raised to normal levels suggested that it may also apply to HM. Indeed, pilot work by Phelps (personal communication July 12, 1991) suggested that HM failed to recall any items under the study conditions of Freed, even though his recognition was in the 85% range. This nonexistent recall is in sharp contrast to what one would consider normal levels of recall under the Freed study conditions, about 30%–40%.

The relatively preserved recognition of amnesics may be tied in complex ways to the means by which recognition is equated. We extended the normals' retention interval to 1 day from amnesics' 1 minute, following the procedure of Mayes and Meudell (1981). Under these conditions, amnesic and normal recognition were again equated, but amnesic recall was significantly worse than that of normals. However, Haist, Shimamura, and

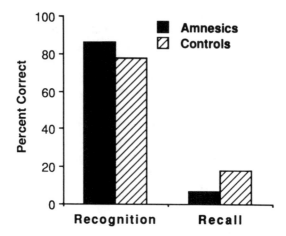

FIG. 2.1   Recognition and recall with amnesics studying the word list twice, 5 seconds per word, and controls studying the list for 0.5 seconds.

Squire (1992) failed to replicate this finding. It is not clear why this discrepancy arose. The density of Haist et al.'s amnesics and our amnesics appear to be comparable. Our amnesics' recognition is at chance levels if they were tested under the same study conditions as normals. Haist and colleagues argued that our patients may have had frontal lobe damage, whereas theirs did not. Frontal lobe damage could lead to a breakdown in strategic encoding and retrieval—a kind of encoding and retrieval more important for successful recall than successful recognition. However, our patients did not show any signs of frontal lobe damage on standardized neuropsychological tests. Clearly, if any frontal lobe damage was present, it was not severe and unlikely to account for the dramatic difference between recall and recognition that we found.

The discrepancy between ours and Haist et al.'s results may signal that relatively preserved recognition is difficult to observe when one equates recognition by increasing normals' retention interval. As far as I know, no one has failed to replicate the finding of relatively preserved recognition when recognition is equated by increasing amnesic study time. Understanding the differences between these two techniques and why one technique should yield more robust results than the other is difficult, and the necessary research has yet to be done. Increasing study time for amnesics could provide them a means of organizing the to-be-remembered list, or it could merely offer them the chance to strengthen the trace or to form multiple traces of the individual words. This latter encoding—that of repetition—would clearly produce a representation that might equate amnesics' and controls' recognition, while leaving amnesics' recall depressed. The amnesic deficit may be such that organizational strategies are ineffective, as I discuss later. If this is the case, amnesics may be able to use the increased study time solely to strengthen the trace or form multiple representation. Increasing study time might yield robust and consistent results, because it has a predictable effect on amnesic encoding.

The story for retention interval is much more complicated. By and large, it is unclear what consequences increased retention interval may have on amnesics' and controls' recognition and recall. The relative difference between recall and recognition and the factors affecting the rate of forgetting will depend on how information was initially encoded and what intervened between study and test. These variables may not be controlled well enough by simply increasing the retention interval to limit the variability in performance.

Whatever the eventual explanation for the discrepancy between the study time manipulation and the retention interval manipulation, clearly under some conditions, amnesic recognition can reliably be relatively well preserved compared to amnesic recall. It does not follow, of course, that there is a subsystem responsible for recall and another subsystem responsible for recognition, only that there is one subsystem more important for successful recall than for successful recognition and another more important for successful recognition than successful recall. The first system is disrupted with amnesia whereas the second system is not.

The finding of relatively preserved recognition indicates that amnesics' memories need not lack the conscious belief in a memory's pastness, as proponents of the distinction between explicit and implicit memory maintain (see Schacter, 1987, for a review). Recognition, after all, requires the conscious belief that the recognized items occurred in the past. Amnesics' ability to recognize past events more accurately than would be expected from their severely depressed recall suggests that their problem may lie more in accessing a memory during recall than in judging its pastness. Memories are encoded and are available with the appropriate cues. It is not the implicitness or explicitness of the memory task but the memory probe provided by the task that determines amnesics' performance.

There are, of course, alternatives to this conclusion. According to one model of priming, a presentation of a word activates entries in semantic memory and thereby facilitates word completion on subsequent tests. Alternatively, prior exposure may make subsequent presentations more perceptually fluent (Jacoby & Dallas, 1981). Yet another model posits that the transfer-appropriate processing required by priming is limited to data processes (Roediger, Weldon, & Challis, 1989). In each case, the mechanism underlying priming is presumed intact in amnesics, thereby accounting for their preserved priming. If recognition judgments can also be swayed by activation or fluency levels or can rest solely on data processing, then amnesics' relatively preserved recognition could be traced to the same mechanism as is priming. The presumed challenge of the finding of relatively preserved recognition could, then, be easily averted.

If the choice was based on activation, fluency level, or data processing alone, confidence ratings might be lower than if the judgment was based on the retrieval of a past event. Under these circumstances, amnesic performance on a recognition test would be better than expected from their free recall (where activation, fluency, or data processing presumably plays a minimal role), but amnesics could not be said to "recognize" the item, in the sense of having a memory belief. However, the few extant studies indicate that amnesics are confident in their correct recognition judgments (Hirst et al., 1988; Shimamura & Squire, 1988; but see also Rozin, 1979). Moreover, amnesics' confidence ratings make sense, in that accurate recognition judgments are given higher confidence ratings than inaccurate ones. When asked if they were guessing about their choice in a recognition test, amnesics often strongly asserted that they were not guessing, but actually remembered "seeing the word before." These observations argue against any attempt to reduce amnesics' relatively preserved recognition to the same mechanisms as their preserved priming.

Nevertheless, we might test more directly whether amnesics' relatively preserved recognition reflects their ability to recollect explicit or episodic memories. If it does, amnesic recognition should remain relatively preserved, even when evidence of priming has disappeared. In a test of this hypothesis, Hirst et al. (in press) varied exposure time for amnesics and normal controls so that two-item, forced-choice recognition was equated at short retention intervals. Hirst et al. also found a clear priming effect for stem completion at this short retention interval. Priming effects, however, disappeared for amnesics as the retention interval was extended (replicating Squire, Shimamura, & Graf, 1987). Despite this disappearance, amnesic recognition was still matched to controls' recognition performance.

In another experiment, Hirst et al. investigated the effect of orienting tasks on amnesic recognition and priming. If the relatively preserved recognition in amnesics is a result of their intact priming, then the properties of amnesic recognition should reflect those of priming, not those of normal recognition. In normals, priming is not affected by the depth of an orienting task during study, whereas recognition is (Graf, Mandler, & Haden, 1982). If the relatively preserved recognition of amnesics depends solely on their intact priming, one might expect that the depth of an orienting task should not affect either amnesic priming or amnesic recognition. On the other hand, if amnesics' relatively preserved recognition reflects in part their ability to search for and retrieve episodic memories, then amnesic recognition may be like normal recognition, that is, affected by the depth of an orienting task. Hirst et al. equated amnesic and control recognition and found no levels of processing effect for priming in amnesics or normals, but a significant effect for amnesic and normal recognition. The results indicate that amnesic recognition and priming are differentially affected by orienting tasks, again suggesting that amnesic priming and amnesic recognition involve distinct processes (see Figure 2.2).

Thus, it appears that amnesics' relatively preserved recognition cannot be attributed to priming in semantic memory. All the evidence suggests that amnesics do indeed remember past events when making their recognition judgments. They can recognize past events better than their depressed recall would suggest, and when they make their recognition, they do not depend solely on activation. Moreover, amnesics appear to be confident of their memory. They assign high confidence ratings, their ratings make sense, and when asked, they claim to be "consciously recollecting" a past event.

The Coherence Model: A Process Approach to Memory

These considerations indicate that amnesics encode and remember some explicit memories. The explicit/implicit memory distinction may not provide a ready explanation of amnesics' relatively preserved ability to recognize past events. The deficit does not revolve solely around issues of

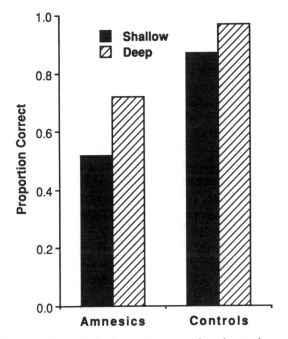

FIG. 2.2   The effects of orienting tasks on amnesic and controls recognition.

conscious memory beliefs. That is, whatever the exact nature of the division of memory suggested by amnesia, it cannot be characterized by the content of the memory, such as conscious belief that the memory occurred in the past. The characterization may have to engage the processes underlying the encoding and retrieval of the memory.

A move away from attempts to classify tasks according to the content of the to-be-remembered material fits into the current emphasis on *transfer-appropriate processing*. According to Roediger et al. (1989), transfer depends on whether the processes engaged at study are present at test, and whether tasks dissociate or show parallel effects when the variable in question affects processes that are shared by the tasks. According to this approach, amnesics should perform well on some tasks but not others, depending on the processes these tasks engage at encoding and retrieval and not solely on the content of the memory.

Several attempts have been made to distinguish types of processes within the framework of transfer-appropriate processing. In particular, many researchers have distinguished between data or perceptual processing and conceptual processing (Roediger et al., 1989). We propose a variant on this distinction.

People encode experience as a connected network of perceptual units. The notion of *perceptual unit* is defined broadly. The individual letters, or the line segments that make up the letters in a word, are probably not the perceptual units of reading; rather, the word itself is (Reicher, 1969). When I look at a chair and see that it is sitable, the chair and its sitability also probably constitute a single perceptual unit (Gibson, 1975). Moreover, when I look at the building in which I work, I do not see, or encode as a separate unit, the building and my workplace. Rather, I see, and encode as a unit, a building that is my workplace. Perceptual units do not involve raw, noncognitive elements of experience, but already highly processed material.

Of course, what constitutes a perceptual unit can differ from individual to individual or situation to situation. An art connoisseur might look at a painting and see a Klee, but a novice may merely see a mass of lines and subtle colors. Similarly, a chess master may see large complex chunks when looking at a chess position, but a novice may see only individual, unrelated pieces (Chase & Simon, 1973). When subjects are shown a large *H* made up of small *S*s, they see not the *S*s as individual units making up the *H* but a large *H* (Pomerantz, 1981). When the *H* is made even larger, so that subjects can focus on only one segment of the *H* at a time, subjects now see the *S*s as individual units making up the *H*. The *H* is no longer an individual unit (Kinchla & Wolfe, 1979).

The findings of relatively preserved recognition in amnesics can be accounted for by assuming that an architectural distinction exists between the processing of perceptual units and the processes that weave these units together into a continuous stream, a proposal I call the Coherence Model (for a related model, see Johnson, 1983; Johnson & Hirst, 1991). This distinction differs from the data- and conceptual-processing distinction in that, as I understand the terms, the processing of a perceptual unit could involve both data and conceptual processing, as in the pick-up of affordances. In distinguishing between the processing of perceptual units and the processing of the relations between perceptual units, I am not positing two separate structural memories — one for the storage and retrieval of perceptual units, and another for the storage and retrieval of the relations between perceptual units. Rather, I am suggesting that there are two distinct kinds of processing — one involved with the processing and encoding of perceptual units, and another for the processing and encoding of the relations among perceptual units. The claim is that amnesics can encode perceptual units but not the connections between them. Their representation of experience is a set of snapshots that have not been glued together into a continuous film. Amnesics' representation of experience, then, differs from normals in its semantic richness and elaboration. Their memories are disjointed and disorganized. The content of each unit or snapshot is encoded, but the context — the unit's relation to other units — is not.

Interestingly, similar claims have surfaced in the animal literature. Eichenbaum, Stewart, and Morris (1990; see also Sutherland & Rudy, 1989), for example, proposed a Relational Representation Theory for hippocampal functioning. They maintained that "hippocampal processing is critical for memory representation of relations among multiple independent cues, but is not required for learning that can be based on adaptations to individual cues" (p. 332). Support for Eichenbaum et al.'s claims came in part from studies of rats in water mazes — a pond of water in which rats must find a hidden platform. They were trained from the same starting position and needed only to have a snapshot of the location of the hidden platform and its surroundings to find it from trial to trial. However, if they were suddenly placed in a new starting spot, a snapshot would be insufficient if they could not reconfigure it to take account of the new starting location. This reconfiguration is possible only if the information was originally encoded relationally, rather than as a single, inflexible, perceptual unit. Eichenbaum and others found that hippocampotized rats could learn to swim directly from a fixed starting point to the platform, but could not then transfer their performance to a new starting point. Obviously, the representation that they formed was merely a perceptual snapshot, not a relational cognitive map.

Consequences of the Coherence Model

A representation along the lines proposed herein has the expected consequences. Recognition, for instance, should be relatively preserved when compared to free recall, inasmuch as recognition is less affected by manipulations of organization, elaboration, and context than recall (see Johnson, 1983, for a discussion of this point). This is not to say that amnesic recognition is phenomenlogically the same as normal recognition. If amnesics cannot place a recognized item into the larger context in which it was experienced in the past, then amnesic memories might be like those when people meet someone whom they know they have met before, but cannot identify when, where, why, or anything else about the person. They recognize the person, but this memory remains isolated from all other memories.

These considerations suggest that confidence of amnesics in their recognition judgments should be weaker than that found in normals, but only when the confidence must be based on information relating to perceptual units rather than on information contained within a perceptual unit. Although little work has been done on this issue, Hirst et al. (1986) found that confidence ratings of amnesics were at normal levels when recognizing items from unrelated word lists but below normal levels when recognizing items from categorizable word lists.

In addition to predicting that amnesic recognition should be relatively preserved when compared to amnesic recall, the Coherence Model also provides a foundation for understanding amnesics' intact priming. Priming tasks do not require subjects to remember when or where material was previously encountered or even how it was related to other material. Rather, it is enough for the item to come to mind, stripped of its episodic context. The impoverished mnenmonic representations amnesics appear to form should be enough to produce such a stripped-down memory; it is transfer-appropriate for priming tasks (Roediger et al., 1989). Moreover, the proposed level of encoding of amnesics should yield the kind of increased activation or perceptual fluency often posited to drive priming.

The Coherence Model also provides another test — that amnesic recognition is relatively preserved when compared to amnesic recall. According to the Coherence Model, the representation amnesics form is impoverished in a way that should render inoperative the principle of encoding specificity, that information is better remembered in the context in which it was originally studied. A relevant study is Cermak (1982), which built on Tulving and Thomson's (1973) examination of the principle of encoding specificity. In the Cermak experiment, amnesics and controls studied paired associates, in which the first item in the pair was either a weak or strong associate of the second. In later testing, subjects were cued with the strong associate. For normals, the strong associate was a less effective cue when the to-be-remembered item was studied in the context of the weak associate than when it was studied in the context of the strong associate. Amnesics did not show this context effect. Moreover, normals benefited from a weak associate cue if the to-be-remembered item was originally studied in the context of the weak associate, whereas amnesics did not benefit from a weak associate cue, regardless of the context of study.

We extended Cermak's (1982) investigation. Our study is more of a direct replication of Tulving and Thomson. In Tulving and Thomson's work subjects studied words in the context of a weak associate and were asked during the testing period to generate words to a strong associate. A recognition test followed in which subjects were asked if any of the generated words had also appeared on the study list. Note here that the memory test occurred in a context that differed from the original study context: Subjects originally studied the word in the context of a weak associate, but were tested in the context of a strong associate. The cued-recall test that followed reintroduced the original study by providing the weak associate as a cue. Tulving and Thomson found, testing only normals, that the normal relations between recognition and recall did not hold under these conditions. According to the principle of encoding specificity, the incompatibility of the study and test contexts drives this reversal of the normal pattern. To the extent that recognition depends on the compatibility of the study and test contexts, it can be depressed to levels below those of cued recall.

The Coherence Model, which emphasizes the loss of context in amnesic memory, predicts that amnesics should not manifest a similar pattern. In our replication of Tulving and Thomson, we verified this claim. We found that amnesic recognition was actually equivalent to control recognition under these testing conditions, even though study time and retention interval for normals and amnesics were identical. Moreover, despite the equated recognition, the amnesic cued recall was significantly worse than the controls' cued recall.

The experiment supplied further support for the claim that recognition is relatively preserved in amnesics. Even though study conditions were identical for amnesics and controls, amnesic recognition was at normal levels, whereas amnesic recall was significantly worse than normals. In the present experiment, we did not have the "unknowns" that plague the study time and retention interval manipulations. We knew what we were manipulating — contextual information. Moreover, the study began to unveil what aspect of memory leads to relatively preserved recognition in amnesics. Specifically, amnesic recognition was at normal levels when context played a crucial and detrimental role in normal recognition. Our findings suggest that context does not play the same role in amnesics. It is likely that contextual information is simply not available to them.

The Coherence Model was motivated to explain amnesics' relatively preserved recognition. It is, however, a less transparent model of memory systems than the declarative/procedural memory distinction or the explicit/

implicit memory distinction, in that it classifies memory not on its content but on the processing that occurs during its acquisition. Consequently, it does not make any claims about the uniform preservation of skills in amnesics. Inasmuch as the Coherence Model posits that amnesics encode perceptual units, one might expect that the acquisition of many skills should be preserved, as long as they do not require the integration of these units. This criterion holds for Cohen and Squire's (1980) mirror-reading task: Subjects merely had to read what was in front of them. The information needed to accomplish the task was contained in the single snapshot of the mirror image of letters.

However, in some instances, acquisition of the skill requires the integration of information contained in separate perceptual units. An example would be solving the Tower of Hanoi. In this puzzle, people are given three pegs with disks of various sizes piled in a conical shape on the first peg. To successfully solve the puzzle, they must move all of the disks to another peg to recreate the cone on that peg. They may move only one disk at a time and never put a larger disk on top of a smaller disk. If subjects are to improve from trial to trial, they must relate each move with previous moves. Otherwise, they are left to trial-by-error, with each move of a disk unrelated to previous moves. According to the Coherence Model, amnesics cannot form relations across perceptual units and, as a corollary, form relations across time. Consequently, they should not be able to learn the Tower of Hanoi at normal rates. As already noted, despite early reports to the contrary, it appears that amnesics cannot learn to solve the Tower of Hanoi at normal rates (Butters et al., 1985).

A task by Broadbent, Fitzgerald, and Broadbent (1986) nicely illustrates the distinction I am making. Subjects were asked to solve a problem concerning a transportation system. There were four variables: (a) the time interval between buses (t), (b) the fee charged in the parking lots (f), (c) the use of the buses as measured by the number of passengers (b), and (d) the utilization of the parking lots (p). These four variables were related to each other according to two simultaneous equations unknown to the subjects. In the experiment, subjects' "knowledge" of the relations was initially assessed, and they were then put into a learning phase. In each trial of this phase, subjects were given the desired values for two of the variables, t and f, and were asked to supply values for the other two variables, b and p, that would produce the desired t and f. For each guess of b and p, the corresponding values of t and f were calculated for feedback. Subjects were then instructed to guess other values of b and p, again in the hope of producing the desired original values of t and f. A trial continued until subjects found the correct values of b and p to produce the desired t and f. Subsequent trials proceeded in the same manner, but with different desired values of t and f. After four trials, subjects' knowledge of the relations among the four variables was again assessed. Although subjects were able to find the desired values with fewer guesses across trials, they evidenced no better conscious under-standing of the relations among variables after the learning phase than before it. They behaved as if they knew the relations, but they could not verbally articulate them.

Phelps (1989) recently showed that amnesics could learn to solve the transportation problem at the same rate as normals, but only under specific learning conditions. In the original Broadbent study, the desired values, subject's guesses, and the feedback remained on the CRT screen throughout a particular learning trial. Thus, subjects had access to their previous guesses and feedback at any time (Phelps's no-memory condition). When a similar external record was kept for the amnesics, they learned to make accurate predictions without later evidencing any verbal knowledge about the relations among variables. Moreover, their rate of learning was the same as that of normals. However, when the two given values and the two subject-generated values were erased after each problem (Phelps's memory condition), amnesics could not learn the relations: They did not improve with practice, nor could they articulate the relations between the variables. Normals, however, learned the correct solution as quickly as they did in the condition in which problem solutions were preserved across trials.

The results illustrate the importance of looking carefully at the task requirements in a skill acquisition or implicit memory task. Success at the transportation task does not depend on whether the acquired knowledge is explicit or implicit, or whether what is acquired is procedural or declarative, but on the nature of processing underlying the acquisition. The memory condition of the task requires subjects to see the relationship between guesses across trials. This comparison may require the explicit retrieval of previous guesses or an implicit formation of the relations. In either case, amnesics appear unable to make the comparison in this condition. When an external trace of past guesses is available to them, amnesics have no difficulty in learning to solve the problem. Difficulty arises only when particulars of past guesses must be remembered (implicitly or explicitly).

Such observations may explain why it is difficult to treat all skills or procedures as uniformly depressed in amnesics. The skills involved in mirror reading, solving the Tower of Hanoi, and the Broadbent tasks differ along a number of dimensions; one relevant dimension may be the type of comparison involved in the two tasks. As already noted, mirror reading does not require a comparison of the particulars of one trial with the next. All of the information needed to read the mirror image of the word is contained in the trial. Successful mastery of Tower of Hanoi requires a comparison across successive moves of the disks: To obtain a clear insight into the procedure needed to solve the problem, one must keep a sequence of moves clearly in mind. Depending on the version of the Broadbent task,

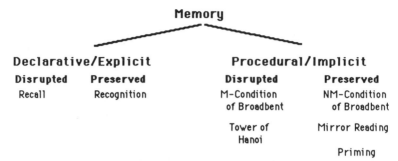

FIG. 2.3   Preserved and disrupted functioning of amnesics.

one may merely attend to information on the screen or must integrate information across trials. Obviously, a closer examination of the process of acquiring a skill, along the lines suggested by the Coherence Model, is needed to fully understand the pattern of preserved and disrupted skill learning in amnesics.

A structural, transparent description of memory systems will simply not account for the evidence. As Figure 2.3 illustrates, some tasks that presumably tap explicit or declarative memory, such as recognition, are relatively preserved with amnesia, whereas others, such as recall, are disrupted. Moreover, tasks that presumably tap implicit or procedural memory, such as stem-completion and mirror-reading skills and some conditions of the Broadbent task, are preserved with amnesia, whereas others, such as the skills involved in some conditions of the Broadbent task and the Tower of Hanoi, are disrupted. Such a complex portrait cannot be described simply in terms of the structural, transparent features of the task. A deeper, process explanation is needed. We suggest that the Coherence Hypothesis may prove viable.

It appears then that, like perception and language, the components of memory are not transparent and may be best captured by a discussion of distinct processes rather than structural systems. I am not sure if I have answered the question George posed. I have only provided a glimmer into the workings of the mind. It is divided into components. These components are rarely transparent; rather, their exact nature is deeply embedded and hidden in behavior. Most tasks draw upon multiple components. And at least for memory, these components are best thought of as distinct processes rather than structural systems that link encoding and retrieval mechanisms.

REFERENCES

Adler, A. (1944). Disintegration and restoration of optic recognition in visual agnosia. *Archives of Neurology and Psychiatry, 51*, 243–259.

Atkinson, R. C., & Shiffrin, R. M. (1968). Human memory: A proposed system and its control processes. In K. W. Spense & J. T. Spence (Eds.), *The psychology of learning and motivation* (Vol. 2 pp. 89–105). New York: Academic Press.

Block, N. (1980). What is functionalism? In N. Block (Ed.), *Readings in Philosophy of Psychology*. (pp. 171–184). Cambridge: Harvard University Press.

Broadbent, D. E., Fitzgerald, P., & Broadbent, M. H. P. (1986). Implicit and explicit knowledge in the control of complex systems. *British Journal of Psychology, 77*, 33–50.

Butters, N., Wolfe, J., Martone, M., Granholm, E., & Cermak, L. S. (1985). Memory disorders associated with Huntington's disease: Verbal recall, verbal recognition, and procedural memory. *Neuropsychologia, 23*, 729–743.

Cermak, L. S. (1982). The long and short of it in amnesia. In L. S. Cermak (Ed.), *Human memory and amnesia* (pp. 43–60). Hillsdale, NJ: Lawrence Erlbaum Associates.

Chase, W. G., & Simon, H. (1973). The mind's eye in chess. In W. G. Chase (Ed.), *Visual information processing* (pp. 215–278). New York: Academic Press.

Churchland, P. S. (1986). *Neurophilosophy*. Cambridge, MA: MIT Press.

Cohen, N. J., Eichenbaum, H., Decadeo, B. S., & Corkin, S. (1985). Different memory systems underlying acquisition of procedural and declarative knowledge. In D. S. Olton, E. Gamzu, & S. Corkin (Eds.), *Memory dysfunctions: An integration of animal and human research from preclinical and clinical perspectives*. (Vol. 444, pp. 54–71). Annals of New York Academy of Science. New York: NY Academy of Science.

Cohen, N. J., & Squire, L. R. (1980). Preserved learning and retention of pattern analyzing skill in amnesia: Dissociation of knowing how and knowing that. *Science, 210*, 207–209.

Eichenbuam, H., Stewart, C., & Morris, R. G. M. (1990). Hippocampal representation in spatial learning. *Journal of Neuroscience, 10*, 331–339.

Fodor, J. (1983). *The modularity of mind*. Cambridge, MA: MIT Press.

Freed, D. M., Corkin, S., & Cohen, N. J. (1984). Rate of forgetting in H. M.: A reanalysis. *Society of Neuroscience Abstracts 10*, 383.

Geschwind, H. (1965). Disconnexion syndromes in animals and man. *Brain, 88*, 237–292, 585–644.

Gibson, J. J. (1975). *The ecological approach to visual perception*. Boston, MA: Hougton Mifflin.

Graf, P., Mandler, G., & Haden, P. (1982). Simulating amnesic symptoms in normal subjects. *Science, 218*, 1243–1244.

Graf, P., Squire, L. R., & Mandler, G. (1984). The information that amnesic patients do not forget. *Journal of Experimental Psychology: Learning, Memory, and Cognition, 10*, 164–178.

Grodzinsky, Y. (1984). The syntactic characterization of agrammatism. *Cognition, 16*, 99–120.

Haist, F., Shimamura, A. P., & Squire, L. R. (1992). On the relationship between recall and recognition memory. *Journal of Experimental Psychology: Learning, Memory, and Cognition, 18*, 691–702.

Hirst, W. (1982). The amnesic syndrome Description and explanations. *Psychological Bulletin, 9*, 435–460.

Hirst, W. (1988). On consciousness, recall, recognition, and the structure of memory. In K. Kirsner, F. Lewandowsky, & J. C. Dunn (Eds.), *Implicit memory* (pp. 33–46). Hillsdale, NJ: Lawrence Erlbaum Associates.

Hirst, W. (in press). *Aspects of a cognitive neuroscience of memory*.

Hirst, W., Johnson, M. K., Kim, J. K., Phelps, E. A., Risse, G., & Volpe, B. T. (1986). Recognition and recall in amnesics. *Journal of Experimental Psychology: Learning, Memory, and Cognition, 12*, 442–451.

Hirst, W., Johnson, M. K., Phelps, E. A., Piers, C., Morral, A., & Volpe, B. T. (in press). *Relatively preserved recognition in amnesics does not depend on intact priming*.

Hirst, W., Johnson, M. K., Phelps, E. A., & Volpe, B. T . (1988). More on recognition and recall in amnesics. *Journal of Experimental Psychology: Learning, Memory, and Cognition, 14*, 758–762.

Hirst, W., & Manier, D. (in press). *On the origins of memory beliefs.*

Huppert, F. A., & Piercy, M. (1977). Recognition memory in amnesic patients: A defect of acquisition? *Neuropsychologia, 15*, 643–652.

Jacoby, L. L., & Dallas, M. (1981). On the relationship between autobiographical memory and perceptual learning. *Journal of Experimental Psychology: General, 100*, 306–340.

Johnson, M. K. (1983). A multiple-entry modular memory system. In G. H. Bower (Ed.), *The psychology of learning and motivation* (Vol. 17, pp. 81–123). New York: Academic Press.

Johnson, M. K., & Hirst, W. (1991). Processing subsystems of memory. In R. G. Lister & H. J. Weingartner (Eds.), *Perspective of cognitive neuroscience* (pp. 197–217). New York: Oxford University Press.

Kinchla, R. A., & Wolfe, J. M. (1979). The order of visual processing: "Top-down," "bottom-up," or "middle-out." *Perception & Psychophysics, 25*, 225–231.

Linebarger, M., Schwartz, M., & Saffran, E. (1983). Sensitivity to grammatical structure in so-called agrammatic aphasics. *Cognition, 13*, 361–392.

Mayes, A. R., & Meudell, P. R. (1981). How similar is the effect of cueing in amnesic and in normal subjects following forgetting? *Cortex, 17*, 113–124.

McGoon, G., Ratcliff, R., & Dell, G. (1986). A cirtical examination of the semantic/episodic distinction. *Journal of Experimental Psychology: Learning, Memory, and Cognition, 11*, 295–306.

Milner, B. (1962). Les troubles de la memoire accompagnant des lesions hippocampiques bilaterales [Memory deficits accompanying bilateral lesions of the hippocampus]. In *Phsysiologie de l'hippocampe* (pp. 257–272). Paris: Centre National de la Recherche Scientifique.

Neisser, U. (1978). Memory: What are the important questions? In M. M. Gruneberg, P. E. Morris, & R. N. Sykes (Eds.), *Practical aspects of memory.* (pp. 3–24). London: Academic Press.

Phelps, E. A. (1989). *Cognitive skill learning in amnesics.* Unpublished doctoral dissertation, Princeton University, Princeton, NJ.

Pomerantz, J. R. (1981). Perceptual organization in information processing. In M. Kubovy & J. R. Pomerantz (Eds.), *Perceptual organization* (pp. 141–180). Hillsdale, NJ: Lawrence Erlbaum Associates.

Reicher, G. M. (1969). Perceptual recognition as a function of meaningfulness of stimulus material. *Journal of Experimental Psychology, 81*, 274–280.

Reid, T. (1969) Essays on the intellectual powers of man. Cambridge: MIT Press.

Roediger, H. L., Weldon, M. S., & Challis, B. H. (1989). Explaining dissociations between implicit and explicit measures of retention: A processing account. In H. L. Roediger & F. I. M. Craik (Eds.), *Varieties of memory and consciousness: Essays in honour of Endel Tulving* (pp. 3–41). Hillsdale, NJ: Lawrence Erlbaum Associates.

Rozin, P. (1979). The psychobiological approach to human memory. In M. R. Rosenzweig & E. L. Bennett (Eds.), *Neural mechanisms of learning and memory* (pp. 3–28). Cambridge, MA: MIT Press.

Sacks, O. (1985). *The man who mistook his wife for a hat.* New York: Summit Books.

Schacter, D. L. (1987). Implicit memory: History and current status. *Journal of Experimental Psychology: Learning, Memory, and Cognition, 13*, 501–518.

Sherry, D. F., & Schacter, D. L. (1987). The evolution of multiple memory systems. *Psychological Review, 94* 439–454.

Shimamura, A. P., & Squire, L. R. (1988). The quality of recall and recognition memory in amnesic patients and normal subjects. *Journal of Experimental Psychology: Learning, Memory, and Cognition, 14*, 763–770.

Squire, L. R. (1992). Memory and the hippocampus: A synthesis from findings with rats, monkeys, and humans. *Psychological Review, 99*, 195–231.

Squire, L. R., Shimamura, A. P., & Graf, P. (1987). Strength and duration of priming effects in amnesic patients and normal subjects. *Neuropsychologia, 25* 195–210.

Sutherland, R. J., & Rudy, J. W. (1989). Configural association theory: The role of the hippocampal formation in learning, memory, and amnesia. *Psychobiology, 17*, 129–144.

Treisman, A., & Gelade, G. (1980). A feature integration theory of attention. *Cognitive Psychology, 12*, 97–136.

Tulving, E., & Thomson, D. M. (1973). *Psychological Review, 80*, 352–373.

Tyler, H. R. (1968). Abnormalities of perception with defective eye movements (Balint's syndrome). *Cortex, 4*, 154–171.

Ungerleider, W., & Mishkin, M. (1982). Two cortical visual systems. In D. J. Ingle, M. A. Goodale, & R. J. W. Mansfield (Eds.), *The analysis of visual behavior*. Cambridge, MA: MIT Press.

Zurif, E. B., & Blumstein, S. E. (1978). Language and the brain. In M. Halle, J. Bresnan, & G. A. Miller (Eds.), *Linguistic theory and psychological reality*. (pp. 229–245). Cambridge, MA: MIT Press.

3 The Role of Language in Cognition: A Computational Inquiry

Jill Fain Lehman
Allen Newell
Thad Polk
Richard L. Lewis
Carnegie Mellon University

We were asked to "tell George Miller how the mind works from our particular standpoint." We have chosen, instead, to answer the question, "What is the role of language in cognition?" We decided not to tell George how the mind works, because one of us has recently composed a statement of considerable length on just that topic (Newell, 1990). Yet, the core of the detailed answer given there, namely, Soar as a unified theory of cognition, seems to many cognitive scientists to be rooted primarily in artificial intelligence (AI) and cognitive psychology, hence, not rooted in language. George would surely object if that were really so. The relationship between language and cognition has been a central concern for George throughout his career. We are sure that he takes an answer to our question as central to any theory of mind—as central to "how the mind works." We agree with him. So much so that we thought the most interesting thing we could do was to tackle that relationship from "our particular standpoint," which is to say, from a standpoint that is grounded in computation and cognition.

Benjamin Lee Whorf (1956) casts a long shadow over questions about the role of language in cognition, much as one might like to have it otherwise. His striking claim was that our habitual language determines our everyday thought, thereby trapping the members of a culture within the world view implicit in their linguistic structures.[1] After it became clear from many attempts at verification that no such determining effect could be discerned (Hoijer, 1954), a distinction was drawn between the original conception of

---

[1]Actually it is difficult to determine to whom to attribute the forcefulness of the statement — Whorf or his mentor Sapir.

linguistic relativity, the Strong Whorfian Hypothesis, and a more modest version, the Weak Whorfian Hypothesis. In the weakest of all its forms, the latter states simply that language has effects on cognition, although exactly what effects remains unclear. That the notion of linguistic relativity is alive and well is attested to by a recent article (Hunt & Agnoli, 1991), which takes the astounding (to us) view that because chronometric psychologists typically take 50-millisecond differences in their experimental results to be significant, any linguistic treatment effect that shows a 50-millisecond difference in a cognitive variable supports the Weak Whorfian Hypothesis. With this criterion in hand, the authors then make a grand tour through the literature of language/cognition experiments and show that language affects cognition almost everywhere.

So the Weak Hypothesis holds pervasively. Yet, surely there is much more to the role of language in cognition. Surely there must be strong effects, if only we knew where to look for them. Surely there are other ways to ask the question.

Our standpoint is computational. It is not to examine or test a hypothesis — here, Whorf, weak or strong. We start with Whorf because we think that helps to provide an overall context for the question, although it is clear that other theories address our question as well (e.g., modularity; (Fodor, 1983). Our methodology in exploring the issue is to reason from the architecture and to examine existing systems, looking for clues about how language and cognition might relate. We begin our discussion of the role of language in cognition by examining the prevailing computational point of view.

LANGUAGE AS TRANSDUCER

A basic tenet of cognitive science is the *internal task-operation* view of mental activity, which states that thinking occurs in internal, task-oriented spaces that use internal, task-oriented operators on internal representations of the situation. This characterization of cognition is one of the field's great contributions. It allowed computation to be brought to the enterprise of understanding the nature of mind. It still allows us to see how thinking could actually occur. Illustrations of its usefulness are everywhere: the work in logic in AI and formal semantics, the formulation in AI of toy tasks such as the blocks world as well as real-world tasks found in expert systems, and the positing of *mentalese*, an internal language of thought, by Fodor (1983). Indeed, the view is essentially coextensive with the *computational view of mind* (Pylyshyn, 1984).

When applied to our question, the internal task-operation view yields the paradigm of *language as transducer*, in which language comprehension and language generation act, essentially, as peripheral processes in the service of cognition (see Fig. 3.1). The process of comprehension transforms utterances from the external world into the internal representation of their meaning that task-oriented operators require. Suitable, goal-oriented manipulations occur; then the complementary process of generation transforms the result of those task operations back into external linguistic forms. Thus, in this view, linguistic processes are peripheral in both the word's senses: existing at the periphery where cognition meets the environment and somehow unessential to the stuff of thinking itself.

The transducer paradigm is as pervasive as the internal task-operation model. In psychological modeling, this is how the UNDERSTAND theory of problem acquisition works (Hayes & Simon, 1975). In AI, the transducer paradigm is epitomized by the natural-language front-end.

What does the transducer paradigm say about the role of language in cognition? It provides a simple and direct answer. Language and cognition share a structure, which we call the *situation model*. By delivering a nonlinguistic representation of the situation.to the task, language has its effect on cognition through the encoding of their shared model and through any subsequent structures added to long-term memory based on that encoding. The transducer paradigm supports a form of the Weak Whorfian Hypothesis: Language influences cognition, but does not determine it. Language's effects are pervasive, just because its encodings provide the starting points for thought. Yet, considering cognition's general force toward veridical and useful encodings, the effects of language per se will only occasionally be crucial. Given this long-standing response to our question, is any other answer possible? We go to the architecture and ask.

THE ARCHITECTURE REPLIES

The Soar architecture has been described elsewhere (Newell, 1990). Figure 3.2 summarizes it briefly. Following the numbers in parentheses, the architecture consists of a long-term *recognition memory* (1) composed of *patterns* that deliver their associations to a *working memory* (2) whenever

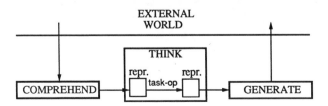

FIG. 3.1. The transducer model.

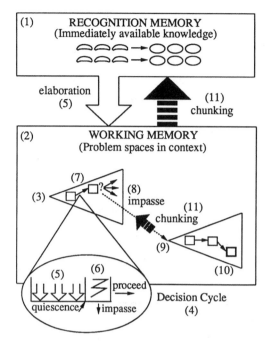

FIG. 3.2.   The Soar architecture.

the current knowledge in working memory matches the pattern.[2] Working memory defines the current problem-solving context. Problem solving itself occurs in *problem spaces*, shown as triangles (3), by a process of state-to-state transition from an initial state to a desired state. Transitions occur via the application of *operators*, one transition per *decision cycle* (4). Long-term patterns match during the elaboration phase of a decision cycle, resulting in the flow of knowledge from recognition memory into working memory (5). This knowledge includes preferences for new problem spaces, operators, or states. Once all patterns have delivered their associations, a fixed decisions procedure is invoked (6). If there is an unequivocal next step, it is taken (7). Otherwise, the architecture *impasses* (8) and a new *goal* is established to attain the knowledge to resolve the impasse. The new goal gives rise to a new problem space (9), and problem solving continues. Once the impasse is resolved by reaching a desired state in the subspace (10), Soar's learning mechanism combines the pattern of conditions that lead to the impasse with the results of problem solving into an association for that pattern. These *chunks* are added to long-term memory (11).

---

[2]These patterns-with-associations are usually described as *productions* in the Soar literature. This is technically correct, but has proven confusing, because productions are often taken in the sense used within the expert systems literature. Productions in Soar form a type of associative memory. Productions in expert systems correspond to the operators of problem spaces.

To understand the architecture's reply to the question of the role of language in cognition, let us first separate cognition from language by reifying the former in a *Task problem space* defined by task operators, and the latter in a *Language problem space* defined by comprehension and generation operators (Figure 3.3). This reification is just shorthand for the sets of problem spaces that actually realize a language or task capability. Of course, some of the Task problem space's task operators will be *transduction operators* to allow information to flow between the Task space and the environment, because doing so is part of the task. These transduction operators are not implemented in the Task space, however; they are only evoked there, for they involve the language capabilities of the system (and so are implemented in the Language space). All of this simply follows from the desire to represent language and thought within the Soar architecture. From this beginning, we can then imagine the typical, hierarchical goal stack that arises in Soar as a result of impasses during problem solving. As shown in Fig. 3.3, within the goal stack we can, in general, find either or both of the two possible relationships between language and thought: A Task space may impasse into a Language space, or a Language space may impasse into a Task space. This is purely a structural reply from the architecture. However, it is not without functional consequences.

An examination of the impasse from Task to Language (Fig. 3.3[A])

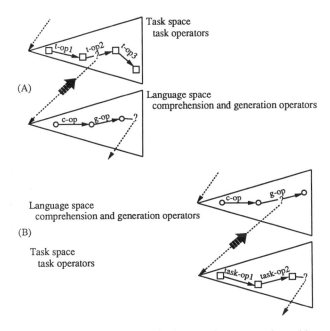

FIG. 3.3.   Possible relationships between language and cognition.

reveals Soar's version of the transducer paradigm. The mapping is straight-forward; we trace it out in Figure 3.4. The Task space, in this case the Blocks-world space, contains task operators that perform task-related transformations on the state. For example, in Panel A task-op1 creates an initial situation model containing red and green blocks on a table. Some of the Task space operators are transduction operators, used when linguistic input appears from the external world. Panel B of the figure shows the application of task-op2 in the context established by the initial situation model. Task-op2 performs a transduction of the sentence *Put the red block on the green block* into its nonlinguistic representation in the situation model. Because the transduction requires linguistic knowledge, task-op2 is implemented by comprehension operators in the Language space, giving an instance of the structural configuration in Fig. 3.3(A). Once the content of the utterance has been transduced, operators in the Task space may continue to transform the state in the service of the task. Panel C of Fig. 3.4 shows task-op3, which actually moves the red block (mentally, if not

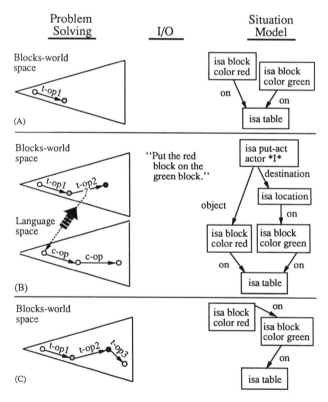

FIG. 3.4.   Language transduction in the blocks world.

through motor commands as well).[3] Of course, a similar process occurs when transduction is required for generation.

The role of language here is essentially ancillary. Granted, a Weak Whorfian view is supported by the architecture, because task operations proceed based on the situation model delivered by Language. However, if there were some other method for generating the relevant piece of situation model (such as remembering it or looking at it), then no impasse would arise, and task operations alone would be adequate to reach a desired state. The Weak Whorfian Hypothesis is weakened further by the observation that, whatever language operations are used, they may occur in the context of, and be influenced by, a preexisting situation model that has resulted solely from task operations.

That the transducer paradigm can be found among the potential behaviors of the Soar architecture should not be surprising. Soar clearly takes the internal task-operation view; it is from this view that the transducer paradigm naturally evolves. The question now becomes whether this is the end of the story. Surprisingly, the structural reply in Fig. 3.3 produces two other functional possibilities, each very different.

FROM TASK TO LANGUAGE:
LINGUISTIC THINKING OPERATORS

In the preceding example, and in the transducer paradigm in general, there are two types of operations: (a) thinking, and (b) transduction. As shown in Fig. 3.4 (A) and (C), thinking operations are carried out by task operators that are proposed and implemented in the Task space using task knowledge to take an existing state into a new state. As shown in Panel B, transduction operators are carried out by a distinct subclass of the task operators, the transduction operators, that are proposed in the Task space, but implemented by linguistic operators in the Language space using linguistic knowledge. Some transduction operators take an existing situation model and a

---

[3]It may seem strange that the act of comprehending the given sentence does not result in the situation model in Panel C. It is important to note that in this example we have separated the act of establishing the meaning of a sentence in context from the act of realizing that meaning; that is, we have separated recognizing a command to perform an act of putting from the actual moving of the block. The act of establishing meaning is the responsibility of comprehension, the realization of the meaning is considered to be outside of comprehension and the responsibility of the task. Later in the chapter, we examine what it would mean to produce the situation model in the bottom panel directly through comprehension and demonstrate how the Soar architecture affords both possibilities.

linguistic input from the external environment into a new situation model; others take an existing situation model and produce a linguistic output.

The characterization of thinking operations as nonlinguistic is an assumption of the transducer paradigm, not the Soar architecture. Indeed, as shown in the second panel of Figure 3.5, the architecture admits the possibility of *linguistic-thinking operators (LTOs)* — task operators implemented in the Language space that use knowledge about language to take existing situation models directly to new situation models without the presence of an external utterance. Of course, we know what linguistic knowledge is needed to implement a transduction. At this point in the discussion, it is unclear what linguistic knowledge is needed to implement an LTO.

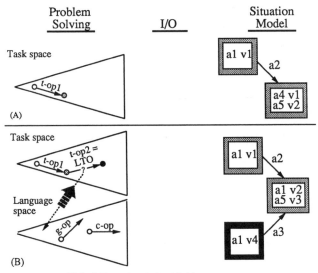

FIG. 3.5.   Linguistic thinking operators.

Observing that the architecture admits the possibility of LTOs is a far cry from either demonstrating that LTOs exist or explaining what LTOs mean. To do so, we must look beyond the architecture's reply and employ our second methodological tool of examining existing Soar systems. Thus, we turn to VR-Soar, a system that solves syllogisms, to find answers.

A Brief Digression:
VR-Soar and the Categorical Syllogism Task

The syllogism task is probably familiar: Given two premises, state a conclusion that relates the terms unique to each premise and that necessarily follows from the premises. Two specific syllogisms and their general forms are shown:

Premise 1: All artists are barbers   All A are B
Premise 2: All barbers are chefs   All B are C
Response: All artists are chefs   All A are C

Premise 1: All artists are barbers   All A are B
Premise 2: Some barbers are chefs   Some B are C
Response: ?   ?

VR-Soar is a computational theory of human syllogistic reasoning.[4] By predicting individual behavior on all 64 premise pairs, the theory seeks to explain both the regularities humans show in syllogistic behavior and their individual differences (Polk & Newell, 1988; Polk, Newell, & Lewis, 1989). As is clear in the examples, some syllogisms are easy and some are not, the latter providing evidence that solving syllogisms is a genuine reasoning task. As such, we expect to find task operators as well as transduction operators. Indeed, computational theories of this task fit the transducer paradigm. One family of theories claims that humans use a *propositional representation* and reason by means of *logical inference operations* (Braine, 1978; Rips, 1983). These theories use content-independent rules to derive additional propositions from the collection that is already available. Another family of theories claims that humans use *mental-model representations* and reason by means of *semantic validity operations* that construct alternative models (in the model-theoretic sense) to show that the results are true in all models of the premises (Johnson-Laird & Bara, 1984; Johnson-Laird & Byrne, 1991). In both families the externally provided premises — which, of course, are linguistic — are encoded into the central representation (propositions or mental models, as the case may be) and manipulated by task operators. The conclusion, formed in the task space, is then generated as a linguistic expression.

VR-Soar is a member of the mental-model family. The general organization of the system is shown in Figure 3.6. The static impasse structure in the figure makes it clear that there are ample opportunities for Task to Language impasses during actual problem solving. The Task space has two task operators, generate-conclusion and negate-conclusion, and two transduction operators, read and respond. The two task operators do not strictly follow our previous definition, because they are not completely implemented in the Task space. Nevertheless, both generate-conclusion and negate-conclusion are task operators. To understand why, observe that in VR-Soar the language generation capability is spread across these two operators and respond. Generate-conclusion produces a nonemitted lin-

---

[4]The version discussed here differs in some ways from the final version, which is still under minor modification and evaluation (Polk, 1992).

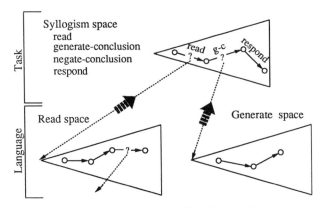

FIG. 3.6. VR-Soar, a system for solving syllogisms.

guistic form that obeys the task constraint of relating the terms unique to each premise. Therefore, it uses task knowledge to change the state by adding to it an internal representation of a linguistic form—it performs both a task operation and a piece of the transduction.[5] Respond then performs the remainder of the transduction by emitting the internal linguistic form to the external world. Negate-conclusion also requires task knowledge that is independent of the operator's participation in the transduction process. It is proposed for the task-specific purpose of checking whether the conclusion necessarily follows from the premises. It changes the state by taking an internal linguistic form and producing a new internal linguistic form. Although generate-conclusion and negate-conclusion perform part of the transduction process in the VR-Soar implementation, this need not have been the case. The transduction effects of these operators could have been separated out and implemented by other operators, but their task effects could not.[6] In short, both generate-conclusion and negate-conclusion have essential roles to play in the thinking part of the syllogism task.

VR-Soar uses two different methods to solve syllogisms: (a) a basic method, and (b) a falsification method. In the basic method, the system simply generates a statement that involves the two unique terms from the cumulative situation model created by reading the premises. Consider the first example we saw and the situation model produced after each premise:

---

[5]The test for the unique premise terms is that part of the operator's implementation that is in the Task space (Newell, Yost, Laird, Rosenbloom, & Altmann, 1991).

[6]We could, for example, have had generate-conclusion simply annotate two elements of the situation model as being the unique terms in the premises, leaving the production of the internal linguistic form connecting those two terms to another operator.

Operators	Situation Model
Read: "All artists are barbers."	[(artist barber)]
Read: "All barbers are chefs."	[(artist barber chef)]
Generate-conclusion: All artists are chefs.	
Respond: "All artists are chefs."	

Reading the first premise produces a model with a single person that has the properties of being both an artist and a barber. Reading the second premise in the context of the existing model augments the single person with the property of being a chef (that is, comprehension of the premise results in every barber already in the model being made a chef). From this cumulative model it is straightforward to generate the conclusion *All artists are chefs* and respond accordingly.

Often the basic method leads to situation models that support conclusions that don't necessarily follow from the premises. Some of these conclusions can be filtered out by the falsification method and its use of the negated-conclusion operator. Falsification will filter out those conclusions whose negations lead to a contradiction in the situation model established by the premises. Consider how this method is used in our second example:

Operators	Situation Models
Read: "All artists are barbers."	[(artist barber)]
Read: "Some barbers are chefs.'	[(artist barber)
	(artist barber chef)]
Generate-conclusion: Some artists are chefs.	
Negate-conclusion: No artists are chefs.	
Read: No artists are chefs.	[(artist barber not-chef)
	(artist barber not-chef)]
(Re)read: All artists are barbers.	no change
(Re)read: Some barbers are chefs.	[(artist barber not-chef)
	(artist barber not-chef)
	(barber chef)]
Respond: "No valid conclusion."	

As in the previous example, reading the first premise creates the model of a single person who is an artist and barber, which is then augmented by reading the second premise. How a person interprets the word *some* is considered a source of individual differences. In the interpretation shown here, the meaning of *some* is that at least one but not all of the barbers that are being talked about are chefs. This interpretation results in the addition to the situation model of a barber/artist who is a chef. From this cumulative model, a conclusion relating the unique terms can be generated: *Some artists are chefs*. At this point in the basic method, VR-Soar would respond with the generated, albeit incorrect, conclusion. Using falsification, however, the next step is, instead, to negate the conclusion. Comprehending the negated conclusion then augments the model further—the artists are no longer chefs. Finally, the system rereads the two premises. The first premise is consistent with the model and produces no changes. The second premise is consistent as well, and augments the model further. Because no inconsistency arises with respect to the situation model during rereading, the system correctly responds *No valid conclusion*.

Several interesting things occur in these two examples. In the first syllogism, solved by the basic method, treating the language processes as transducers was sufficient for the task. In fact, transduction processes alone were enough to accomplish most of the task. In the second syllogism, however, falsification required two additional thinking operations: (a) incorporating the negated conclusion into the situation model, and (b) testing that situation model against the premises. These thinking operations were accomplished using language processes. This is exactly what LTOs are all about.

LTOs: Reprise

Before the digression, we established two features of LTOs:

1. We defined an LTO as a task operator implemented in the Language space.
2. We noted that an LTO is distinct from a transduction operator because it does not require input from the external environment in order to produce a change to the state.

At that point in the discussion, it remained unclear how LTOs could be implemented in the Language space, whether they really exist, and, most importantly, what they mean.

If we look closely at the series of task events that take place in VR-Soar during problem solving by the falsification method, we find two instances of LTOs. The first occurs in the sequence of operations that transforms the initial situation model produced by reading the premises into the new situation model that incorporates the negated conclusion. As required, this sequence of operations changes the situation model through linguistic means, but without the existence of an utterance from the external environment. Specifically, the change comes about through a piece of language generation followed by a piece of language comprehension. The generation is performed jointly by the generate-conclusion and negate-conclusion operators; the comprehension is performed by read.[7]

The second (and third) instance of an LTO can be found in the rereading operations that test the validity of the cumulative situation model. Here there is one LTO for each premise tested, and the acts of generation and comprehension are performed during the implementation of a single operator. These LTOs are a bit harder to recognize for two reasons. First, the regeneration of each premise happens via reading, which seems to be a case of bringing in an utterance from the external environment, and, therefore, is not a case of an LTO. Functionally, however, the rereading is an internal activity — that the premises are read was necessary the first time (the transduction), but that they are read is incidental the second time. They could, for example, have simply been remembered. To make the point a bit differently, suppose we had heard the premises initially and written them down. The act of writing them down is functionally equivalent to memorizing them. Thus, if recovering them in the latter case is an internal act of generation, then it is functionally internal in the former case as well. The second difficulty in recognizing the rereading operations as LTOs is that in the first rereading there is no apparent change to the situation model, as required by our definition (the second rereading is fine in this respect). Again, we must look past the implementation details to the functional issues being played out. Although no change to the content of the model occurs, the observation that the premise is not in contradiction with the model must nevertheless leave some mark (or how else can we know we have performed a test?).

We have found two examples of LTOs in VR-Soar and discovered their implementation in Language to consist of an act of generation followed by an act of comprehension. What, to answer our final question, do LTOs mean? By virtue of performing task operations that are not mere transductions, using LTOs is truly thinking in language. Do LTOs therefore vindicate the Strong Whorfian Hypothesis that language determines thought? If LTOs were the only kind of thinking operator available, the answer would be yes. Clearly, if all thinking had to be done via language, then the structure of the language would have strong effects on thinking. Yet we have not established how widely LTOs can be used, and there are certainly many nonlinguistic spaces for tasks as well. Spaces based on the

---

[7]It should not be considered problematic that the LTO whose purpose is to incorporate the negated conclusion appears in VR-Soar as a sequence of operators rather than a single operator. Operators can generally be realized atomically or as a composition of suboperations. Expressed differently, operators can usually be implemented as methods, and methods can usually be implemented as single operators. To understand this structural distinction in the current context, consider a version of Fig. 3.6 in which the task space contains an incorporate-negated-conclusion operator that is implemented in a lower space by the operators generate-conclusion, negate-conclusion, and read.

visual world are available from the very beginning. We also teach ourselves many spaces for calculation, diagram interpretation, and so on. All these spaces are filled with nonlinguistic thinking operators. Thus, whereas LTOs may take their rightful place in the cognitive repertoire, they are but one of the techniques available for thinking.

FROM LANGUAGE TO TASK: TASKIFICATION

In looking at the blocks world example and VR-Soar, we found two functional implications of the structural configuration produced by an impasse from Task to Language. Language can influence thinking by being the transducer of knowledge from linguistic form into the situation model — the Weak Whorfian Hypothesis. Alternatively, language can actually perform the task; that is, thinking can occur in language — what we might call the LTO–Whorfian Hypothesis. The impasse from Task to Language being only half the story, we now turn our attention to the other half of the architecture's reply.

Consider the configuration shown previously in Fig. 3.3(B). There, an operator in the Language space (in this case a comprehension operator) gives rise to an impasse that can only be resolved through task knowledge. To understand how such a configuration can occur, and what taskification means, we must digress once again, this time to understand how language comprehension occurs in Soar.

A Brief Digression:
NL-Soar and the Language-Comprehension Task

NL-Soar is the current realization of Soar's Language space. It is the set of problem spaces and operators that provide Soar with a comprehension capability that responds to the real-time constraint of 200 to 300 milliseconds per word (Lehman, Lewis, & Newell, 1991a, 1991b). In the mapping of Soar onto human cognition (Newell, 1990), the real-time constraint corresponds to a processing constraint of two to three operators per word. Meeting this processing constraint requires *recognitional comprehension* via total integration of the relevant knowledge sources: syntax, semantics, pragmatics, and discourse. This total integration is achieved in NL-Soar by a *comprehension operator* that is learned automatically through chunking, thereby also becoming recognitional.

A graphical trace of the operation of NL-Soar is shown in Figure 3.7. Comprehension is recognitional whenever the comprehension operator contains the knowledge of what to do with the given word in the given context. Under those circumstances, all knowledge is brought to bear in a single

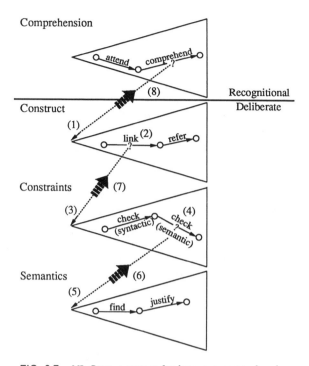

FIG. 3.7.   NL-Soar, a system for language comprehension.

operator application, incrementally augmenting NL-Soar's utterance and situation models. The utterance model captures the structure of the incoming utterance, whereas the situation model captures its meaning. When the comprehension operator is inadequate for the current context, an impasse arises, and the remaining problem spaces in NL-Soar implement the comprehension operator through deliberate problem solving. The problem spaces accessible via the impasse bring syntactic, semantic, and pragmatic knowledge to bear by the sequential application of relevant operators. When the impasse is resolved, chunks are built that avoid the impasse in analogous contexts in the future. These chunks become part of the comprehension operator, integrating in a single operation all the knowledge that was applied sequentially during the problem solving to resolve the impasse.

Suppose NL-Soar is given the sentence *The artist is a barber* and assume the comprehension operator is undefined for *barber* in the context created by *The artist is a*. Following the numbers in parentheses in Fig. 3.7, consider the processing done by the system for that word when it is encountered in that context. Extrapolating from the examples previously discussed, we know that at the point that *barber* is processed, the situation model contains only a single person with the property of being an artist. The lack of comprehension operator knowledge for *barber* creates an impasse in the Comprehension space (1). As a result, a link operator is proposed in the Construct space to tie *barber* into the utterance model as a predicate nominative (2). Before the link can be established, it must meet certain syntactic, semantic, and pragmatic conditions. Thus, another impasse arises leading to further processing in the Constraints space (3). In Constraints, NL-Soar performs a number of syntactic checks, for example, to make sure there is number agreement between the subject and the predicate nominative. Then the system must make certain that the link makes sense, that is, that artists are, in fact, the sorts of things that can be barbers (4).

Suppose that the knowledge that satisfied this semantic constraint is unavailable in the Constraints space. Then an impasse arises (5), and operators in the Semantics space are brought to bear that show this constraint to be satisfied.[8] All of this processing has assembled the knowledge that the proposed link for *barber* can be made. Yet, assembling that knowledge is only the first half of the process. As each impasse resolves, chunking occurs. Through chunking, knowledge from Semantics becomes immediately available in Constraints in analogous contexts in the future (6). Similarly, as the impasse from Construct to Constraints is resolved, chunking moves syntactic, semantic, and pragmatic knowledge into the higher space (7). Once the situation model has been augmented by the refer operator in Construct, the impasse from Comprehension to Construct is resolved, and chunking creates a new piece of the comprehension operator for *barber* (8). The association that is learned during this last impasse resolution tests for all the conditions that determined the word's meaning in the general context, including the semantic condition that justified making the artist a barber. When those conditions are present in the future, the comprehension-operator chunks will produce their changes to the utterance and situation models directly, including the change that adds the property of being a barber. In other words, chunking has moved linguistic knowledge from the lower spaces up into recognitional comprehension. Because chunking is a general, uniform mechanism, the integration of any knowledge source into the comprehension process is accomplished in the same way. This is exactly what the impasse from Language to Task is all about.

Taskification: Reprise

Before our second digression, we raised two questions regarding the impasse from Language to Task: How could it arise? What would it mean? The NL-Soar example shows the process by which independent knowledge sources become part of the conditions of the comprehension operator, and,

---

[8]Although it is not obvious from the discussion, pragmatic knowledge is brought to bear in Semantics as well.

thus, part of the relevant context for assigning a particular meaning. Because this process is essentially invariant over knowledge sources, we are now in a position to answer our questions: A Language to Task impasse arises whenever the task constrains the meaning of a word. The result of such an event is the incorporation of task-specific knowledge into the comprehension operator, a process we call *taskification*.

To make the idea of taskification concrete, let us consider two examples. In our first example, we reconsider the second premise of the second syllogism discussed in Section 3.1, *Some artists are chefs*. It is certainly possible to assume, as we did implicitly earlier, that the interpretation a person gives to *some* in this task is whatever the meaning of *some* would normally be for that person. It is also possible, however, to instruct someone to use a particular meaning of *some*, as in, *by "some" we mean that there is at least one that is not*. How could these instructions be used by someone who did not, naturally, interpret *some* in this way? Figure 3.8 demonstrates.

The instruction defining the meaning of *some* creates a task constraint that is part of the context of the syllogism task. Reading the premise occurs as a regular transduction in this context (1). If the comprehension operator is already sensitive to this context, comprehension for *some* proceeds recognitionally, otherwise an impasse occurs (2). The action proposed in

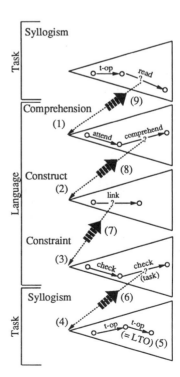

FIG. 3.8. The taskification of language.

Construct is the normal one for *some*: to link the word via the qualifier role to an expectation in the utterance model. The expectation simultaneously holds a place for the subsequent head noun and its referent and acts as a repository for constraints that the head noun and its referent must meet. The proposed link must undergo constraint checking as part of the normal deliberate processing (3), and the task constraint must be passed just like all of the linguistic constraints. The proposal of this constraint causes an impasse (4), just as the semantics constraint did. This time, however, the Language space does not have the knowledge to resolve the impasse. Because the Task space does have the knowledge, the impasse that arises goes from Language to Task. Once the Task space has done whatever is needed to satisfy the task constraint (e.g., by using an LTO to change the proposed situation model to include two referents [5]), the Language-to-Task impasse is resolved and the goal stack itself begins to unwind. As we follow chunking back up the problem-space hierarchy ([6] through [8]), task knowledge will move up into the Language space. When we resolve the final impasse (9), the new piece of the comprehension operator for *some* will implement the variant form of the situation model directly.

As a second example of taskification, we reconsider the transition from Panel B to Panel C in the blocks-world example of Fig. 3.4. During our previous discussion, we noted the distinction between establishing the meaning of a sentence in context and acting to realize that meaning. In response to this distinction, we argued that the situation model in Panel B was the proper result of comprehension, requiring an additional task operation beyond the transduction to arrive at the situation model in Panel C. We also noted, however, that the Soar architecture affords the possibility of producing the model in Panel C directly during comprehension. It is now clear how that could occur — through a Language-to-Task impasse during constraint checking. If such an impasse were to occur, the task space could, in response, perform exactly the transformation shown in the figure, but perform it on the *proposed* situation model. By bringing task knowledge to bear within the comprehension process (rather than after it), the subsequent knowledge added to the comprehension operator via chunking would directly realize the mental action.

What these examples do not quantify is the limits of taskification. Given the real-time character of comprehension, there is simply not enough time for arbitrary numbers of task operations (arbitrary amounts of thinking) during the process. The question that remains — how much work can the task do in influencing comprehension? — is a natural one for which we have, as yet, no response.[9] Nevertheless, we can make a more general statement

---

[9]Although we observe that it seems, in general character, quite similar to the question of how much inference can occur during the process of bringing semantic constraints to bear during comprehension.

about what taskification means in cases in which the task does constrain meaning. As more task contexts arise, more and more of the task will move up into the Language space. Over time, the comprehension operator will contain more and more task-specific knowledge for the vocabulary of the task. Thus, as the taskification of the person's language proceeds, the apparent modularity between Task and Language disappears.

BEYOND WHORF:
PREDICTIONS FROM THE ARCHITECTURE

We began our exploration of the role of language in cognition by observing that the current practice is to view language as merely a transducer, distinct from cognition and with limited potential for influencing cognition's path. We then countered this Weak Whorfian view by appealing to the architecture. What we found — LTOs and taskification — predicts a decidedly more active role for language than the common view allows.

In essence, LTOs show us that thinking in language is possible. This, in itself, appears noteworthy. Although we have not done an exhaustive scan of the literature, it is our impression that no one else has described how thinking in language is possible — though it is assumed in many contexts. Indeed, the transducer model claims thinking in language is not possible, because there must always be task operations to do the work of thinking.

Although LTOs might seem to lead to a dominating role for language in cognition — the Strong Whorfian Hypothesis that language determines thought — that simple conclusion is unwarranted. LTOs are not required for thought; they are only one possible method for performing task operations. To the extent that nonlinguistic means are used during problem solving, language will have only the weak influence it has as a transducer. Thus, the existence of LTOs creates the potential for a determining role for language: the LTO-Whorf Hypothesis, stronger than the Weak Whorfian view but weaker than the Strong.

How much stronger? How much weaker? In part, taskification decides. If we assume that an LTO is used only when it can do the job, then the more taskified the language is, the more often LTOs are applicable and the stronger the influence of language on cognition. At the same time, taskification means that the language through which the LTOs are implemented is, itself, partly task dependent, once again weakening language's role. The role of the language in thinking is also limited by the structure of language, that is, by the kind of changes comprehension can make in a situation model. The nature of these limits is hardly apparent from our discussion. What we have shown in this chapter is only a provocative beginning for the full story of thinking in language.

What the Soar architecture tells us, then, is twofold: Language can, in fact, determine thought, but its power to do so independent of the task itself varies over time and context. It is not clear that such conclusions would follow from other architectures. Strong modularity, for example, precludes the possibility of taskification and is essentially antithetical to the idea that Task and Language slowly blend into one. Thus, the architecture yields two novel predictions. These do not fully answer the question we posed at the beginning: "What is the role of language in cognition?". Yet, they open up the question to new avenues of investigation. They also show that an architecture grounded in both AI and cognitive psychology can contain fundamental insights about language: Cognitive Science need not be split forever into its core disciplines of AI, Linguistics, and Cognitive Psychology. George Miller would surely approve of that.

REFERENCES

Braine, M. D. S. (1978). On the relation between the natural logic of reasoning and standard logic. *Psychological Review, 85* (1), 1–21.

Fodor, J. A. (1983). *Modularity of mind: An essay on faculty psychology.* Cambridge, MA: MIT Press.

Hayes, J. R., & Simon, H. A. (1975). Understanding written problem instructions. In L. W. Gregg (Ed.), *Knowledge and cognition* pp. 167–200. Hillsdale, NJ: Lawrence Erlbaum Associates.

Hoijer, H. (Ed.). (1954). *Language in culture: Conference on the interrelations of language and other aspects of culture.* Chicago, IL: University of Chicago Press.

Hunt, E., & Agnoli, F. (1991). The Whorfian hypothesis: A cognitive psychology perspective. *Psychological Review, 90*(3), 377–389.

Johnson-Laird, P. N., & Bara, B. G. (1984). Syllogistic inference. *Cognition, 16,* 1–61.

Johnson-Laird, P. N.,& Byrne, R. M. J. (1991). Deduction. Hillsdale, NJ: Lawrence Erlbaum Associates.

Lehman, J. F., Lewis, R. L., & Newell, A. (1991a). Integrating knowledge sources in language comprehension. *Proceedings of the Thirteenth Annual Conference of the Cognitive Science Society* pp. 461–466.

Lehman, J. F., Lewis, R. L., & Newell, A. (1991b). *Natural language comprehension in Soar* (Tech. Rep. CMU-C5-91-117). Pittsburgh, PA: Carnegie Mellon University.

Newell, A. (1990). *Unified theories of cognition.* Cambridge, Mass: Harvard University Press.

Newell, A., Yost, G., Laird, J. E., Rosenbloom, P. S., & Altmann, E. (1991). Formulating the problem-space computational model. In R. F. Rashid (Ed.), *CMU computer science: A 25th anniversary commemorative* (pp. 255–293). New York: ACM Press Anthology Series.

Polk, T. A., (1992). *A verbal reasoning theory for categorical syllogisms* (Tech. Rep. CMU-CS-92-178). Pittsburgh, PA: Carnegie Mellon university.

Polk, T. A., & Newell, A. (1988). Modeling human syllogistic reasoning in Soar. *Proceedings of the 10th Annual Conference of the Cognitive Science Society,* 181–187.

Polk, T. A., Newell, A., & Lewis, R. L. (1989). Toward a unified theory of immediate reasoning in Soar. *Proceedings of the 11th Annual Conference of the Cognitive Science Society,* 506–513.

Pylyshyn, Z. W. (1984). *Computation and cognition: Toward a foundation for cognitive science.* Cambridge, MA: Bradford Books, MIT Press.

Rips, L. J. (1983). Cognitive processes in propositional reasoning. *Psychological Review, 90*(1), 38–71.

Whorf, B. L. (1956). *Language, thought, and reality: Selected Writings.* Cambridge, MA: Technology Press of MIT.

4 The Central Problem for the Psycholinguist

Steven Pinker
Massachusetts Institute of Technology

Many scientists can trace a lifelong interest in a problem to the writings of a single author encountered as a student. For me the author was George Miller, and I encountered him through his papers "Some Preliminaries to Psycholinguistics" (Miller, 1965) and "The Psycholinguists" (Miller, 1967). The first of these papers presented a list—seven items long, of course—of "preliminary admonitions to anyone contemplating language as a potential subject for his psychological ratiocinations" (pp. 17–18):

1. Not all physical features of speech are significant for vocal communication, and not all significant features of speech have a physical realization.
2. The meaning of an utterance should not be confused with its reference.
3. The meaning of an utterance is not a linear sum of the meanings of the words that comprise it.
4. The syntactic structure of a sentence imposes groupings that govern the interactions between the meanings of the words in that sentence.
5. There is no limit to the number of sentences or the number of meanings that can be expressed.
6. A description of a language and a description of a language user must be kept distinct.
7. There is a large biological component to the human capacity for articulate speech.

In the other paper, Miller focused on his fifth admonition. Human language is one of the wonders of the natural world, because it is an infinite system mastered by creatures with finite brains. Languages are infinite in the mathematical sense that there is no longest sentence: One can always add *He thinks that I think that* . . . to the beginning of an English sentence to get an even longer sentence. Even if there is some actual limit on the length of a sentence that a mortal speaker or listener can process, languages are so vast that they are infinite for all practical purposes. Miller noted (1967, p. 82) that if a speaker is interrupted at a random point while uttering a sentence, there are on average about 10 words that can extend the string as part of a grammatical and meaningful sentence. (At some points, only one word is possible, and at others, thousands are; ten is the average.) A 20-word sentence is not at all atypical for an ordinary human speaker, so one can estimate that speakers know how to deal with at least 10^{20} sentences. It would take 100,000,000,000 centuries (2,000 times the age of the earth) to hear them all. Clearly, speakers have not memorized all the sentences they are capable of producing or hearing, but possess some mental machinery capable of creating or analyzing an unlimited number of novel word combinations. Miller argued that this ability—productivity—sets "the central problem for the psycholinguist" (1967, p. 80).

Productivity posed an especially striking problem for the psychology of the time, because the only mental mechanisms acknowledged to give rise to novel behavior were the laws of associative generalization: If an organism experiences A and B together frequently, then thereafter, when it is presented with A, it will expect B; stimuli similar to A will also elicit expectations of B to an extent related to the degree of similarity. This law appeared in various forms in the stimulus–response theory of Hull and Skinner, in the neurophysiological theorizing of Hebb, and in the mathematical learning models used to explain data on "verbal learning" experiments. In essence they were variants of the mechanisms described two centuries earlier by Hume (1748/1966) pp. 97, 107):

> There appear to be only three principles of connection among ideas, namely, *resemblance, contiguity* in time or place, and *cause or effect*. . . . [Experience] shows us a number of uniform effects, resulting from certain objects. . . . When a new object, endowed with similar sensible qualities, is produced, we expect similar powers and forces, and look for a like effect. From a body of like color and consistence with bread we expect like nourishment and support.

Associationist learning theorists were a main target of Miller's admonitions in "Preliminaries." Half the article was spent dissecting a sentence from a contemporary textbook on the psychology of learning that managed to flout all seven. Miller, borrowing in part from his collaborator Chomsky (1957, 1959, 1965; Miller & Chomsky, 1963), showed that people's interpretation of novel English sentences calls for a psychological mechanism very different from associative generalization. The mere fact that languages embrace indefinitely long sentences ("5. There is no limit to the number of sentences or the number of meanings that can be expressed") is difficult to explain under any theory that says that new sentences are understood by analogy to similar old ones. Moreover, sentence interpretation does not seem to depend on generalizations of frequently occurring combinations of elements. Chomsky's famous sentence, *Colorless green ideas sleep furiously*, illustrates this point in two ways. The word string is easily recognizable as a possible sentence of English, and thereby is discriminated from other unfamiliar strings, such as *Furiously sleep ideas green colorless*. Moreover, speakers can assign a grammatical structure to the string that allows them to give it a definite interpretation. They can answer questions such as "What slept, and how?" "What did the ideas do?" and "What kind of ideas were they?" ("4. The syntactic structure of a sentence imposes groupings that govern the interactions between the meanings of the words in that sentence."). Yet these abilities cannot depend on previously trained associations. They certainly cannot depend on associations between one word and the next. The sentence was crafted so that each pair of successive words — *colorless green, green ideas, ideas sleep,* and *sleep furiously* — occur as adjacent words in English texts with a frequency of zero. Nor can understanding the sentence depend on prior associations between real-world experiences and the word strings that express them. It is a safe bet that no one, before hearing this sentence, had encountered green ideas that were colorless and the furious manner in which they slept ("2. The meaning of an utterance should not be confused with its reference.").

Finally, it is clear that dimensions of acoustic, phonetic, and lexical similarity among sentences do not map smoothly onto similar sets of meanings. The following pair of sentence types from Chomsky makes this clear:

John appeared to Marsha to be brave.
John appealed to Marsha to be brave.

The two sentences are, on the surface, as similar as it is possible for sentences to be: They differ in a single phonological feature in a single segment in a single word. But their meanings are not at all similar: In the first sentence, John is the brave one, in the second, Marsha; in the second sentence, John is doing something, in the first, he is not ("3. The meaning of an utterance is not a linear sum of the meanings of the words that comprise it.").

Clearly, when people deal with a new sentence, they are not generalizing on the basis of its similarity to familiar word pairs, familiar meanings, or even familiar whole sentences. Miller, promoting an approach to human intelligence that was soon to take over cognitive psychology and linguistics (Miller, Galanter, & Pribram, 1960), argued that they were not generalizing on the basis of similarity to familiar entities at all. Rather, they were doing mental computation, using a discrete combinatorial system that in the case of language is called a grammar. By possessing a finite set of rules that concatenate symbols in certain orders and hierarchical relationships, people could produce and comprehend brand new sequences of words without having to have heard similar word sequences in the past.

In particular, possession of the mental equivalent of rules, such as "a sentence is composed of a subject noun phrase followed by a verb phrase," and "a verb phrase is composed of a verb followed by an optional object noun phrase and an optional complement clause," together with structured dictionary entries for words (Chomsky, 1965), could give the speaker all the productive abilities that these sentences called for. Infinite sentences can be interpreted and produced, because a speaker possesses one rule that allows a sentence to contain a verb phrase, and another that allows a verb phrase to contain a sentence. This finite pair of rules can be iterated any number of times to generate an arbitrarily long sentence. Moreover, the principles of formation that give rise to that infinity are of a certain, highly interesting type. Many behaviors are potentially infinite; walking, for example, is an unlimited iteration of steps. But the infinity of languages is a product of a different kind of mechanism. Rather than iterating a single kind of item, grammars concatenate items into sequences, name them, and then allow one kind of sequence to be inserted inside another. The recursive structure thereby defined is what allows the meaning of the whole sentence to be extracted from the arrangement of its parts, and it implies that humans possess a special kind of processor that can find and keep track of that structure during sentence comprehension and production. Indeed, it is the kinds of structures and processes defined by the rules of language that really inform us about human psychology; the fact that the language as a mathematical object is infinite under certain idealizations, such as unlimited memory, is an interesting by-product of that psychology ("6. A description of a language and a description of a language user must be kept distinct.").

Rules of language, moreover, specify the order of the formal symbols "subject" and "verb," rather than the order of one word and another. This allows the speaker to plug any noun, such as *ideas*, into the subject slot, and any verb, such as *sleep*, into the verb slot. The process can proceed despite the fact that the two particular words have never been experienced together, or that the meaning they define is bizarre.

Finally, the words *appear* and *appeal* are not learned as sounds to which other information is associated. In such an arrangement, if two words share a sound component, they share any meaning component linked to it unless trained otherwise. Rather, words are stored as abstract entries in the mental dictionary. Each entry is a distinct slot or address to which a sound and a meaning are linked as separate data fields. Because sounds and meanings are not associated to each other, but to the entry, the words' phonological similarity does not cause their meanings to be smeared. One part of the entry for *appear* says "my subject is perceived to be in a state," and another part says "I am pronounced [əpir]." One part of the entry for *appeal* says "my subject is communicating a desire," and another part says "I am pronounced [əpil]."

A PRESCIENT EXAMPLE

Productivity permeates language. One need not even examine the complex syntax of phrases and sentences to see its importance; the structure of simple words will do. When Miller defined productivity as the central problem for the psycholinguist in "The Psycholinguists," he illustrated the phenomenon with a vivid example involving a single word. The problem encapsulated fundamental issues concerning competing explanations for productivity; indeed, the discussion that follows uncannily foreshadows a scientific debate that would take place 20 years later:

> For several days I carried in my pocket a small white card on which was typed UNDERSTANDER. On suitable occasions I would hand it to someone. "How to you pronounce this?" I asked.
>
> He pronounced it.
>
> "Is it an English word?"
>
> He hesitated. "I haven't seen it used very much. I'm not sure."
>
> "Do you know what it means?"
>
> "I suppose it means one who understands."
>
> I thanked him and changed the subject.
>
> Of course, understander *is* an English word, but to find it you must look in a large dictionary where you will probably read that it is "now rare". Rare enough, I think, for none of my respondents to have seen it before. Nevertheless, they all answered in the same way. Nobody seemed surprised. Nobody wondered how he could understand and pronounce a word without knowing whether it was a word. Everybody put the main stress on the third syllable and constructed a meaning from the verb "to understand" and the agentive suffix *-er*. Familiar morphological rules of English were applied as a matter of course, even though the combination was completely novel.

Probably no one but a psycholinguist captured by the ingenuous behavioristic theory that words are vocal responses conditioned to occur in the presence of appropriate stimuli would find anything exceptional in this. Since none of my friends had seen the word before, and so could not have been "conditioned" to give the responses they did, how would this theory account for their "verbal behavior"? Advocates of a conditioning theory of meaning—and there are several distinguished scientists among them—would probably explain linguistic productivity in terms of "conditioned generalizations". They could argue that my respondents had been conditioned to the word understand and to the suffix -er; responses to their union could conceivably be counted as instances of stimulus generalization. In this way, novel responses could occur without special training.

Although a surprising amount of psychological ingenuity has been invested in this kind of argument, it is difficult to estimate its value. No one has carried the theory through for all the related combinations that must be explained simultaneously. One can speculate, however, that there would have to be many different kinds of generalization, each with a carefully defined range of applicability. For example, it would be necessary to explain why "understander" is acceptable, whereas "erunderstand" is not. Worked out in detail, such a theory would become a sort of Pavlovian paraphrase of a linguistic description. Of course, if one believes there is some essential difference between behavior governed by conditioned habits and behavior governed by rules, the paraphrase could never be more than a vast intellectual pun. (Miller, 1967, pp. 80–82)

Twenty years later, Rumelhart and McClelland (1986, 1987) took up the challenge to work out such a theory in detail. By then, Miller's framing of the central problem for the psycholinguist had become so entrenched that Rumelhart and McClelland, like most psychologists, had no need to cite him directly, but their goals were strikingly defined by Miller's (1967) essay. They chose his simple example of productivity, namely, people's ability to suffix words productively, focusing on the inflectional past-tense suffix -ed that turns *walk* into *walked*, essentially similar to the the derivational agentive suffix -er that turns *understand* into *understander*. The past-tense suffix was an apt choice, because productive mastery had been demonstrated in children as young as 4 years old. When children are given leads such as "Here is a man who knows how to *rick*; he did the same thing yesterday; he ....," they supply the appropriate novel from *ricked*. Rumelhart and McClelland's goal was to account for the phenomenon using the theory of stimulus generalization that Miller was so skeptical of. They recognized that the main hurdle was, as Miller had put it, to "carry the theory through for all the related combinations that must be explained simultaneously," and to implement "many different kinds of generalization, each with a carefully defined range of applicability." The English past-tense system makes this requirement especially acute, because it requires many different kinds of generalization. Alongside the thousands of regular verbs that add *-ed* to form the past tense, there are about 180 irregular verbs of varying degrees of systematicity, such as *come–came, feel–felt,* and *teach–taught.*

Why did it take two decades for someone to take up Miller's challenge? The key development was the reemergence in the mid-1980s of neural network modeling in cognitive psychology, now called *parallel distributed processing* or *connectionism.* The key idea was that language and other cognitive processes were to be explained not in terms of rules, but in terms of massive networks of densely interconnected simple processing units. In such networks, an input is usually represented as a pattern of activation in a large vector of units, each corresponding to a feature of the input item (this is called a *distributed representation*). An output is represented as a pattern of activation on a second vector of units. Each input unit is connected to each output unit by a link whose weight is modifiable by training; sometimes one or more layers of "hidden" units mediate input and output. Though the networks have hundreds of thousands or millions of connections, this apparent lack of parsimony was no longer held to be a liability. The nets are held to be a metaphor for the brain's massively parallel circuitry, and advances in computer technology made their complex dynamics easy to simulate. Most important, such architectures appear to be ideal for computing many different kinds of related generalizations simultaneously — Miller's main challenge. As such they are a high-tech implementation of the associationist principle of stimulus generalization, as this quote, an echo of Hume's, makes clear:

> People are good at generalizing newly acquired knowledge. . . . If, for example, you learn that chimpanzees like onions you will probably raise your estimate of the probability that gorillas like onions. In a network that uses distributed representations, this kind of generalization is automatic. The new knowledge about chimpanzees is incorporated by modifying some of the connection strengths so as to alter the causal effects of the distributed pattern of activity that represents chimpanzees. The modification automatically changes the causal effects of all similar activity patterns. So if the representation of gorillas is a similar activity pattern over the same set of units, its causal effects will be changed in a similar way. (Hinton, McClelland, & Rumelhart, 1986, p. 82)

Rumelhart and McClelland's particular accomplishment was a parallel distributed processing model that was successfully trained to acquire the past-tense forms of hundreds of verbs and that generalized properly to dozens of new verbs that it had not been trained on. More strikingly, the model appeared to manifest a number of phenomena previously known to characterize children's behavior as they learn the English past-tense system, most notably, their "overregularization" of irregular verbs in errors such as *breaked* and *comed*. But the model had no explicit representation of words or rules; it simply mapped from units standing for the sounds of the verb stem to units standing for the sounds of the past-tense form. Its apparent success led Rumelhart and McClelland to conclude that they had answered Miller's challenge that nothing but a rule system could account for the kind of linguistic productivity seen in people's ability to produce and understand novel-affixed words:

> We have, we believe, provided a distinct alternative to the view that children learn the rules of English past-tense formation in any explicit sense. We have shown that a reasonable account of the acquisition of past tense can be provided without recourse to the notion of a "rule" as anything more than a *description* of the language. We have shown that, for this case, there is no *induction problem*. The child need not figure out what the rules are, nor even that there are rules. (Rumelhart & McClelland, 1986, p. 267)

> We suggest instead that implicit knowledge of language may be stored in connections among simple processing units organized into networks. While the behavior of such networks may be describable (at least approximately) as conforming to some system of rules, we suggest that an account of the fine structure of the phenomena of language use and language acquisition can best be formulated in models that make reference to the characteristics of the underlying networks. (Rumelhart & McClelland, 1987, p. 196)

Given the widespread acceptance of Miller's arguments for the computational theory of mind, the model's apparent success was nothing short of revolutionary. Rumelhart and McClelland said, "We view this work on past-tense morphology as a step toward a revised understanding of language knowledge, language acquisition, and linguistic information processing in general" (Rumelhart & McClelland, 1986, p. 268). One reviewer (Sampson, 1987), writing in the *Times Literary Supplement*, called the implications "awesome," because "to continue teaching [linguistics] in the orthodox style would be like keeping alchemy alive."

Revolutionary manifestos aside, the Rumelhart–McClelland model and its successors (see MacWhinney & Leinbach, 1991; Plunkett & Marchman, 1991) irrevocably changed the study of human language. Miller's challenge has been answered, and it is no longer possible to treat the mere existence of linguistic productivity as evidence for rules in the head. To determine whether modern, sophisticated associative networks are "no more than a vast intellectual pun," or whether, as Rumelhart and McClelland suggest, it is the linguist's rule system that is the pun, more fine-grained experimental and linguistic investigations are needed. It is necessary to seek subtle effects that distinguish the kind of productivity provided by rules from the kind of productivity provided by associative networks.

EMPIRICAL EVIDENCE DISTINGUISHING BETWEEN ASSOCIATIVE AND RULE-DRIVEN PRODUCTIVITY

I have been looking for the fine-grained evidence that would help decide between Miller's rule-based account of affixation and the associationist challenge that he adumbrated 25 years ago. In the rest of this chapter I discuss some of the evidence obtained so far and the conclusions it leads to. I find the conclusions particularly interesting, because they vindicate both Miller and his latter-day challengers. If I am right, neither rules alone nor networks alone seem adequate to account for people's capacity for linguistic productivity. Nor is it true that productivity involves some nebulous intermediate capacity that is rulelike in some respects and networklike in others. Rather, the morphological system breaks down into two subsystems: one using rules, and one using a network, and the two subsystems appear to be qualitatively distinct. One subsystem underlies productivity with regular verbs; the other underlies productivity with irregular verbs. But to reach this conclusion, we must examine, in some detail, the regular and irregular subsystems and the theories that have been proposed to account for the difference between them.

Traditional theories of grammar offer the following first approximation of the difference. Regular inflection is fully predictable, and hence could be computed by a rule that concatenates the affix -d to the verb stem. As Miller's game with the *understander* card shows, this allows an adult to inflect an unlimited number of new verbs, and Berko's (1958) experiment shows that the ability is developed even in preschoolers. In contrast, irregular verb forms are unpredictable: Compare *sit–sat* and *hit–hit*, *sing–sang* and *string–strung*, and *feel–felt* and *tell–told*. Therefore they must be individually memorized. Retrieval of an irregular form from memory ordinarily blocks application of the regular rule, although in children retrieval occasionally fails, yielding overregularization errors such as *breaked* (Ervin, 1964; Kuczaj, 1977; Marcus et al., 1992).

The rule–rote theory, although appealingly straightforward, is inadequate. Rote memory, if thought of as a list of slots, is designed for the very rare verbs with unrelated past-tense forms, such as *be–was* and *go–went*. But for all other irregular verbs, the phonological content of the stem is largely preserved in the past form, as in *swing-swung* and *creep-crept* (Chomsky & Halle, 1968; Pinker & Prince, 1988). Moreover, a given irregular pattern such as a vowel change is typically seen in a family of phonetically similar items, such as *sing-sang, ring-rang, spring-sprang, shrink-shrank*, and *swim-swam*, or *grow-grew, blow-blew, throw-threw*, and *fly-flew*. The rote theory cannot explain why verbs with irregular past forms come in similarity families, rather than belonging to arbitrary groups, which would be just as easy to memorize and store in a memory list. Finally, irregular pairs are psychologically not a closed list, but their patterns can sometimes be extended to new forms on the basis of similarity to existing forms. All children occasionally use forms such as *bring-brang* and *bite-bote* (Bybee & Slobin, 1982; Pinker & Prince, 1988; Xu, Pinker, Marcus, & Ullman, 1992). A few irregular past forms have entered the language historically under the influence of existing forms: *Quit, cost, catch* are from French, and *fling, sling, stick* have joined irregular clusters in the last few hundred years (Jespersen, 1961). Such effects are obvious when dialects are compared (for example, *help-holp, rise-riz, drag-drug*, and *climb-clome*; Mencken, 1936). Such analogizing can be demonstrated in the laboratory: Faced with inflecting nonsense verbs such as *spling*, many adults produce *splung* (Bybee & Moder, 1983; Kim, Pinker, Prince, & Prasada, 1991; Prasada & Pinker, 1993).

The partial systematicity of the irregulars has been handled in opposite ways by modern rule and associationist theories. One version of the theory of Generative Phonology (Chomsky & Halle, 1968) posits irregular rules (for example, change *i* to *a*) alongside regular ones. The theory is designed to explain the similarity between verb stems and their past-tense forms: If the rule just changes a specified segment, the rest of the stem comes through in the output untouched, by default, just as in the fully regular case. But such rule theories do not address the similarity among different verbs in the input set and people's tendency to generalize irregular patterns. If an irregular rule is restricted to apply to a list of words, the similarity among the words in the list is left unexplained. But if a common pattern shared by the words is identified, and the rule is restricted to apply to all and only the verbs displaying that pattern, (e.g., change *i* to *a* when it appears after a consonant cluster and precedes *ng*), the rule fails, because the similarity to be accounted for is one of family resemblance rather than necessary or sufficient conditions (Bybee & Slobin, 1982; Pinker & Prince, 1988). Such a rule, while successfully applying to *spring, shrink*, and *drink*, would incorrectly apply to *bring-brought* and *fling-flung* and would fail to apply to *begin-began* and *swim-swam*, to which it should apply.

Connectionist theories also propose that regular and irregular patterns are computed by a single mechanism, but in this case the mechanism is the kind of pattern associator network employed in the Rumelhart-McClelland model. As noted, the model consists of an array of input units, an array of output units, and a matrix of modifiable weighted links between every input and every output. None of the elements or links corresponds exactly to a word or rule. The stem is represented by turning on a subset of input nodes, each corresponding to a sound pattern in the stem. This sends a signal across each of the links to the output nodes, which represent the sounds of the past-tense form. Each output node sums its incoming signals and turns on if the sum exceeds a threshold; the output form is the word most compatible with the set of active output nodes. During the learning phase, the past-tense form computed by the network is juxtaposed with the correct version provided by a "teacher," and the strengths of the links and thresholds are adjusted so as to reduce the difference. By recording and superimposing associations between stem sounds and past sounds, the model improves its performance and can generalize to new forms to the extent that their sounds overlap with old ones. This process is qualitatively the same for regular and irregular verbs: *Stopped* is produced because input *op* units were linked to output *opped* units by previous verbs; *clung* is produced because *ing* was linked to *ung*. As a result, such models can imitate people's analogizing of irregular patterns to new forms.

Upon close examination, however, the connectionist model turns out to be inadequate in other ways (Sproat, 1992; Lachter & Bever, 1988; Pinker & Prince, 1988). The precise patterns of inflectional mappings in the world's languages are unaccounted for: The network can learn input–output mappings found in no human language, such as mirror-reversing the order of segments, and cannot learn mappings that are common, such as reduplicating the stem. The actual outputs are often unsystematic blends such as *mail–membled* and *tour–tourder*. Lacking a representation of words as lexical entries, distinct from their phonological content, the model cannot explain how languages can contain homophones with different past-tense forms such as *lie–lied* (prevaricate) and *lie–lay* (recline), *ring- -rang* and *wring–wrung*, and *meet–met* and *mete–meted* ("1. Not all physical features of speech are significant for vocal communication, and not all significant features of speech have a physical realization"). A common reaction to this failing is to suggest that past-tense formation is an association to semantic as well as phonological features, but the structure of English shows this not to be true. Past-tense marking is not systematically sensitive to lexical semantics; the regular–irregular distinction does not correlate with any feature of verb meaning. For example, *hit–hit, strike- struck*, and *slap–slapped* have similar meanings, but three different past-tense forms; *stand–stood, stand me up–stood me up*, and *understand– understood* have unrelated meanings, but identical past-tense forms. As in the case of *appear* and *appeal*, words' forms (in this case, past-tense forms) and their meanings are buffered from one another by an abstract index or lexical entry that defines the words' wordhood; form and meaning are not directly associated with each other.

These problems, Prince and I argued (Pinker, 1991; Pinker & Prince, 1988 1991), call for a theory of language with both a computational component, containing specific kinds of rules and representations, and an associative memory system, with certain properties of connectionist models. In such a theory, regular past-tense forms are computed by a rule that concatenates an affix with a variable standing for the stem, much as Miller proposed for *understander* in 1967. Irregulars are memorized pairs of words, but the linkages between the pair members are stored in an associative memory structure fostering some generalization by analogy (Bybee & Slobin, 1982). Although *string* and *strung* are represented as separate, linked words, the mental representation of the pair overlaps in part with similar forms such as *sling* and *bring*, so that the learning of *slung* is easier and extensions such as *brung* can occur as the result of noise or decay in the parts of the representation that code the identity of the lexical entry.

Because it categorically distinguishes regular from irregular forms, the rule-association hybrid predicts that the two processes should be dissociable from virtually every point of view. With respect to the psychology of language use, irregular forms, as memorized items, should be strongly affected by the properties of associative memory discussed by Hume and by Hinton, Rumelhart, and McClelland (1986), such as sensitivity to frequency and similarity; regular forms should not. With respect to language structure, irregular forms, as memory-listed words, should be available as the input to other word-formation processes; whereas regular forms, being the final outputs of such processes, should not. With respect to implementation in the brain, because regular and irregular verbs are subserved by different mechanisms, it should be possible to find one system impaired while the other is spared. The predictions can be tested with methods ranging from psycholinguistics experiments to the grammatical analysis of languages to the study of child development and language disorders.

EFFECTS AND NONEFFECTS OF ASSOCIATIVE LAWS ON INFLECTIONAL MORPHOLOGY

Frequency. If irregular verbs are memorized items, they should be better remembered the more they are encountered. Indeed, children make errors such as *breaked* more often for verbs their parents use in the past tense less frequently (Bybee & Slobin, 1982; Marcus et al., 1992). To adults, low-frequency irregular pasts such as *smote*, *bade*, *slew*, and *strode* sound odd or stilted and often coexist with regularized counterparts such as *slayed* and *strided* (Bybee & Slobin, 1982; Pinker, 1991 Pinker & Prince, 1988). As these psychological effects accumulate over generations, they shape the language. Old English had many more irregular verbs than Modern English, such as *abide–abode, chide–chid,* and *gild–gilt*; the ones used with lower frequencies have become regular over the centuries (Bybee, 1985). Most surviving irregular verbs are used with high frequencies, and the 13 most frequent verbs in English—*be, have, do, say, make, go, take, come, see, get, know, and find*—are all irregular (Francis & Kucera, 1982).

Although any theory positing a frequency-sensitive memory can account for frequency effects on irregular verbs (with inverse effects on their corresponding regularized versions), the rule-associative-memory hybrid model predicts that regular inflection is different. If regular past-tense forms can be computed online by concatenation of symbols for the stem and affix, they do not require prior storage of a past-tense entry and thus need not be harder or stranger for low-frequency verbs than for higher ones.

Judgments made by native English speakers of the naturalness of word forms bear this out. Unlike irregular verbs, novel or low-frequency regular verbs, though they may sound unfamiliar in themselves, do not accrue any increment of oddness or uncertainty when put in the past tense: *Infarcted* seems as natural a past-tense form of *infarct* as *walked* is of *walk* (Pinker & Prince, 1988). The contrast can be seen clearly in idioms and clichés, because they can contain a verb that is not unfamiliar itself but that appears in the idiom exclusively in the present or infinitive form. Irregular verbs in such idioms can sound strange when put in the past tense: Compare *You'll excuse me if I forgo the pleasure of reading your paper before it's published* with *Last night I forwent the pleasure of reading student papers; I don't know how she can bear the guy* with *I don't know how she bore the guy; and I dig The Doors, man!* with *In the 60s, your mother and I dug The Doors, son.* In contrast, regular verbs in nonpast idioms do not sound worse when put in the past: Compare *She doesn't suffer fools gladly* with *None of them ever suffered fools gladly.* Similarly, some regular verbs such as *afford* and *cope* usually appear with *can't,* which requires the stem form, and hence have common stems but very low-frequency past-tense forms (Francis & Kucera, 1982). Yet, the uncommon *I don't know how he afforded it (coped)* does not sound worse than *He can't afford it (cope).*

These effects can be demonstrated in quantitative studies (Ullman & Pinker, 1991). Subjects' ratings of regular past-tense forms of different verbs correlate with their ratings of the corresponding stems (.62) but not with the frequency of the past form (-.14, partialing out stem rating). In contrast, ratings of irregular past-tense forms correlate less strongly with their stem ratings (.32) but significantly with past frequency (.35, partialing out stem rating).

Experiments on how people produce and comprehend inflected forms in real time confirm this difference. When subjects see verb stems on a screen and must utter the past form as quickly as possible, they take significantly less time for irregular verbs with high past frequencies than irregular verbs with low past frequencies (stem frequencies equated), but show no such difference for regular verbs (Prasada, Pinker, & Snyder, 1990; Seidenberg & Bruck, 1990). When recognizing words, people are aided by having seen the word previously on an earlier trial in the experiment; their mental representation of the word has been "primed" by the first presentation. Presenting a regular past-tense form speeds up subsequent recognition of the stem no less than presenting the stem itself, suggesting that people store and prime only the stem and analyze a regular inflected form as a stem plus a suffix. In contrast, prior presentation of an irregular form is significantly less effective at priming its stem than presentation of the stem itself, suggesting that the two are stored as separate but linked items (Kempley & Morton, 1982; Stanners, Neiser, Hernon, & Hall, 1979).

Similarity.   Irregular verbs fall into families with similar stems and similar past-tense forms, partly because the associative nature of memory makes it easier to memorize verbs in such families. Indeed, children make fewer overregularization errors for verbs that fall into families with more numerous and higher-frequency members (Bybee & Slobin, 1982; Kuczaj, 1977; Marcus et al., 1992). As mentioned, speakers occasionally extend irregular patterns to verbs that are highly similar to irregular families (*brang*), and such extensions can be seen in dialects (Mencken, 1936). The effects can also be demonstrated experimentally: Subjects frequently convert *spling* to *splung* (based on *string*, *sling*, etc.), less often convert *shink* to *shunk*, and rarely convert *sid* to *sud* (Bybee & Moder, 1983; Prasada & Pinker, 1993).

The rule-associative-memory theory predicts that the ability to generate regular past-tense forms should not depend on similarity to existing regular verbs: The regular rule applies as a default, treating all nonirregular stems as equally valid instantiations of the mental symbol "verb." Within English vocabulary we find that a regular verb can have any sound pattern, rather than falling into similarity clusters that complement the irregulars (Pinker & Prince, 1988). For example, *need-needed* coexists with *bleed-bled* and *feed-fed*, and *blink-blinked* with *shrink-shrank* and *drink-drank*. Regular-irregular homophones, such as *lie-lay—lie-lied*, *meet-met—mete-meted*, and *hang-hung—hang-hanged* are the clearest examples. Moreover, verbs with highly unusual sounds are easily provided with regular pasts. Although no English verb ends in *-ev* or a neutral vowel (Francis & Kucera, 1982), novel verbs with these patterns are readily inflectable as natural past-tense forms, such as *Yeltsin out-Gorbachev'ed Gorbachev* or *We rhumba'd all* *night.* Children are no more likely to overregularize an irregular verb if it resembles a family of similar regular verbs than if it is dissimilar from regulars, suggesting that regulars, unlike irregulars, do not form attracting clusters in memory (Marcus et al., 1992). Adults, when provided with novel verbs, do not rate regular past forms of unusual sounds like *ploamphed* as any worse, relative to the stem, than familiar sounds such as *plipped* (similar to *clip, flip, slip,* etc.), unlike their ratings for irregulars (Prasada & Pinker, 1993). In contrast, in associationist models both irregular and regular generalizations tend to be sensitive to similarity. For example, the Rumelhart–McClelland model could not produce any output for many novel regular verbs that did not resemble other regulars in the training set (Pinker & Prince, 1988; Prasada & Pinker, 1993); this is true of more sophisticated descendents of the model as well (Sproat, 1992).

ORGANIZATION OF GRAMMATICAL PROCESSES

Grammars divide into fairly autonomous submodules in which blocks of rules produce outputs that serve (or cannot serve) as the input for other blocks of rules. Linguistic research suggests that the information flow is from the lexicon to derivational morphology (complex word formation) to regular inflection, with regular and irregular processes encapsulated within different subcomponents (Kiparsky, 1982). If irregular past-tense forms are stored in memory as entries in the mental lexicon, like other stored words they should be the *input* to rules of complex word formation. If regular past-tense forms are computed from words by a rule acting as a default, they should be formed from the *outputs* of complex word-formation rules. Two phenomena illustrate this organization.

Earlier I used homophones such as *lied/lay* to illustrate Miller's admonition that "not all significant features of speech have a physical realization." Such examples can be generated productively, because the regular process can apply to any sound whatsoever, no matter how tightly associated with an irregular pattern. An excellent illustration of this ability is the phenomenon of "regularization-through-derivation": Verbs intuitively perceived as derived from nouns or adjectives are always regular, even if similar or identical to an irregular verb. Thus, one says *grandstanded*, not *grandstood*; *flied out* in baseball (from *a fly ball*), not *flew out*; *high-sticked* in hockey, not *high-stuck* (Kim, Pinker et al., 1991; Kiparsky, 1982). The explanation is that irregularity consists of a linkage between two word roots, the atomic sound-meaning pairings stored in the mental lexicon; it is not a link between two words or sound patterns directly. *High-stuck* sounds silly, because the verb is tacitly perceived as being based on the noun root *(hockey) stick*, and noun roots cannot be listed in the lexicon as having any past-tense form (the past tense of a noun makes no sense semantically), let alone an irregular one. Because its root is not the verb *stick*, there is no data pathway by which *stuck* can be made available; to obtain a past-tense form, the speaker must apply the regular rule, which serves as the default. In our experiments, we find that subjects presented with novel irregular-sounding verbs (for example, *to line-drive*) strongly prefer the regular past-tense form (*line-drived*) if it is understood as being based on a noun ("to hit a line drive"), but not in a control condition for unfamiliarity where the items were based on existing irregular verbs ("to drive along a line"). In this case the usual irregular form is preferred (Kim, Pinker et al., 1991).

The effect, moreover, occurs in experiments testing subjects with no college education (Kim, Pinker et al., 1991) and preschool children (Kim, Marcus, Hollander, & Pinker, 1991). This is consistent with the fact that many of these lawful forms entered the language from vernacular speech and were opposed by language mavens and guardians of "proper" style (Kim, Pinker et al., 1991; Mencken, 1936). "Rules of grammar" in the psycholinguists' sense, and their organization into components, are inherent to the computational systems found in all humans, not just those with access to explicit schooling or stylistic injunctions. These injunctions, involving a very different sense of "rule" as something that "ought to" be followed, usually pertain to minor differences between standard written and nonstandard spoken dialects.

The effects of the organization of grammar on productive word forms can also be seen in lexical compounds. Such compounds sound natural when they contain irregular noun plurals, but not when they contain regular noun plurals: Compare *mice-infested* with *rats-infested*, *teethmarks* with *clawsmarks*, and *men-bashing* with *guys-bashing* (Kiparsky, 1982; Senghas, Kim, Pinker, & Collins, 1991). Assume that this compounding rule is fed by stored words. Irregulars are stored words, so they can feed compounding; regulars are computed at the output end of the morphology system, not stored at the input end, so they cannot feed the compounding process. This constraint has been documented experimentally in 3- to 5-year-old children (Gordon, 1985). When children who knew the word *mice* were asked for a word for a "monster who eats mice," they responded with *mice-eater* 90% of the time; but when children who knew *rats* were asked for a word for a "monster who eats rats," they responded with *rats-eater* only 2% of the time.

Interestingly, the children could not have learned the constraint by recording whether adults use irregular versus plurals inside compounds. Adults do not use such compounds often enough for most children to have heard them: The frequency of English compounds containing any kind of plural is close to zero (Francis & Kucera, 1982; Gordon, 1985). Rather, the constraint may be a consequence of the innate organization of the children's grammatical systems.

CROSSLINGUISTIC CORROBORATION

Of course one cannot draw strong conclusions about the human mind from the study of English and English speakers. English has a number of peculiarities. Relative to other languages, it is inflectionally poor, with only a single productive past-tense inflection *(-ed)*, compared to dozens in some languages. Moreover, that inflection applies to the vast majority of verbs in the language (perhaps 95%); whereas, other languages may lack a dominant inflection or have one that applies to a small majority or plurality of words, with far greater irregularity. Thus, a skeptic could wonder whether the putatively qualitative differences between irregular and regular forms in English simply reflect the learning history of English speakers exposed to its lopsided vocabulary. Since the regular past-tense ending applies to the vast majority of verbs, it might behave differently from the irregulars not because it taps a different psychological process, but because speakers have heard it with so many different English verbs, and thereby associate many different stem properties with the *-ed* suffix.

As a first test of this possibility, we sought a language that is similar enough to English to have recognizable counterparts to its regular and irregular affixes, but with different vocabulary statistics. This would allow the qualitative and quantitative differences between regular and irregular systems to be teased apart. German presents an interesting comparison, because it has homologues to both the English *-ed* ending and the regular noun plural ending *-s*, but the ratio of regular to irregular forms is dramatically different in each case. For example, the fully productive plural ending *-s* applies to a tiny *minority* of nouns in German, perhaps 50, making it far less frequent than the other plural inflections found in the language. German has a very common plural form *(-en)* that is also productive, though not in the same way as truly regular affixes, and a large number of words conforming to a variety of irregular patterns.

Despite these differences, there are a number of striking qualitative parallels between the German and English regular–irregular distinction. For example, German regular plurals formed with *-s* do not appear inside compounds, just as in English, even though such plurals are a minority in the language. The *-en* inflection, which behaves like a productive derivational (word-formation) process and not like a productive inflectional (syntactic) process, does appear inside compounds. Strikingly, some German-speaking children appear to misinterpret the *-en* ending as if it was a fully productive inflection, like *-s*. The misinterpretation manifests itself in exactly the two ways predicted by the theory that there is a psychologically distinct rule-application process, but it would be a sheer coincidence in other theories. German children studied by Clahsen, Rothweiler, Woest, and Marcus (1992) overregularize -en to nouns that do not allow it, *and* they refuse to allow it to appear inside compounds, despite evidence available to them that it can do so in the adult language. Most interestingly, the two abilities go together: the more often a particular child overregularizes -en, the more often he or she omits it from compounds in which it belongs.

Marcus et al. (1993) also conducted an experiment on adult German speakers' behavior in forming plurals of novel nouns. Earlier experiments (e.g., Koepcke, 1988) had suggested that German speakers tend to do so on the basis of analogy, consistent with a uniform inflectional architecture influenced only by vocabulary statistics. For example, the plural of *Hund* is *Hunde*, and so, using analogy, subjects often produce *Punde* as the plural of the novel word *Pund*. However, none of these experiments tested subjects in circumstances constituting crucial "default" cases. One such case is found when a novel noun fails to resemble any existing one (as in the English experiments reported by Prasada and Pinker, 1993). Another can be found when a novel noun is derived from some other category such as a name, and thus, because it is not listed as a noun root in the lexicon, it is ineligible for the analogization of existing stored irregular patterns (this is the phenomenon studied in the experiments reported by Kim, Marcus et al., 1991, and Kim, Pinker et al., 1991). Studying 16 adult German speakers, Marcus et al. found that three distinct types of circumstances did in fact lead German speakers to give high naturalness ratings to nouns affixed with the default plural -s form. First, the -s plural improves relative to the irregular plurals in words that do not rhyme with existing words (and hence cannot be given a non-s form by analogy), in comparison to words that do rhyme with existing nouns. Second, the -s plural also improves relative to the irregular plurals when a novel noun is presented as being borrowed from a foreign language (e.g., a set of cars referred to by their manufacturer's name, as in the English *Toyotas*). This is a circumstance that, like derivation from a name or another category such as a verb, seals off listed irregular roots and hence requires a default operation. Finally, the -s plural improves relative to the irregular plurals when the novel word is presented as a proper name, as in the English *We're having the Manns over for dinner*, even when the novel noun rhymes with an existing irregular noun and hence should be especially prone to analogizing. It seems then, that under circumstances in which analogy is inadequate, German speakers use a default plural rule, namely, one that affixes -s to a stem, despite its relative rarity in the language.

German speakers also behave like English ones in their treatment of their language's participle system. In German, the regular participles, formed with the suffix -*t* (e.g., *kaufen-gekauft* "bought"), do not vastly outnumber the irregular participles, formed with idiosyncratic stem changes and the suffix -*en* (e.g., *singen-gesungen* "sing"). Adult German speakers are sensitive to the morphological derivation of novel verbs, just as English speakers are (cf. Kim, Pinker et al., 1991; Kiparsky, 1982). Marcus et al. (1993) elicited the present-perfect forms of these verbs in contexts that encouraged the subjects to interpret the verbs either as having a verb root, or as being derived from a noun, such as *bepfeifen* with the meaning "to put pipes on" (based on the noun *Pfeife*, "pipe"). Subjects produced significantly more regularly inflected forms for verbs derived from nouns than for verbs with pure verb roots. (As in the Kim, Pinker et al., 1991, study, all verbs were presented in a metaphorical or extended usage; therefore, centralness of meaning or degree of familiarity cannot account for the differences observed.) Once again, the distinction between regularity and irregularity does not appear to depend on a strong difference between the type frequency of regular and irregular verbs, such as we find in English. Even in the notoriously complicated system of German plural and participle inflection, distinct psychological mechanisms may be necessary to account for the differences between regularity and irregularity.

DEVELOPMENTAL AND NEUROLOGICAL DISSOCIATIONS

If regular and irregular patterns are computed by different subsystems, they should dissociate in special populations. Individuals with undeveloped or damaged grammatical systems and intact lexical memory should be unable to compute regular forms, but should handle irregulars. Conversely, individuals with intact grammatical systems and atypical lexical retrieval should handle regulars properly, but be prone to overregularizing irregulars. Such double dissociations, most clearly demonstrated in detailed case studies, are an important source of evidence for the existence of separate neural subsystems. Preliminary evidence suggests that regular and irregular inflection may show such dissociations.

Childhood.   One conspicuous phenomenon in language development is the appearance of overregularizations such as *comed*. Such errors constitute a worsening of past marking with time; for months beforehand, all overtly marked irregular past forms are correct (Cazden, 1968; Ervin, 1964; Marcus et al., 1992). The Rumelhart–McClelland model's most famous empirical success is its apparent ability to duplicate this transition without any shift in mechanism from rote to rule. Rumelhart and McClelland explained the effect as follows: Because most high-frequency verbs in English are irregular, if children learn a few high-frequency verbs first, they will possess a vocabulary of idiosyncratic singletons, each with its own mapping to output past-tense forms. If vocabulary acquisition then undergoes a burst of expansion, lower-frequency, predominantly regular verbs will flood in, and the shared mapping from stem patterns to the nodes representing the -ed ending will temporarily overwhelm the idiosyncratic connections, resulting in overregularization errors. In examining the speech of three children and their parents, however (Marcus et al., 1992), we found no increase in the proportion of verb tokens that were regular, presumably because the high-frequency irregulars such as *come, go, do, see, take, give,* and so on, dominate conversation at any age; when new, lower-frequency regulars such as *abscond* or *defenestrate* are acquired, they compete among themselves for air time in speech, rather than displacing irregulars. When children's vocabulary types were examined, they did show an increase in the number and proportion of regular verbs over time (inevitable, given the small number of irregulars and their essentially finite number), but this increase did not correlate with children's overregularization rates over time: Regular verbs are learned most quickly in the early stages of acquisition, before children begin to overregularize.

Thus, the onset of overregularization is not due to the child becoming temporarily overwhelmed by the regular pattern because of an influx of regular verbs, as connectionist theories predict. Instead it accompanies the appearance of the regular tense-marking process itself: Overregularizations appear when the child ceases using bare stems such as *walk* to refer to past events (Kuczaj, 1977; Marcus et al., 1992). The explanation of children's apparent regression in development is simple. Memorization of irregular verb forms from parental speech can take place as soon as words of any kind can be learned. But deployment of the rule system must await the abstraction of the English rule from a set of word pairs juxtaposed as nonpast and past versions of the same verb. The young child can possess memorized irregulars, produced probabilistically but without overt error, and no rule; the older child, possessing the rule as well, would apply it obligatorily in past-tense sentences whenever he or she failed to retrieve the irregular, resulting in occasional errors.

Aphasia.   A syndrome sometimes called agrammatic aphasia can occur after extensive damage to Broca's area and nearby structures in the left cerebral hemisphere of the brain. Labored speech, absence of inflections and other grammatical words, and difficulty comprehending grammatical distinctions are frequent symptoms. Agrammatics have trouble reading aloud regular inflected forms: *Smiled* is pronounced as *smile, wanted* as *wanting.* Nonregular plural and past forms are read with several orders of magnitude greater accuracy, controlling for frequency and pronounceability (Marin, Saffran, & Schwartz, 1976; Ullman, Hickok, & Pinker,

1992). For example, regular *misers*, *clues*, and *buds* were read by three agrammatic patients less accurately than phonologically matched plurals that are not regular because they lack a corresponding singular, such as *trousers*, *news*, and *suds* (45% versus 90%), even though a phonologically well-formed stem is available in both cases. In the Hickok et al. study, when verbs matched for past and base frequencies and pronounceability were presented to an agrammatic patient, he read 56% of irregular pasts and 18% of regular pasts successfully. This is predicted if agrammatism results from damage to neural circuitry that executes rules of grammar, including the regular rule necessary for analyzing regularly inflected stimuli, but leaves the lexicon relatively undamaged, including stored irregulars which can be directly matched against the irregular stimuli.

Specific Language Impairment (SLI).   This refers to a syndrome of language deficits not attributable to auditory, cognitive, or social problems. The syndrome usually includes delayed onset of language, articulation difficulties in childhood, and problems in controlling grammatical features such as tense, number, gender, case, and person. Recent case studies (Gopnik, 1990; Gopnik & Crago, 1991) suggest that one form of SLI may especially impair aspects of the regular inflectional process. Natural speech includes errors such as "We're go take a bus; I play musics; One machine clean all the two arena." In experiments, the patients had difficulty converting present sentences to past (32% SLI vs 78% sibling controls). The difficulty was more pronounced for regular verbs than irregulars. Regular past forms were virtually absent from the children's spontaneous speech and writing, although irregulars often appeared. In the writing samples of two children examined quantitatively, 85% of irregular pasts, but 30% of regular pasts, were correctly supplied. The first written regular pasts were for verbs with past-tense frequencies higher than their stem frequencies; subsequent ones were acquired one at a time in response to teacher training, with little transfer to nontrained verbs. Adults' performance improved and their speech began to sound normal, but they continued to have difficulty inflecting nonsense forms such as *zoop* (47% SLI, 83% controls). It appears as if their ability to apply inflectional rules is impaired relative to their ability to memorize words: Irregular forms are acquired relatively normally, enjoying their advantage of high frequencies; regulars are memorized as if they were irregular.

SLI appears to have an inherited component. Language impairments have been found in 3% of first-degree family members of normal probands, but 23% of language-impaired probands (Tallal, Ross, & Curtiss, 1989; Tomblin, 1989). The impairment has been found to be 80% concordant in monozygotic twins and 35% concordant in dizygotic twins (Tomblin, personal communication, March 1991). One case study (Gopnik, 1990;

Gopnik & Crago, 1991) investigated a 3-generation, 30-member family, 16 of whom had SLI; the syndrome followed the pattern of a dominant, fully penetrant autosomal gene. This constitutes evidence that some aspects of the use of grammar have a genetic basis.

Williams Syndrome.   Williams syndrome (WS), associated with a defective gene expressed in the central nervous system involved in calcium metabolism, causes an unusual kind of mental retardation (Bellugi, Bihrle, Jernigan, Trauner, & Doherty, 1990). Though their IQ is measured at around 50, older children and adolescents with WS are described as "hyperlinguistic" with "selective sparing of syntax," and grammatical abilities are close to normal in controlled testing (Bellugi et al., 1990). This is one of several kinds of dissociation in which language is preserved despite severe cognitive impairments, suggesting that the language system is autonomous of many other kinds of cognitive processing (Curtiss, 1989).

WS children retrieve words in a deviant fashion (Bellugi et al., 1990). When normal or other retarded children are asked to name some animals, they say *dog*, *cat*, and *pig*; WS children offer *unicorn*, *tyrandon*, *yak*, and *ibex*. Normal children speak of *pouring water*; WS children speak of *evacuating a glass*. According to the rule-associative-memory hybrid theory, preserved grammatical abilities and deviant retrieval of high-frequency words are preconditions for overregularization. Indeed, some WS children overregularize at high rates (16%) — their only noticeable grammatical error (Bellugi et al., 1990; Klima & Bellugi, personal communication, March 1991). Currently, Ullman and I are testing this logic on other neuropsychological patients with relatively spared grammatical abilities but defective word-finding abilities, such as patients with Alzheimer's disease; we find that they inflect regular and novel verbs correctly, but often overregularize irregular verbs, just as predicted (Ullman, Hickok, & Pinker, 1992).

CONCLUSION

One of Miller's lasting gifts to psychology was his challenge to the ever-popular idea that the mind is a homogeneous system whose complexity comes from the complexity of environmental correlations as recorded by a general-purpose learning mechanism. Miller (1965, 1967; Miller et al., 1960) argued that the structure of language and the productivity of language speakers called for a very different conception of the human mind, in which the mind is treated as a computational device in which rules operate on symbolic data structures. Remarkably, a simple example that Miller chose for illustrative purposes — the psychological process of interpreting a novel-affixed form such as *understander* — turned out, 20 years later, to encapsulate these rival conceptions succinctly. Although neoassociationist researchers rose to Miller's challenge to duplicate human behavior with a more complex associative mechanism, at best they have found that the memory system used in language acquisition and processing has some of the properties of an associative network, and that such properties can replace rules in the limited domain of the learning and sporadic generalization of irregular forms. But this will not do for more systematic regular affixes such as -ed and -er, which appear to require classic symbolic rules.

Indeed, what we have learned about productive affixation has even broader implications, for it appears to vindicate Miller's seventh (and thereby most important) preliminary to psycholinguistics in which he wrote:

> Finally, it is important to remember that there is a large innate component to our language-using ability. Not just any self-consistent set of rules that we might be able to invent for communicative purposes could serve as a natural language. All human societies possess language, and all of these languages have features in common — features that are called "language universals", but are in fact prelinguistic in character. It is difficult to imagine how children could acquire language so rapidly from parents who understand it so poorly unless they were already tuned by evolution to select just those aspects that are universally significant. There is, in short, a large biological component that shapes our human languages. (Miller, 1965, p. 17)

The studies I reviewed, although focusing on a single rule of grammar, bear out this preliminary admonition. For the regular affixational system appears to be autonomous of real-world meaning, nonassociative (unaffected by frequency and similarity), sensitive to abstract formal distinctions (for example, root versus derived, noun versus verb), more sophisticated than the kinds of "rules" that are explicitly taught, qualitatively similar across languages with large differences in superficial vocabulary statistics, developing on a schedule not timed by environmental input, and organized by principles that could not have been learned, possibly with a distinct neural substrate and genetic basis.

ACKNOWLEDGMENTS

Preparation of this chapter was supported by NIH Grant HD 18381 and NSF Grant BNS 91-09766. I thank Paul Bloom, Gary Marcus, and Alan Prince for comments on an earlier draft. I am also grateful to my collaborators on the research reported in this chapter: Chris Collins, Marie Coppola, Greg Hickok, Michelle Hollander, John J. Kim, Sandeep Prasada, Alan Prince, Annie Senghas, Karin Stromswold, Michael Ullman, and Fei Xu.

REFERENCES

Bellugi, U., Bihrle, A., Jernigan, T., Trauner, D., & Doherty, S. (1990). Neuropsychological, neurological, and neuroanatomical profile of Williams Syndrome. *American Journal of Medical Genetics Supplement, 6*, 115-125.

Berko, J. (1958). The child's learning of English morphology. *Word, 14*, 150-177.

Bybee, J. L. (1985). *Morphology*. Philadelphia: Benjamins.

Bybee, J. L., & Moder, C. L. (1983). Morphological classes as natural categories. *Language, 59*, 251-270.

Bybee, J. L., & Slobin, D. I. (1982). Rules and schemas in the development and use of the English past tense. *Language, 58*, 265-289.

Cazden, C. B. (1968). The acquisition of noun and verb inflections. *Child Development, 39*, 433-448.

Chomsky, N. (1957). *Syntactic structures*. The Hague: Mouton.

Chomsky, N. (1959). A review of B. F. Skinner's "verbal behavior." *Language, 3*, 26-58.

Chomsky, N. (1965). *Aspects of the theory of syntax*. Cambridge, MA: MIT Press.

Chomsky, N., & Halle, M. (1968). *The sound pattern of English*. New York: Harper and Row.

Clahsen, H., Rothweiler, M., Woest, A., & Marcus, G. F. (1992). Regular and irregular inflection in the acquisition of German noun plurals. *Cognition, 5*, 225-255.

Curtiss, S. (1989). The independence and task-specificity of language. In A. Bornstein & J. Bruner (Eds.), *Interaction in human development* (pp. 105-137). Hillsdale, NJ: Lawrence Erlbaum Associates.

Ervin, S. M. (1964). Imitation and structural change in children's language. In E. H. Lenneberg (Ed.), *New directions in the study of language* (pp. 163-189). Cambridge: MIT Press.

Francis, N., & Kucera, H. (1982). *Frequency analysis of English usage*. Boston: Houghton Mifflin.

Gopnik, M. (1990) Dysphasia in an extended family. *Nature, 344*, 715.

Gopnik, M., & Crago, M. B. (1991). Familial aggregation of a developmental language disorder. *Cognition, 39*, 1-50.

Gordon, P. (1985). Level-ordering in lexical development. *Cognition, 21*, 73-93.

Hinton, G. E., McClelland, J. L., & Rumelhart, D. E. (1986). Distributed representations. In D. E. Rumelhart, J. L. McClelland, & the PDP Research Group (Eds.), *Parallel distributed processing: Explorations in the microstructure of cognition: Vol. 1. Foundations*. Cambridge, MA: Bradford Books/MIT Press.

Hume, D. (1966). Enquiry concerning human understanding. In L. W. Beck (Ed.), *18th Century philosophy* (pp. 93-125). New York: Free Press.

Jespersen, O. (1961). *A modern English grammar on historical principles, VI*. London: George Allen & Unwin Ltd.

Kempley, S. T., & Morton, J. (1982). The effects of priming with regularly and irregularly related words in auditory word recognition. *British Journal of Psychology, 73*, 441-454.

Kim, J. J. Marcus, G. F., Hollander, M., & Pinker, S. (1991). Children's inflection is sensitive to morphological structure. *Papers and Reports in Child Language Development, 30*, 39-46.

Kim, J. J., Pinker, S., Prince, A., & Prasada, S. (1991). Why no mere mortal has ever flown out to center field. *Cognitive Science, 15*, 173-218.

Kiparsky, P. (1982). Lexical phonology and morphology. In I. S. Yang (Ed.), *Linguistics in the morning calm*. (pp. 3-91). Seoul, Korea: Hansin.

Koepcke, K. -M. (1988). Schemas in German plural formation. *Lingua, 74*, 303-305.

Kuczaj, S. A. (1977). The acquisition of regular and irregular past tense forms. *Journal of Verbal Learning and Verbal Behavior, 16*, 589-600.

Lachter, J., & Bever, T. G. (1988). The relation between linguistic structure and associative theories of language learning–A constructive critique of some connectionist learning models. *Cognition, 28*, 195-247.

MacWhinney, B., & Leinbach, J. (1991). Implementations are not conceptualizations: Revising the verb learning model. *Cognition, 40*, 121-157.

Marcus, G. F. (1992, April 10-12). *Regularity and irregularity in German plural formation.* Paper presented at the 21st Annual University of Wisconsin-Milwaukee Linguistics Symposium.

Marcus, G. F., & Brinkmann, U., Clahsen, H., Wiese, R., Woest, A., & Pinker, S. (1993). *German inflection: The exception that proves the rule. MIT Center for Cognitive Science Occasional Paper #47.*

Marcus, G. F., Pinker, S., Ullman, M., Hollander, M., Rosen, T. J., & Xu, F. (1992). Overregularization in language acquisition. *Monographs of the Society for Research in Child Development, 57 (228).*

Marin, O., Saffran, E. M., & Schwartz, M. F. (1976). Dissociations of language in aphasia: Implications for normal function. In S. R. Harnad, H. S. Steklis, & J. Lancaster (Eds.), *Origin and evolution of language and speech. Annals of the New York Academy of Sciences, 280*, 868-884.

Mencken, H. (1936). *The American language.* New York: Knopf.

Miller, G. A. (1965). Some preliminaries to psycholinguistics. *American Psychologist, 20*, 15-20.

Miller, G. A. (1967). The psycholinguists. In G. A. Miller (Ed.), *The psychology of communication (pp. 70-92).* London: Penguin Books.

Miller, G. A., & Chomsky, N. (1963). Finitary models of language users. In R. D. Luce, R. Bush, & E. Galanter (Eds.), *Handbook of mathematical psychology* (Vol. 2, pp. 419-491). New York: Wiley.

Miller, G. A., Galanter, E., & Pribram, K. H. (1960). *Plans and the structure of behavior.* New York: Holt, Rinehart, and Winston.

Pinker, S. (1991). Rules of language. *Science, 253*, 530-535.

Pinker, S., & Prince, A. (1988). On language and connectionism: Analysis of a Parallel distributed processing model of language acquisition. *Cognition, 28*, 73-193.

Pinker, S., & Prince, A. (1991). Regular and irregular morphology and the psychological status of rules of grammar. *Proceedings of the 17th Annual Meeting of the Berkeley Linguistics Society (pp. 230-251).* Berkeley, CA: Berkeley Linguistics Society.

Plunkett, K., & Marchman, V. (1991). U-shaped learning and frequency effects in a multi-layered perceptron: Implications for child language acquisition. *Cognition, 38*, 43-102.

Prasada, S., & Pinker, S. (1993). Generalizations of regular and irregular morphology. *Language and Cognitive Processes, 8*, 1-56.

Prasada, S., Pinker, S., & Snyder, W. (1990, November 23-25). *Some evidence that irregular forms are retrieved from memory but regular forms are rule-generated.* Paper presented to the Annual Meeting of the Psychonomic Society, New Orleans.

Rumelhart, D.E., & McClelland, J.L. (1986). On learning the past tenses of English verbs. In J. L. McClelland & D. E. Rumelhart (Eds.), *Parallel distributed processing* (Vol. 2, pp. 216-271). Cambridge, MA: MIT Press.

Rumelhart, D. E., & McClelland, J. L. (1987). Learning the past tenses of English verbs: Implicit rules or parallel distributed processing? In B. MacWhinney (Ed.), *Mechanisms of language acquisition.* Hillsdale, NJ: Lawrence Erlbaum Associates.

Sampson, G. (1987, June 12). A turning point in linguistics. *Times Literary Supplement*, p. 643.

Seidenberg, M., & Bruck, M. (1990, November 23-25). *Consistency effects in the generation of past tense morphology.* Paper presented to the Annual Meeting of the Psychonomic Society, New Orleans.

Senghas, A., Kim, J. J., Pinker, S., & Collins, C., (1991, October 18-20). *Plurals-inside-compounds: Morphological constraints and their implications for acquisition*. Paper presented at the Sixteenth Annual Boston University Conference on Language Development, Boston.

Sproat, R. (1992). *Morphology and computation*. Cambridge, MA: MIT Press.

Stanners, R. F., Neiser, J. J., Hernon, W. P., & Hall, R. (1979). Memory representation for morphologically related words. *Journal of Verbal Learning and Verbal Behavior, 18,* 399-441.

Tallal, P., Ross, R., & Curtiss, S. (1989). Familial aggregation in Specific Language Impairment. *Journal of Speech and Hearing Disorders, 54,* 167-173.

Tomblin, J. B. (1989). Familial concentration of language impairment. *Journal of Speech and Hearing Disorders, 54,* 287-295.

Ullman, M., Hickok, G., & Pinker, S. (1992, May 20-22). *Irregular and regular morphology in an aphasic*. Paper presented at the Theoretical and Experimental Neuropsychology/ Neuropsychologie Experimentale et Theoreticale (TENNET) Conference, University of Quebec at Montreal.

Ullman, M., & Pinker, S. (1991, March 26-28). *Connectionism versus symbolic rules in language: A case study*. Paper presented at the Spring Symposium Series of the American Association for Artificial Intelligence, Stanford.

Xu, F., & Pinker, S. (1993). *Weird past tense forms*. Unpublished manuscript, Department of Brain and Cognitive Sciences, MIT, Cambridge, MA.

5 The Social in Cognition

Edward E. Jones
Princeton University

A number of historians who have tried to characterize the past 25 years in American psychology have referred to the cognitive revolution. Indeed, George Miller deserves a major amount of credit for helping to wean mainstream psychology away from rat mazes, pigeon boxes, and hours of deprivation. Yet to the social psychologist, the idea of a "cognitive revolution" can inspire an ironic chuckle. As my good friend Bob Zajonc (1980b) claimed a decade ago, social psychology has always been cognitive. Indeed, how could it be otherwise? If we define social psychology in terms of responses to a social environment—that is, an environment of people in action and of the symbolic products of their action—it is impossible to avoid the basic assumption of "subjectivism." We deal in social situations, and the only meaningful way to describe a social situation is to try to get a handle on how that situation is perceived and interpreted by the actors in it.

The origins of this recognition, of the recognition that a social psychology must be grounded in social perception and social cognition, are numerous and diverse. Some 65 years ago, Thomas and Thomas (1928) introduced the term *definition of the situation* arguing that "if men define situations as real, they are real in their consequences" (p. 572). For psychologists in general and for social psychologists in particular, Bartlett provides a more recent starting point. His 1932 book *Remembering* is certainly a major precursor of contemporary cognitive psychology. It specifically set the stage for studies of the role of motivation and expectancy in perception, celebrated in the so-called "new look" of the Bruner and Postman experimental program immediately after World War II. Although Bartlett's claim that people interpret complex verbal material in terms of experienced-based schemata would hardly have surprised the even earlier students of the psychology of testimony or rumor, Bartlett nevertheless brought such considerations into the mainstream of psychological research and provided a number of useful descriptive labels for summarizing common tendencies for assimilation to a preestablished cognitive framework.

Bruner and his colleagues (e.g., Bruner, 1951) added explicit motivational and psychodynamic factors to the mix, at the same time emphasizing the idea that we can be affected by situations without being aware of how they are affecting us. Then we come to those giants who had such an enormous impact on the evolution of social psychology: Lewin and Heider. It is important to note that although both recognized the great value of phenomenal reports by others, each was careful to permit a vague and unspecified arena of situational influence lying outside phenomenal awareness. For Lewin (e.g., 1951), the lifespace or the psychological field was completely deterministic, but not all elements of the lifespace were contained in the phenomenal awareness of the individual. Similarly, Heider's (1958) analysis of naive psychology was viewed as an important tool of method, but he also wanted to leave room for influences outside the phenomenal awareness of the person. Heider's approach really involved a kind of semantic psycholinguistics: He sought wisdom in the accepted meanings of, and the relations between, a limited number of everyday concepts such as desire, ability, effort, envy, dislike, own, benefit, or owe.

Lewin, as all good psychologists are supposed to know, contrasted the Aristotelian and Galilean approaches to scientific understanding. The Aristotelian approach led in the direction of trait psychology and those formulations in the field of personality emphasizing past experience and correlation approaches to interpretive factors or clusters. Lewin didn't look kindly on efforts in that direction. The Galilean approach that Lewin favored has clearly won out in the social psychological mainstream. His focus on the "lifespace" — essentially a psychological environment full of valences and pressures and opportunities and boundaries — and his metatheory depicting a field of psychological forces, set the stage for an experimental approach, and thus the controlling aspects of situational contexts became focal mediating research constructs.

The experimental game to be played — the game that was made implicit by Lewin and made more explicit by his student Festinger — involves the imaginative construction of situations that have roughly the same significance — the same meaning with reference to their goals or concerns or motives — for a chosen sample of subjects (who usually happen to be, for matters of convenience, college students). It is not easy to characterize exactly how this game is played in some simple string of sentences, but as experimental social psychology has evolved, one central research theme has been the discovery of subtle and important situational influences that occur outside the awareness of our subjects. Indeed, if people were more routinely aware of the situational influences that affect their behavior, social psychology would be a less important, or at least a very different, discipline. The "induced compliance" paradigm in cognitive dissonance research (e.g., Festinger & Carlsmith, 1959), Milgram's (1974) obedience research, studies of the nonintervening bystander (Latane & Darley, 1970), just to cite a few famous and familiar examples, seem to require that subjects share a certain profound innocence concerning the constraining structure of the situation.

Psychology's cognitive revolution has its counterpart in a more modest minirevolution within social psychology celebrated under such labels as social cognition or information processing. Some very bright and industrious people are attempting to push beyond the earlier notions of attribution theory to characterize the ways in which socially relevant information is selected, encoded, stored, structured, and retrieved. I admire many of these sophisticated efforts, efforts that can involve very elaborate flow charts and that generate research contributing to our understanding of how things are remembered and retrieved. Nevertheless, these approaches have yet to convince me that they indeed can handle what is truly social about social cognition. So, in spite of the recent upsurge in information-processing approaches within social cognition, much of social psychological research and theorizing remains strongly flavored by the phenomenal causality approach of naive psychology.

In other words, there is still plenty of mileage to be gained by trying to capture the naive psychology of causal attribution based on the assumption that if we can characterize the ways in which people perceive causes and effects in their everyday environment, we can understand why they behave the way they do. This is not at all incompatible with an information-processing approach, but it does tend to focus more on situational inputs and interpretive response outputs than on the delineation of intervening cognitive transformations. Gilbert (1989, p. 191) put it rather dramatically: "None [of the attribution theories] . . . specifies what actually happens when an attribution is made—which chutes open, which bells go 'ding,' which lights wink on and off."

But, there is a paradox lurking. If we join Lewin, Heider, and many others in realizing that naive psychology is not to be equated with phenomenal awareness, then how much does it help to know how people think the environment is organized in cause-and-effect terms? Well, of course, the naive psychology of causal attribution does carry us a long way—there is considerable overlap between how we perceive the environment and how it is in fact "structured for our use." However, where can we fit the realization that our dearly beloved field of experimental social psychology thrives on just those patterns of situational influence of which the individual remains unaware?

A further dose of some recent history may be useful at this point. The attributional approaches promoted by Heider (1958), Kelley (1967), and myself (Jones & Davis, 1965) were originally attempts to characterize the ways in which people actually think about and respond to the ongoing social situation. In a very broad and rather crude sense the theories were quite successful in enabling the prediction of large classes of behavior. They appeared to capture a sizable chunk of common sense. However, as the attributional approach held sway during much of the 1970s and the 1980s, it was the failures of prediction that became more intriguing. What started out to be deductive theories often became normative baselines against which the "irrationality" of individual actors could be identified. The most prominent example of a predictive failure involves the robust tendency toward dispositionalism—a tendency that seems to push away from the appropriate recognition of situational determinants of another's behavior toward a clearly biased emphasis on individual differences. If perceivers see a person acting completely in line with situational constraints, in a way that even they realize could be entirely determined by those constraints, they nevertheless are inclined to make a dispositional attribution and to assume that some individual propensity contributed to the individual's actions. This has been variously called the "fundamental attribution error" (Ross, 1977) and "correspondence bias" (Jones, 1990b), the latter term referring to the fact that we tend to see behavior tends to be seen as corresponding to a disposition while tending to underplay the role of situational influences.

So it can be said that attribution theories were partly true, and when they weren't true they should have been true. When our theories failed to predict, we could say, "Ah ha! This is a normative baseline and isn't it intriguing that people don't respond the way they logically should." So we attributionists in a sense had our cake and could eat it too. As the attribution literature began to expand in the 1970s, the identification of various attributional biases began to merge with substantial evidence of decision-making heuristics that often resulted in logical or arithmetic errors of judgment. Nisbett and Ross (1980), much influenced by the work of heuristics of Tversky and Kahneman (1974), captured many of these vagaries of human inference in an important book about 10 years ago.

More recently, the interests of social psychologists in those areas of behavioral influence that lie outside of awareness have begun to focus on phenomena that are strongly reminiscent of the distinction between automatic and controlled processing. They also seem to remind us that "subliminal perception" is alive and healthier than ever. The following are a few examples of how this distinction seems to be affecting contemporary social psychology.

Personal/Cultural Theories, Stereotypes, and Unconscious Ideologies

Some 15 years ago the work of Nisbett and Wilson (1977) attempted to make clear the role of implicit personal and cultural theories in the interpretation of behavior. They provided a number of intriguing demonstrations of the different contexts in which people are influenced by subtle environmental arrangements while remaining unaware that these demonstrable influences were in fact present. Just to pick one simple example, women faced with four identical sets of panty hose arranged on a table in front of them had a strong tendency to evaluate the right-hand set as the most attractive. When asked whether their ratings were affected by the positions of the panty hose, virtually all subjects denied such influence and were often annoyed with the researcher for even suggesting such a factor.

More recently, there has been considerable interest and concern with the role of unconscious ideologies and of the influence of stereotypes, again operating below or outside the level of awareness. It is fairly easy to generate anecdotal evidence regarding the operation of unconscious ideologies — for example, assumptions about gender differences or race differences. The following is a now familiar puzzle:

> A father and his son were driving to a ball game when their car stalled on the railroad tracks. In the distance a train whistle blew a warning. Frantically, the father tried to start the engine, but in his panic, he couldn't turn the key, and the car was hit by the onrushing train. An ambulance sped to the scene and picked them up. On the way to the hospital, the father died. The son was still alive, but his condition was very serious and he needed immediate surgery. The moment they arrived at the hospital, he was wheeled into an emergency operating room, and the surgeon came in, expecting a routine case. However, on seeing the boy, the surgeon blanched and muttered, "I can't operate on this boy — he's my son."

Of course, in this enlightened age most of us catch on quickly that the surgeon is the boy's mother, but a decade or so ago, this case proved to be a puzzling riddle even for presumably liberated academics. The general point thus remains an important one, even though underlying stereotypes and ideologies can clearly change in content and accessibility.

Some recent research by Devine (1989) even suggests that nonprejudiced people are quite aware of the stereotypes underlying racism and in fact are influenced by racist ideology in important if subtle ways — even though they would vigorously deny the validity of the ideology and would score low on any prejudice scale.

After establishing that both high- and low-prejudiced subjects (as identified by a scale measuring "implicit racism") were equally aware of a stereotype concerning Black Americans, Devine exposed both highs and lows to a subliminal version of the stereotype. Specifically, subjects were asked to identify the quadrant of a tachistoscope on which a stimulus appeared over a series of trials. Each "stimulus" was in fact a word. In one condition, 80% of the words were taken from the Black American stereotype. Examples were: Blacks, negroes, poor, lazy, athletic, musical, busing, and oppressed. In another condition, only 20% of the words were derived from this stereotype. Subsequent memory probes made it clear that those words were in fact presented below the level of reportable awareness.

This procedure was followed by a "second experiment" in which the same subjects were asked to form an impression of Donald, a well-traveled target person in other experiments on priming, who was briefly described in "ambiguously hostile" terms. For example, one sentence described him as demanding money back from the clerk immediately after his purchase. Another noted that he refused to pay rent until his apartment was painted.

In conveying their impression of Donald, subjects in the 80% condition tended to rate him as more "hostile," "dislikeable," and "unfriendly," than subjects in the 20% condition. Whether the raters were high or low in prejudice made no difference. Thus, when subjects were primed below the level of awareness with many features of the Black American stereotype, even nonprejudiced subjects were inclined to see the innocent Donald in very negative terms.

In a further study, when asked to list their conscious associations to the category *Black Americans*, high- and low-prejudiced subjects behaved very differently. High-prejudiced subjects were quite willing to generate a number of negative traits; low-prejudiced subjects were much more inclined toward positive labels and corrective beliefs.

Thus, Devine seemed to show that people are affected by their knowledge of stereotyped content, even when they disagree with the validity of the stereotype. This is a little scary (and it deserves to be replicated). It points to the discrepant functioning of automatic and controlled processing in a crucial area of social judgment.

Peripheral Models of Attitude Change

In the area of attitude-change theory and research, the elaboration likelihood model of Petty and Cacioppo (1986) is an explicit recognition that attitude change can occur in two contexts or perhaps on two levels. One context involves explicit awareness and the rational consideration of relevant information; the other context involves symbols such as the good looks or the irrelevant fame of the communicator that primes and triggers reactions outside of the level of awareness. An example in one textbook (Worchel, Cooper, & Goethals, 1989) is that of the commercial in which Robert Young, who played Marcus Welby on television, advises people to drink decaffeinated coffee, saying explicitly, "I'm not a doctor, but I play one on TV." If anyone was influenced to switch to the advertised brand of coffee, they would be hard-put to provide a rational explanation for this behavior.

Dual Theories of Attribution

A number of intriguing dual theories of attribution have recently emerged that essentially distinguish between the identification of perceived behavior in attribution-relevant terms and the subsequent cranking up of the attribution process itself. For example, McArthur and Baron (1983) borrowed heavily from Gibson's (1979) emphasis on the analysis of stimulus structures to argue that much of the information contained in the social environment is also prestructured to convey immediately the stable meaning of events. There is a strong evolutionary flavor to their reasoning as they suggest that certain kinds of information are critically important in a given ecological niche. Because it is so adaptive to differentiate male from female and friend from foe in the social environment (just as animals need to distinguish prey from predator), such information comes to us in prestructured forms as a consequence of its adaptive importance over a long sequence of generations.

Trope (1986) made a more explicit distinction between the identification and cognitive labeling of an observed action event — and the causal attribution of why it is occurring and what underlying motive or disposition it may represent. People label an overture as "friendly" through an immediate, automatic act of identification. Then, perhaps, they tackle the problem of deciding whether this is a real friendly guy or just a dedicated used-car salesman. Neither the individual nor the psychologist looking at the individual can clearly explain exactly why this automatic identification process occurs.

Along these same lines, one can hardly help but be intrigued by the research of Johansson (1973) and his colleagues who showed how perceivers can identify males and females, dancers and walkers, and other patterns of mundane motor activity, from extremely limited information conveyed by pin-points of light attached to target persons who are otherwise in complete darkness. This is no calculated inference; it is an immediate apprehension.

The Role of Priming in "Unintended Thought"

Social cognition has been much affected by the legacy of procedures from cognitive science. Therefore, it is not surprising that the varied and diverse operations of cognitive priming have reached into and had effects on social psychology. A recent volume by Uleman and Bargh (1989) entitled *Unintended Thought* summarized many of these priming studies—studies showing the automatic or unwitting influence of exposure to information in the recent past that helps to frame interpretation of events in the present. Earlier work of Higgins (Higgins, Rholes, & Jones, 1977) and more recent work of Bargh (1982, 1989) warned that impressions of a new acquaintance at one moment in time may be heavily influenced by supposedly unrelated recent experiences—experiences that make certain interpretations about the acquaintance more accessible than others. There are many other intriguing chapters in this volume that provide a helpful summary of the amount of work that's going on in the area of automatic thought processes. These include, for example, chapters on the role of affect, the consequences of attempting not to think of something, implications of reduced or strained cognitive resources for social inferences, and the evidence for spontaneous trait inferences.

Bargh (1989) raised the interesting question of whether people must simply give in and be passive victims of these automatic processes and comes up with an interesting metaphor: "that of the ambitious royal advisor upon whom a relatively weak king relies heavily for wisdom and guidance. The actual power of decision always rests with the king, who by no means has to follow the preferred advice; yet the counselor who 'has the king's ear' wields the real power over decisions and the policy of the kingdom" (p. 40). I'm not sure whether this is better than Freud's metaphor of the Id and the Ego, but I present it as a possible contemporary alternative.

Mental Control and the Return of the Suppressed

In a recent paper on the social foundations of mental control, Wegner and Erber (1992) discussed some of the many instances in which private thoughts diverge from their public expression. The linkage between behavioral control and thought control is fascinating and problematic. Usually, there are felt pressures on the individual to bring his or her thoughts in line with behavior—to make the behavior more "authentic"—so people try to concentrate on thoughts that support socially appropriate actions and suppress thoughts and emotions that undermine such actions. Unfortunately, Wegner's research on thought suppression indicates how difficult it is not to think about something—as in "don't think about a white bear," or "try not think about sex." One of Wegner and Erber's main conclusions is that in trying to suppress thoughts in the interests of social accommodation or the avoidance of depressed mood, people tend to become obsessed with the very thoughts they are trying to suppress.

Without disputing this tendency of voluntarily suppressed thoughts to rebound or resurface, our own research (Jones, 1990a) does point to some subtle conditions under which uncharacteristic actions — such as responding in a very self-deprecating manner in an interview — can carry over at least temporarily to a depressed private view of the self. This occurs when the interviewee is cajoled (subtly induced rather than required) to present himself or herself unfavorably, suggesting the operation of cognitive-dissonance reduction processes at work once again.

Cognitive and Behavioral Features of the "Self-Fulfilling Prophecy" in Social Interaction

Finally, to return to the more purely social, there is the so-called "self-fulfilling prophecy" in social interaction. This effect occurs when a perceiver's expectancy or a hypothesis about another person leads to actions by the perceiver that elicit confirmatory actions in the target person. If I wanted to mention one single feature that helps to distinguish the social psychological approach from "mainstream" cognitive science, I would mention the extent to which people participate in producing or creating their own social reality — not just by imagining or perceptually distorting it in some congenial way, but by adding their own behavior to everything else that is going on. A moment's thought makes clear that, in the real world, people provide part of the stimulus environment to which others are responding. They can, thus, produce very different environments in a family gathering or a faculty meeting by responding pessimistically or optimistically, by acting aggressively or passively, by being gauche or tactful, or by smiling or frowning.

Much of our own recent research indicated that people are terrible at dealing with the implications of their own contributions to the social environment (e.g., Gilbert and Jones.) Each should, as lay students of human behavior, show some signs of discounting the diagnostic significance of reactions to their own constraining remarks or actions. Our data emphasize that people are dispositionalists even here — that they tend to take at face value, and make dispositional attributions to account for, actions of others that they have clearly brought about by their own influence.

The following is a striking experimental example of the perceiver's failure to discount his or her own constraining influence, as described by Jones (1986, p. 234):

In a simulated interview situation, 26 Princeton undergraduate subjects believed that their roles as interviewers were to signal interviewees to read answers to questions concerning social or political issues. On each of several trials, the subject, in an isolation booth, asked a question and then pressed a button to signal for either a liberal or a conservative response. It was made clear to the interviewer that the statements on each issue had been previously prepared for the experiment and that the interviewee was merely complying with instructions in reading them verbatim. The results showed a strong tendency toward correspondence bias: even though the perceivers were obviously aware that they had induced the responses they heard, they tended to attribute to the interviewee attitudes consistent with the opinions expressed. On a 15-point scale anchored at the end points by the phrases "extremely liberal" and "extremely conservative," 10 out of 13 subjects faced with a predominantly conservative responder rated him on the conservative side, whereas the predominantly liberal responder was rated on the liberal side by 10 out of 13 subjects in that condition. Thus the subjects, who could and logically should have distributed their responses around the midpoint, gave ratings systematically biased in the direction of the responses they had induced and heard.

Gilbert, a collaborator in the experiment, has gone on to document the importance of attentional allocation in such failures to discount situational requirements. In a series of studies (Gilbert, 1989), he showed that people are particularly prone to attribute constrained behavior to a personal disposition of the actor when operating under "cognitive load." Subjects who must keep strings of digits in mind, or who must anticipate their own impending action, or who must exert mental control over their negative feelings — such "cognitive loaded" subjects — do an especially poor job of discounting the influences of strong situational pressures when evaluating a highly constrained role player performing on video- or audiotape. Gilbert (1991) cited this as an instance of a broad and fundamental cognitive tendency to believe-as-we-encode, prior to a subsequent stage of certification (acceptance), rejection, or skeptical adjustment — which can be, and often is insufficient, in any event. When this subsequent, more inferential stage is disrupted by cognitive load, perceived action is taken at face value and attributed to a correspondent disposition. Thus, Gilbert has become a shameless Spinozan while rejecting the Cartesian view that perception and evaluation are totally separate processes.

The failure to recognize one's own constraining influence is essential to the role of "behavior confirmation" in the self-fulfilling prophecy. If I very tentatively expect a male acquaintance to be especially friendly, for example, I will probably approach that person with a smile and nonverbal warmth cues that follow from my expectancy. Even if the other fellow does not really have a characteristically friendly disposition, he may — indeed he probably will — respond with the friendliness initially expected. The problem arises when I take his response as independent verification of my tentative expectancy, so that behavioral confirmation now locks in the erroneous impression. If I were wise enough to say to myself, "well, he seems like a friendly person, but he's probably just responding to my friendly overture," the expectancy of friendliness would at least not receive the strong added impetus conferred by behavior that unequivocally confirms the expectancy.

Where does all this seem to be leading? Probably more than in any other domain of psychology, social psychologists have been intrigued more by the mysteries of mental functioning than by attempts to characterize what happens in a systematic or rigorous way. To understand why this is so, one has to understand the socialization of social psychologists. We all have to cope with the fact that everyone is a social psychologist, or thinks he is (a fact noted by Krech and Crutchfield as long ago as 1948). Each of us has his or her own theory of social events and of individual behavior and personality. When a social psychologist reports a research conclusion, two common reactions are: "Of course, that's so obvious! Why would anybody want to waste his good time studying something we already know," or alternatively, "That's ridiculous, you couldn't possibly be right. Cherchez le fluke or le artifact." Most of us would rather hear the latter than the former. We are deathly afraid of being accused of "bubba psychology"— the psychology of what one's grandmother knew—and most are therefore pushed perhaps unduly toward a seeming preoccupation with errors, biases, failures to predict, and so on—the little and not-so-little pathologies of everyday life.

A more benign way of putting it is that we social psychologists are pushed in the direction of intriguing mysteries. It is almost as if we are more interested in deepening the mystery than reducing it. The information-processing approach mentioned briefly in the beginning of this chapter may lead us out of the wilderness, perhaps with the aid of computer stimulation models, but thus far this approach is saddled (and tethered) with the charge that the procedures pay too heavy a price of foregoing social relevance in order to obtain methodological rigor.

I should not, of course, imply that social psychology can be equated with social cognition. Yet certainly the more that we can learned about social cognition, the better off we shall be in trying to understand such things as close relationships or interdependence, mixed motive negotiations, attitude change and social conformity, and so on. I share with the social cognition students a basic interest in the perception of persons, an interest I have pursued in various ways for 40 years. It does seem to me that if we can understand how persons are perceived, then many of the other problems of social psychology would fall into place. This, at least, is the justifying premise of my recent book, *Interpersonal Perception* (1990b). I would like to think that our own work featuring the perceiver as an actor, as part of the ongoing social situation, is an attempt to move beyond those sterile social cognition approaches—approaches that feature word lists and scenarios— in order to capture the early stages of relationship development. Once again, I am particularly intrigued by the distinctive feature of social psychology, namely, that people create their own social reality. The behavior of others cannot be conveniently separated from whatever is done to elicit it.

After rambling over this rocky terrain, I now focus more specifically on the topic that I accepted as my particular assignment—namely, how the mind is treated in social psychology. I have, of course, implicitly been talking about this, but perhaps a few summarizing statements are in order:

1. *Level of Abstraction: Staying Close to Phenomenal Experience.* Most social psychologists resist the kinds of fine-grain analyses that lend themselves readily to physiologizing or to computer simulation. Most of us have lived with a felt necessity for such molar concepts as categories, expectancies, goals, inferences, reasons—in short, terms borrowed from the naive vocabularly of persons who are asked to explain themselves, to explain their actions, their beliefs, or their preferences. Most of us take for granted that psychologists, like real people, can account for sizable proportions of human behavior by such an appeal to naive psychology and the phenomenal experience of others.

2. *Capitalizing on Information-Processing Errors.* The mind doesn't always work the way grandma thought. Just as perception psychologists have learned much through the analysis of illusions and perceptual breakdowns, social psychologists have studied and been intrigued by instances in which mental processes get derailed and generate socially consequential errors and gaffes. Once more, though the derailments are systematic and predictable, they are not always well understood. In many cases one is stuck with a kind of functionalism. Thus, heuristic biases such as availability and representativeness are explained as the misapplications of normally useful and efficient (energy-saving) information-processing tactics.

3. *Automaticity and Primitive Constructs.* Beyond the reaches of phenomenal causality analysis are the many routine instances of social perception or "identification" that almost seem hardwired. Functional explanations, in this case, are often joined with notions of experiential repetition as well as evolutionary presumptions. There are those who want to build more and more functional wiring into the human propensity to navigate successfully in the social environment. How does the perceiver know that Johansson's revolving lights represent a woman and not a man walking? How do perceivers process anger and friendliness before trying to interpret the behavior in some explanatory context? Or how, in Zajonc's (1980a) terms, are people wired to evaluate and emote before they fully cognize?

4. *Serving as the Conscience of the Field.* Social psychologists have continually forced perception psychologists and cognitive psychologists to take account of context. To many laborers in the cognitive science vineyard this is just an annoying and burdensome source of inexplicable complexity.

To us it is the essential ingredient of a true understanding of mental processing and we are sustained by the challenge of social, temporal, and personal expectancy contexts as they affect cognitive interpretations of the social reality in which all of us live.

REFERENCES

Bargh, J. A. (1982). Attention and automaticity in the processing of self-relevant information. *Journal of Personality and Social Psychology*, *43*, 425–436.

Bargh, J. A. (1989). Conditional automaticity: Varieties of automatic influence in social perception and cognition. In J. S. Uleman & J. A. Bargh (Eds.), *Unintended thought (pp. 3–51). New York: Guilford.*

Bartlett, F. C. (1932). *Remembering*. Cambridge: Cambridge University Press.

Bruner, J. S. (1951). Personality dynamics and the process of perceiving. In R.R. Blake & G. B. Ramsey (Eds.), *Perception: An approach to personality (pp. 121–147). New York: Ronald Press.*

Devine, P. G. (1989). Stereotypes and prejudice: Their automatic and controlled components. *Journal of Personality and Social Psychology*, *56*, 5–18.

Festinger, L., & Carlsmith, J. M. (1959). Cognitive consequences of forced compliance. *Journal of Abnormal and Social Psychology*, *58*, 203–211.

Gibson, J. J. (1979). *The ecological approach to visual perception*. Boston: Houghton Mifflin.

Gilbert, D. T. (1989). Thinking lightly about others: Automatic components of the social inference process. In J. S. Uleman & J. A. Bargh (Eds.), *Unintended thought* (pp. 189–211). New York: Guilford.

Gilbert, D. T. (1991). How mental systems believe. *American Psychologist*, *46*, 107–119.

Higgins, E. T., Rholes, W. S., & Jones, C. R. (1977). Category accessibility and impression formation. *Journal of Experimental Social Psychology*, *13*, 141–154.

Heider, F. (1958). *The psychology of interpersonal relations*. New York: Wiley.

Johansson, G. (1973). Visual perception of biological motion and a model for its analysis. *Perception and Psychophysics*, *14*, 201–211.

Jones, E. E. (1986). Interpreting interpersonal behavior: The effects of expectancies. *Science*, *234*, 41–46.

Jones, E. E. (1990a). Constrained behavior and self-concept change. In J. Olson & M. Zanna (Eds.), *Self-inference process*: *The Ontario Symposium*, (Vol. 6, pp. 69–86). Hillsdale, NJ: Lawrence Erlbaum Associates.

Jones, E. E. (1990b). *Interpersonal perception*. New York: Freeman.

Jones, E. E., & Davis, K. E. (1965). From acts to dispositions: The attribution process in person perception. In L. Berkowitz (Ed.), *Advances in experimental social psychology* (Vol. 2, pp. 219–266). New York: Academic Press.

Kelley, H. H. (1967). Attribution theory in social psychology. *Nebraska Symposium on Motivation*, *14*, 192–241.

Krech, D., & Crutchfield, R. S. (1948). *Theory and problems of social psychology*. New York: McGraw-Hill.

Latane, B., & Darley, J. M. (1970). *The unresponsive bystander: Why doesn't he help?* New York: Appleton-Century-Crofts.

Lewin,K. (1951). *Field theory in social science* (D. Cartwright, Ed.). New York: Harper & Bros.

McArthur, L. Z., & Baron, R. M. (1983). Toward an ecological theory of social perception. *Psychological Review*, *90*, 215–238.

Milgram, S. (1974). *Obedience to authority*. New York: Harper and Row.

Nisbett, R. E., & Ross, L. (1980). *Human inference strategies and shortcomings of social judgment*. Englewood Cliffs, NJ: Prentice-Hall.

Nisbett, R.E., & Wilson, T. D. (1977). Telling more than we can know: Verbal reports on mental processes. *Psychological Review, 84,* 231-259.

Petty, R. E., & Cacioppo, J. T. (1986). The elaboration likelihood model of persuasion. In L. Berkowitz (Ed.), *Advances in experimental social psychology* (Vol. 19 pp. 123-205). New York: Academic Press.

Ross, L. (1977). The intuitive psychologist and his shortcomings: Distortions in the attribution process. In L. Berkowitz (Ed.), *Advances in experimental social psychology* (Vol. 10, pp. 174-221). New York: Academic Press.

Thomas, W. I., & Thomas, D. S. (1928). *The child in America: Behavior problems and programs*. New York: Knopf.

Trope, Y. (1986). Identification and inference processes in dispositional attribution. *Psychological Review, 93,* 239-257.

Tversky A., & Kahneman, D. (1974). Judgment under uncertainty: Heuristics and biases. *Science, 185,* 1124-1131.

Uleman, J. S, & J. A. Bargh (Eds.). (1989). *Unintended thought*. New York: Guilford.

Wegner, D. M., & Erber, R. (1992). The hyperaccessibility of suppressed thoughts. *Journal of Personality and Social Psychology, 63,* 903-912.

Worchel, S., Cooper, J. & Goethals, G. R. (1989). *Understanding social psychology* (4th ed.). Pacific Grove, CA: Brooks/Cole.

Zajonc, R. B. (1980a). Cognition and social cognition: A historical perspective. In L. Festinger (Ed.), *Restrospections on social psychology* (pp. 180-204). New York: Oxford.

Zajonc, R. B. (1980b). Feeling and thinking: Preferences need no inferences. *American Psychologist, 35,* 151-175.

6 Rules, Reasoning, and Choice Behavior

Richard E. Nisbett
University of Michigan

I was delighted to be asked to contribute to this volume in honor of George Miller. And I was very pleased about the theme of it too—the notion of having people from a wide range of disciplines discuss how they think the mind works. I'm sure that to most psychologists today that's the most natural kind of topic imaginable for a psychology volume, but one of Miller's biggest contributions is that he made it seem so natural that this is the question that psychologists ought to be asking. When I was an undergraduate, that wasn't the question that psychologists thought they should be asking at all. It would have been considered eccentric and soft-headed to be asking, "How does the mind work?" The topic you were supposed to be studying was "What makes people—or rather organisms—behave as they do?" Behavior was supposed to be explained with reference to what came after it, namely, reinforcement, an external event. If absolutely necessary, one could resort to explaining behavior by what came before, namely, a stimulus. One was not supposed to be concerned with what the organism, let alone its mind, was doing in between.

Now, as a fledgling social psychologist, I always knew this couldn't be right. As Abelson pointed out, social psychology is the only branch of psychology that could never be behaviorized. This is because it's just so obvious that what guides social behavior is people's cognitions about the social world. Nevertheless, behaviorism influenced social psychologists in many ways. My imagery of life as a social psychologist in those days was that it was like being on a beach, and you were the 98-pound weakling. A behaviorist bully could come along at any moment and kick sand in your face. Then you'd brush it off and creep away to your cabana. The

99

intimidation had two different kinds of insidious effects. Some social psychologists actually went so far as to try to show that their work really could be understood in terms of learning theory. This was sort of like the Soviet Union in the bad old days when one had to start an article by showing how a proper reading of Marx made it clear that the theory about to be presented was politically correct. Although more often it took the form of spending a great deal of time and emotional energy explaining why it was that the learning theorists couldn't explain the phenomenon. Anybody over a certain age has wasted a lot of time in those kinds of exercises.

For me, the point when I didn't have to do that anymore came after reading the text called *Psychology: The Science of Mental Life* (1962), by George Miller. The title at the time was audacious, and I sort of waited for them to get him. But they didn't get him! And that changed my life. I realized one could get away with things that I had never dreamed of. Shortly after that I encountered the seminal papers on attribution theory by Jones and Davis (1965) and by Kelley (1967), and it was clear to me that I was going to spend the next period of my life (25 years to this point, as it's turned out) working on issues of reasoning about social behavior in the context of the kind of framework that the Miller book presented.

The work I describe is in that tradition of cognitive social psychology. For the last few years, I've been looking at three questions. First, do reasoning and choice make use of abstract rules? By that term I mean rules of the kind that can never be imagined by a traditional behaviorist, who is required to assume that particular responses are called forth by particular stimuli. These include rules at the level of formal logic, causal relations at the deep level of necessity and sufficiency, mathematical notions like the law of large numbers, and what I discuss in most detail, the microeconomic rules of choice. Do such rules actually inform reasoning and choice in everyday life, such as a decision as to where to have lunch or a judgment as to whether Joe is a nice guy? Secondly, I ask whether, if there are abstract rules, it is possible to change them. If they can be changed, do they have to be changed by the behaviorist's mechanism of reinforcement, in which the rule is altered only if some other rule seems to be doing a better job? Or, instead, can rules be altered more easily, by simple insertion at the top, with subsequent alteration of specific inferences by a kind of trickle-down epistemology? Third, supposing the answer to the first two questions is yes, that is, people do use abstract rules to reason about the world, and the rules can be changed easily with insertion, is it a good idea to change the rules people use? Should we do it? Is there any reason to assume that scientists and scholars have any business altering the rules that people have spent the last 3 million years of evolution developing?

Interestingly enough, prior to the 20th century the answer to all three of these questions was yes. The questions weren't even much debated until this century. Yes, there are abstract rules for reasoning and choice. Yes, they can be inserted. (The process is called education.) And yes, it's a good idea to do so. This is essentially the outline of Plato's original formulation, now called formal discipline. Plato felt that you could improve people's reasoning by teaching them arithmetic, and the Romans added logic and grammar to the list of useful formal rules. The medieval scholastics added the syllogism, and then those rules, together with literature and history, essentially set the curriculum for western education until the end of the 19th century when the Germans began to introduce modern language and science as a part of the higher education curriculum.

An attack on this cognitivist pedagogy was one of the chief activities of the behaviorists early in the century. They argued that people didn't have abstract rules and derided the notion that they could be made to have them by instruction. Even William James, no behaviorist himself, was a leader in criticizing the notion that there could be transfer effects across different kinds of mental activity ("exercising the muscles of the mind"). The question of whether it would be a good idea for people to have such rules was of course moot, given the impossibility of the thing.

Now, by the time I came to study reasoning, I had long since given up most of the behaviorist ideology I might have unwittingly picked up, but like most psychologists, I wasn't really prepared to believe that people used abstract rules at the level of logical and mathematical rules. So I was quite surprised at what was found. The first work I did was on social reasoning, starting with a problem I had mulled over for many years—the correspondence bias or fundamental attribution error (Jones & Davis, 1965; Nisbett & Ross, 1980; Ross, 1977). This involves a tendency to assume that the actor has a trait that corresponds to behavior that's been witnessed. One way of understanding the correspondence bias is to regard it as a failure of statistical reasoning. Behavior is more variable than we realize it is; that is, everyone's behavior, along almost any dimension one cares to name, is more variable than we tend to assume. So there's a kind of statistical failing in making the error. The variability that characterizes each individual forbids the correspondent inference. When we see a single behavior and make a correspondent inference on the basis of it, we're violating the law of large numbers, because we ought to have a larger sample than that before we assume that we know the "population value."

In work with Krantz, Fong, and Kunda, I began to look at these aspects of statistical reasoning and how readily they can be changed (Fong, Krantz, & Nisbett, 1986; Nisbett, Krantz, Jepson, & Kunda, 1983). We found that one can change people's reasoning dramatically by higher education in statistics. Our best example of this is a problem in which we (Fong et al., 1986) told subjects that there was a woman who was a manufacturer's representative. She loved her work, which took her all over the country. The only problem was that she had to eat out a lot, and because she was something of a gourmet, this was a bit of a burden to her. Whenever she went to a restaurant where she got an excellent meal, she went back as often as possible while she was in that town. But she was usually disappointed. Subsequent meals were rarely as good as the first. Why do you suppose this is? If you pose this question to an undergraduate who's never had a statistics course, you will almost never get a statistical answer, reflecting anything about the partially random nature of the events in question. They'll say, "Well, maybe the chefs change a lot," or "Maybe her expectations get so high that subsequent meals just can't live up to them." A single statistics course results in about 20% of the subjects giving a statistical answer — usually not a very good one, but at least one that's informed by statistical notions. They may say, "Well, maybe it's just by chance she got such a good meal the first time," which is right as far as it goes. If you ask this question of graduate students — first-year graduate students at the University of Michigan, most of whom have had a couple of courses in statistics — about 60% will give you a statistical answer. They often incorporate much better rationales. For instance, "Well, there are probably more restaurants where you can get an excellent meal some of the time than all of the time. And if that's true, odds are that she's gone to that first kind of restaurant, so there's no place to go but down." This is a very good qualitative analysis of the problem, and of course it's statistical. Finally, we gave this problem to the PhD-level staff at Bell Labs, 85% of whom gave a statistical answer (usually with graphs and formulas).

Of course, there's a confound in this demonstration, because these are self-selected populations. So we started laboratory studies in which we discovered two facts. First, there does seem to be such a thing as defining the law of large numbers as an abstract rule and inserting it at a very high level so that it operates for potentially any kind of problem that deals with uncertainty. In our abstract rule conditions, the rule was defined qualitatively for subjects, saying essentially that the rule just means that more evidence is better than less evidence, and that's particularly important when there is lot of variability in the population. The concepts of *population*, *sample*, *parameter*, and *variability* were all defined for them, as well as the qualitative relations among them. Then we gave subjects problems involving subjective judgments such as the manufacturer's representative one, as well as problems about more objectively codable events such as sports problems, and problems about randomizing devices, for which most people would be inclined to give a statistical answer even in the absence of training. The consequence of training is that more and better statistical answers for all kinds of problems are given.

Even more striking are the results of teaching problems within a given domain. In these concrete example-training conditions we never taught in the abstract about the rule at all, we just gave problems such as the manufacturer's representative problem and worked through them for the subjects, showing how a statistician would answer them, giving essentially the kind of answer that I previously gave as typical for graduate students. You get a good deal of improvement in the domain you train in, but, remarkably, you get just as much improvement in domains that you don't train in. It is hard to see how such results could be obtained unless subjects were generalizing what they learned up to a very high level—one qualitatively equivalent to the law of large numbers. This abstraction then makes possible the solution of problems in all domains in which the rules would be applicable (Fong & Nisbett, 1991).

I think there is also evidence that some causal rules, at the level of pragmatic logical rules of the kind that Cheng and Holyoak (Cheng & Holyoak, 1985; Cheng, Holyoak, Nisbett, & Oliver, 1986) discussed, are also of this type. That is, they exist—there are abstract rules at that very formal level—and training can influence people's use of them (Morris & Nisbett, 1992).

Most recently we (Richard Larrick, James Morgan, and I) started looking at choice rules, which would impress an old-fashioned behaviorist much more, because as long as you are looking at judgments, the S-R folks would be inclined to say this is just paper-and-pencil stuff.

What are the abstract rules that might govern people's actual behavior? The candidate rules are ones developed not by psychologists but by economists. These are the microeconomic rules of choice. There are lots of ways of stating these rules, but one arbitrary way that is as good as any to start with is the fundamental net-benefit principle. This holds that when there are several actions to choose from people pick the one that is going to give them the best outcome defined as the greatest positive difference between benefits and cost. Now to make this principle work in any concrete context two subrules have to be added: one is an uncertainty rule, which specifies that all of the assigned cost and benefit weights have to be modified by the probability of their occurrence, including the probability of incurring the cost and the probability of getting the benefit given that the action is taken. A comparable unit rule of some kind is also necessary; that is, the principle can't be applied if there isn't some way of converting everything to the same units, which can be either money or some other invented construct such as "utils," but a common unit is needed. (Incidentally, there's a comparable requirement for the application of the law of large numbers. If the unit can't be defined, the law of large numbers cannot be used. Sometimes in getting people to use the law of large numbers, instruction in how to unitize the events in a problem is crucial, and once this is done, application of the law is easy and automatic.)

Microeconomic choice theory, as a set of descriptive propositions, has taken progressively worse and worse beatings over the years. Simon (1955) was the first to raise a question about the descriptive accuracy of the microeconomic rules of choice by pointing out that people probably don't optimize as required by the rules, but instead "satisfice." That is, they put enough energy into the decision-making process to make their decisions good *enough*, given the importance of the possible outcomes. Actually, that turns out to be descriptively a little too generous. People don't seem to weight decisions by importance at all. If one examines how much time people spend on decisions, it turns out that they spend as much time picking a shirt as picking an appliance. This scarcely fits even a watered-down principle like satisficing. In addition, people are highly risk-averse. Early work indicated that people are generally willing to pay a very high premium for certainty, foregoing gains of a high likelihood for much lower gains that are certain.

Yet the really serious blows against the theory came in the late 1970s when Kahneman and Tversky (1979) argued that the cost–benefit rules are not even a good first approximation to a descriptive theory of choice. People are risk-averse for gains, they maintained, but they're risk-seeking for losses, preferring a substantial chance of losing a great deal to the certainty of losing a moderate amount. Moreover, decisions are subject to severe framing effects: People calculate value with respect to their current state, not with respect to an absolute state of wealth as required by cost-benefit theory. People don't use probabilities at all, they use something that maps only rather imperfectly onto probabilities (which Kahneman & Tversky call decision weights). They proposed an alternate theory, namely Prospect Theory, which has very little in common with the explicit rules of microeconomic theory and which paints people as using loose heuristics and perceptual judgments rather than rules.

More recently, economists have joined in on the fun of bashing the descriptive theory. They've focused on two additional principles. One is the sunk-cost principle, which holds that people should consider only future benefits and costs when making a decision. Once they've expended some cost — energy, money, or whatever — they have to forget about it. Subsequent behavior should no longer be influenced by that expenditure. To see how we tend to violate that sometimes, imagine that a month ago you bought tickets to a basketball game, paying $40 for them. Tonight's the night of the game, but the star is not playing because he's sick, and the game is 45 minutes away, and it's starting to snow. Should you go? For many people there is a strong temptation to say, "Yes, you should go; otherwise you're wasting the 40 dollars." To which the economist says: "Wrong. You've already wasted the 40 dollars. You're not getting that back. So the smart thing to do is to avoid wasting further resources, which in this case means going to the game — if it's not going to be something you expect to enjoy." Economists have nice thought experiments, which help you to find out if you're really being suckered by the sunk-cost trap. In this case, you should imagine that you didn't have tickets to the game, but instead a friend calls, and says, "I've got tickets to the game tonight, do you want to go?" If your answer would be "You've got to be kidding—the star isn't playing and it's snowing and it's 45 minutes on the freeway"—then you definitely shouldn't go to the game.

The remaining principle that people tend to violate is the opportunity-cost principle. This I find to be the most depressing of all microeconomic principles. It holds that people ought to be thinking all the time about whether there is some better course of action they might be pursuing. For example, if you're sitting listening to a lecture, you should be aware that you could be out strolling or reading a book or washing the car. Attention to the alternative courses of action is the mark of a good decision maker. A classic example of this, in which it is easy to see its importance and how it could be overlooked, concerns the older couple whose kids are grown, and who are rattling around in a five-bedroom house. If one were to suggest to them that they might sell the house and move into an apartment, the answer is quite likely to be, "Well no, that would be ridiculous, because the house is paid for." The economist will point out that they're paying opportunity costs for remaining, because they can sell the house, and, possibly on the interest alone, get a two-bedroom apartment, have lots of money to travel all over the world, and give the money to their grandchildren or whatever.

So people are inclined to violate all of the major principles of microeconomic theory. This raises the question of whether they're the right rules. If the rules are so bad descriptively, maybe they're not correct normatively. It could be that people violate these rules because they have better ones. When pressed on this point, the economists' defense of these rules is not very convincing to most psychologists. The major defense is mathematical, pointing out that it can be shown that the rules would maximize utility. Yet, psychologists want to be shown that in the world they actually live in, with the constraints that exist on people's time and cognitive capacities, they're better off actually using these rules. When pressed for an empirical answer, the best that economists can do is to point out that corporations pay for the advice of decision makers who use these microeconomic rules. Now there are lots of things psychologists can get paid for too, including handwriting analysis, lie detection, and so on. So naturally this isn't very convincing. In addition to trying to show that people do actually make use of the microeconomic rules, or at least can be taught to do so, we tried to show that there are some empirical reasons for believing that people are actually better off using these rules.

Our first approach (Larrick, Morgan, & Nisbett, 1990) was to try to see if we could teach people the microeconomic rules. We thought it would be a good idea to work with people who would be highly motivated to learn these rules, namely, middle-aged professional people who have financial responsibilities and are seeking to learn how to manage their affairs. It turned out to be very difficult to do this. In addition to teaching the abstract microeconomic principles, which is much more difficult than the law of large numbers, because it's a more complicated system, one has to know a lot about interest rates, and taxation, and inflation, and financial entities. It is difficult to estimate how much time it would actually take to give people what they would really need in order to be able to manage their own financial affairs sensibly, certainly more than the six hours of training we gave them.

We decided to switch to people who have been taught the rules more extensively than we could ever achieve. We studied economists to see if they actually think about events in everyday life differently from other people (Larrick, Nisbett, & Morgan, in press). We called the University of Michigan professors of economics, the biologists, and a sample of humanists in various disciplines. The phone call was made in the guise of an ISR survey about choices that were facing the university. We said we'd like to ask them also about some personal choices that they would be making.

One kind of university choice question that we posed informed the subjects that some financial planners at the university anticipated that jobs for young people could soon be more plentiful than in the recent past, for the simple reason that a much smaller fraction of the population is in the younger age group. One implication was that pay would increase for entry-level jobs, in all kinds of industries. The argument had been made that the university should respond to this situation by offering more money for scholarships in order to lure low-income students away from starting work and toward continuing their education. We assumed the economists would be likely to see this as an opportunity-cost question and to agree that this should be done.

We also asked people about their personal decisions, such as how often in the past year they had discontinued some activity for which they had incurred a sunk cost. We asked, for example, whether in the past 5 years they had ever started any of the following and then not finished it: a movie, a restaurant meal, a rented video cassette, an athletic game. We also asked questions about personal decisions involving sunk costs or opportunity costs, for example, whether subjects had ever dropped a research project because it wasn't proving worthwhile. (A control question asked whether they had ever dropped a research project because it hadn't been funded.) Finally, we asked questions about the opportunity costs of time—whether subjects did any maintenance on their own car, mowed their own lawn, and so on. (Economists are very liberating in this case. They believe: "Don't ever do any menial work at all, and own every time-saving appliance you possibly can.")

We also wanted to examine whether normative choices are associated with better outcomes. One type of outcome which everyone could agree that people care about is how much money they make. So we asked whether the differential use of these rules is associated with differential income for university professors. (It was possible to do this study at the University of Michigan, because faculty salaries are published in the student newspaper!) If an association were found between the use of the rules and salary, this would imply that people are better off using these rules—that the use of the rules is normative in the sense of making people more effective and hence more highly paid. Of course, this would not be a strong implication of such a finding, because it could be simply that smarter people are more effective, and smarter people are also more likely to know the rules, or that more motivated people are more productive, and more motivated people bother to find out what these rules are, and so on. Yet, things would look bad for the microeconomic normative position if there weren't an association between the use of these rules and better outcomes. Economists have been telling us for decades that if you're smart and use these rules you'll be rich. So if it's not the case that people who use the rules are richer, that would be destructive to the normative case.

What we found is that for both the policy questions and the reported personal behavior questions, the economists were substantially more likely to use the microeconomic rules than people in biology or the humanities. Economists chose the policies dictated by microeconomic theory; they were more likely to report discontinuing activities and foregoing activities that they've already invested in, and more of their personal decisions reflected a recognition of sunk-cost traps and opportunity costs. Finally, use of the rules was associated with higher salaries, *especially for the noneconomists*. Therefore, use of the rules is indeed associated with the superior outcome of better salaries.

The next question was whether laypeople could be taught some of this. We decided to start on our second effort by teaching just a single rule—the sunk-cost rule. It seemed to us that an application of the rule doesn't require an understanding of a number of auxiliary rules or financial facts about the world. We trained undergraduates on the sunk-cost rule, using either purely financial examples involving dollar costs and benefits or examples that didn't involve money in any way, either on the input or the output side. We found that there was a greater likelihood of avoiding sunk-cost traps as a result of training. In addition, the effects of training were domain-independent; that is, the training effect didn't depend at all on what domain they had been trained in. If they were trained in the financial domain, they improved just as much in the nonfinancial as in the financial domain, and vice versa.

We decided next to see whether the effects of training could be shown after a delay of a month or so, out of the original context. So we taught the rule, using both abstract-rule training and concrete-example training. We then called subjects in the guise of an ISR consumer survey a month later, asking questions with very different formats, including reports about their behavior in the interim. Trained subjects were somewhat more likely to report walking out on bad meals, bad movies, boring sports events, and so on, even though we'd never given them those specific examples as guides. We also found a significant increase in the use of the sunk-cost rule for reasoning about consumer issues confronting both themselves and the university.

The final study was one asking the question of whether better outcomes for students were associated with the use of the microeconomic rules. The outcome that students care about, of course, is grades. So we asked whether it is the case that the students who used these rules had higher grades. We looked at three variables in relation to the use of these rules in guiding behavior and in understanding how economists would analyze various choice problems. We examined whether or not the subjects had taken any economics, what their IQ was as indicated by verbal SATs, and what their grade-point average (GPA) was. Not surprisingly, having had some economics was associated with recognizing the economist's position for our sample of choice problems. Economics training, however, did not affect students' reported behavior. The same pattern was true for verbal intelligence. It was related to recognizing what the economist's position would be, but not to reported behavior. These points all held for the zero-order correlations and for regression analyses that examined simultaneously the effects of all three variables. Grade-point average behaved quite differently. It was highly correlated with reported behavior, though not with recognition of economists' position. The regression coefficient for reported behavior was actually higher than the zero-order correlation. Thus, grade-point average net of verbal IQ and economics training was very strongly associated with reported use of microeconomic rules. In effect, it was the *over*achiever who was particularly likely to report being guided by the microeconomic rules in daily behavior. These data, I argue, are much more consistent with the notion that application of microeconomic rules in everyday life is driving effectiveness, that is, GPA, than with the notion than intelligence is driving both effectiveness and GPA. In fact, verbal intelligence just isn't associated with reported use of the rules in one's own life.

To summarize, I think that people do use abstract rules — for reasoning and for choice. It's just unparsimonious to assume that economists have one rule for helping poor students and another rule for abandoning research projects and so on. Instead, they've got an abstract rule system that tells them how to recognize sunk costs, how to scan for opportunity costs, how to focus on maximizing outcomes, and so on. In addition, we found that there is relative domain-independence of the training effect. We train in one domain and get effects in a different domain, a pattern hard to explain without using the notion that people have abstract rules. We found retention of these rules after an interval over novel content and in new contexts. Finally, use of the rules was associated with better outcomes, that is, higher salaries for faculty who use the rules and higher GPA for students who use the rules.

So the behaviorists got it quite wrong, here as elsewhere. The core notions of traditional formal discipline theory are correct: People have abstract rules for reasoning, they can be altered with quite "top-down" procedures, and there is good reason to believe that some rules are better than others. On the other hand, the behaviorists weren't wrong about everything. They were probably right to criticize formal discipline as it was practiced in the schools. I doubt that the 19th-century curriculum did much to improve students' reasoning or choice. Formal logic, the syllogism, grammar, and mathematics don't provide the sort of pragmatic reasoning tools that the law of large numbers and the microeconomic rules of choice do. It's just that in this case, as in so many others, they threw the baby out with the bath water.

Hats off to George Miller for directing our attention to damp infants!

REFERENCES

Cheng, P. W., & Holyoak, K. J. (1985). Pragmatic reasoning schemas. *Cognitive Psychology, 17*, 391–416.

Cheng, P. W., Holyoak, K. J., Nisbett, R. E., & Oliver, L. M. (1986). Pragmatic versus syntactic approaches to training deductive reasoning. *Cognitive Psychology, 18*, 293–328.

Fong, G. T., Krantz, D. H., & Nisbett, R. E. (1986). The effects of statistical training on thinking about everyday problems. *Cognitive Psychology, 18*, 253–292.

Fong, G. T., & Nisbett, R. E. (1991). Immediate and delayed transfer of training effects in statistical reasoning. *Journal of Experimental Psychology: General, 120*, 34–45.

Jones, E. E., & Davis, K. E. (1965). From acts to dispositions: The attribution process in person perception. In L. Berkowitz (Ed.), *Advances in experimental psychology* (Vol. 2). New York: Academic Press.

Kahneman, D., & Tversky, A. (1979). Prospect theory: An analysis of decision under risk. *Econometrica, 47*, 263–291.

Kelley, H. H. (1967). Attribution theory in social psychology. In D. Levine (Ed.), *Nebraska Symposium on Motivation*. Lincoln: University of Nebraska Press.

Larrick, R. P., Morgan, J. N., & Nisbett, R. E. (1990). Teaching the use of cost-benefit reasoning in everyday life. *Psychological Science, 1*, 362–370.

Larrick, R. P., Nisbett, R. E., & Morgan, J. N. (in press). Who uses the cost-benefit rules of choice? Implications for the normative status of economic theory. *Organizational Behavior and Human Decision-Making*.

Miller, G. A. (1962). *Psychology: The science of mental life* (1st ed.). New York: Harper & Row.

Morris, M. W., & Nisbett, R. E. (1992). Deformation professionelle: Reasoning schemas taught in psychology and philosophy. In R. E. Nisbett (Ed.), *Rules for reasoning*. Hillsdale, NJ: Lawrence Erlbaum Associates.

Nisbett, R. E., Krantz, D. H., Jepson, C., & Kunda, Z. (1983). The use of statistical heuristics in everyday inductive reasoning. *Psychological Review, 90*, 339–363.

Nisbett, R. E., & Ross, L. D. (1980). *Human inference: Strategies and shortcomings of social judgment*. Englewood Cliffs, NJ: Prentice-Hall.

Ross, L. (1977). The intuitive psychologist and his shortcomings. In L. Berkowitz (Ed.), *Advances in experimental social psychology* (Vol. 10). New York: Academic Press.

Simon, H. A. (1955). A behavioral model of choice. *Quarterly Journal of Economics, 69*, 99–118.

7 Can Science Understand the Mind?

Gilbert Harman
Princeton University

DAS VERSTEHEN

Dilthey (1883/1989) distinguished between the physical sciences and the cognitive sciences, including history and literary criticism (the *Geisteswissenchaften*). The physical sciences approach things objectively, determining what objects are made of, how they work, and what their function is. The physical sciences aim to describe laws and other regularities involving things and their parts, in this way achieving an understanding of things, as we might say, "from the outside." But, according to Dilthey, cognitive phenomena admit also of a different sort of understanding from the inside. Cognitive phenomena have content or meaning of a sort that cannot be appreciated within an entirely objective approach. Reasons, purposes, feelings, and experiences can only be understood "from within," via sympathy or empathy.

Dilthey referred to understanding from within as *das Verstehen,* which is just the German word for understanding. Some commentators write of "the method of das Verstehen." Others refer to a "hermeneutical method." But talk of a special method is misleading.

For one thing, Dilthey and others who take the same view do not deny the need for experiment, objective methods, and the search for regularities in cognitive science. They claim, rather, that mental phenomena have a subjective "inside" and so admit to a kind of understanding that plays no role in physics. There is no subjective inside to a molecule. Physics does not need to know "what it is like" to be an electron, it is sufficient to understand how an electron functions. But, although an objective functional approach

111

is needed in cognitive science, another kind of understanding is also needed that is neither needed nor available in physics.

Whether cognitive phenomena admit of a different sort of understanding from that available in the physical sciences is highly controversial. Positivists like Comte (1830–42) deny it. Among the many people on the positivistic side of the dispute are behaviorists like Watson (1913) and Skinner (1974), physicalists like Place (1956) and Smart (1959), and defenders of purely computational accounts of the mind like Newell (1990), Simon and Kaplan (1989), and Pylyshyn (1984).

Many people in addition to Dilthey are on the Verstehen side of the issue, including Weber (1978), Quine (1960), and Nagel (1974). (I explain later why I put Quine on the Verstehen side.)

Let me repeat that the issue is not whether imaginatively putting oneself in someone else's shoes is a good *method* for figuring out what is going on. Both sides can agree that uncontrolled imagination is almost certain to arrive at the wrong answer. If one person tries to figure out what another is going to do by imaginatively putting oneself in the other person's shoes, the first person might very well be completely mistaken. If one person thinks he or she understands what it is like for another person to have a certain experience, the first person may very well be misled. Both sides agree that imagination is not a way to read minds or foresee the future.

Nor do proponents of das Verstehen put it forward as a method of discovery or a method of confirming or testing hypotheses that have already been formulated. Das Verstehen is not supposed to be either one of those things. It is rather supposed to be needed in order to understand certain hypotheses in the first place. So, for example, to understand hypothesis or theory about pain (where pain is not just a functionally defined state, but real pain) requires knowing what pain is, understanding what it is like to feel pain. The objective story about pain has been pursued in biology, neuroscience, and psychology, where much has been learned about how pain is caused and what things pain causes (e.g., Melzack & Wall, 1983). It seems that someone might completely understand this objective story without knowing what it is like to feel pain. Suppose that Oscar is one of those unfortunate souls who does not feel pain and is therefore not warned by pain feelings of burning or other injury (Cohen, Kipnis, Kunkle, & Kubsansky, 1955). Suppose further that Oscar is strictly protected by anxious parents, receives a college education, becomes a neuroscientist, and comes to learn all there is to learn about pain. But can that really be supposed? Can Oscar learn *all* there is to learn about pain? It seems he could not. It seems that he could not learn the most important thing—what pain is, what it is like to experience pain—because, at least according to advocates of das Verstehen, that's one thing science cannot teach.

Notice that what Oscar lacks is not a method. It's not that he needs some sort of ESP. The point is rather that he does not understand something, where failing to understand something is different from lacking a method for finding or confirming theories.

On this occasion, except for the present paragraph, I do not discuss the additional claim that das Verstehen plays a crucial role in understanding people's reasons for their beliefs or behavior. One argument for this claim notes that we lack any objective account of reasons; we do not know any general principles of logic, but principles of logic are principles of implication, not principles of reasoning. Principles of logic have neither a normative nor a psychological subject matter and so say nothing about inference and reasoning. We cannot understand another person's inference, reasoning, or reasons by bringing them under general principles, because we do not know any general principles of the relevant sort. The best we can do at present is to consider what we would think if we were in the other person's situation. I discussed this idea elsewhere (Harman 1986a), which I believe is relevant also to the topic of Bruner's essay in the present volume. In any event, in this chapter I concentrate on the claim that das Verstehen is needed to understand certain psychological hypotheses, even when we do have knowledge of objective principles.

Recent defenders of the need for das Verstehen sometimes refer to an example using color: a person blind from birth who knows everything there is to know from an objective standpoint about color and people's perception of it without knowing what red things look like to a normal observer. Jackson (1982, 1986) developed a variant of the example in which a woman named Mary had been brought up in a totally black-and-white environment, never seeing any colors. We are to suppose that she remained normally sighted. (The example involved a certain amount of science fiction.) Mary did graduate work in color perception, on a National Science Foundation Young Investigator's award, and came to know everything that science could say about color perception, all without leaving her black-and-white room. Yet, she did not yet know what color perception was like from the inside. Because of her passionate interest in this, she was finally allowed to leave her room and for the first time she saw things in color. Pointing to a ripe apple, her companion aid, "This is red." (I hope her companion told the truth.) Mary thought to herself, "So that is what it is like to see something red; that is what red is." She had then learned something about color and color perception that she didn't know before when she knew everything that science could say about color. So, it would seem that something important about color perception cannot be learned from science.

Science approaches matters objectively from the outside. It seems that we go beyond this objective outside view when we understand what it is to see things in color. It seems appropriate to say that we understand from the inside what color perception is like. Mary too came to know from the inside what it is like to see something red. At that point, she knew something she didn't know before, something that wasn't accessible from the outside from a purely objective point of view.

Discussion of "black-and-white Mary" is one way in which the das Verstehen issue has been addressed in the recent philosophical literature. In this guise it is an issue that some philosophers have worried a great deal about.

I should say that the das Verstehen issue is sometimes connected with another issue, the issue of *qualia*. Qualia are supposed to be (a) intrinsic properties of conscious experiences, (b) properties that are essential to the experiences being the conscious experiences that they are, (c) properties of experiences that are part of "what it is like to have the experience," and (d) properties of which one is in some sense aware. It is controversial whether there are qualia in this sense, that is, properties satisfying all four of these conditions. Many writers take it to be obvious that there are qualia in this sense (Block, 1990; Shoemaker, 1982). But whether there are qualia depends in part on exactly what is meant by *intrinsic, essential*, and so on, and on just what it is one is aware of when one has conscious experiences. I and others expressed skepticism about qualia (Dennett, 1991; Harman, 1990).

At the Princeton conference responsible for the present volume, Block reacted to my skepticism about qualia by accusing me of not believing in consciousness, which I guess means that I don't believe his theory about consciousness. It would be equally fair, I suppose, for me to reply that *he* doesn't believe in consciousness, because he doesn't believe my theory! As this small exchange illustrates, the controversy about qualia often involves dramatic charges that one's opponent is denying the obvious.

Fortunately, in this chapter, I am not concerned with qualia, but with a (possibly related) issue concerning das Verstehen, an issue that can be discussed without appeal to intrinsic, essential properties, and so on. It is an issue about meaning.

MEANING

One standard philosophical approach to meaning (e.g., Grice, 1957) started from the idea that language is used in the expression of thought, so that the meaning of a word or phrase has something to do with the thought that the word or phrase is used to express. Of course, that leaves the problem of accounting for the content of thoughts or ideas. An alternative approach (e.g., Burge, 1979) holds that at least sometimes we need to explain the content of thoughts or ideas in terms of the meanings of the words that are used to express them. Of course, that leaves the problem of explaining the meaning of those words! What's needed is a combined account of the content of ideas and the meaning of words that does not simply reduce one to the other, which is left unexplained.

There are three leading kinds of semantic theory of this sort. One seeks to explain the content of thoughts and the meanings of words in terms of truth conditions. A second seeks to explain meaning and content in terms of the way words are used or the way the corresponding concepts or thoughts function in a person's psychological economy. The third holds that the content of someone else's words and ideas can only be explained by translating them into one's own.

In the first view, the content of a full thought or statement is to be identified with the conditions under which that thought or statement would be true. Truth conditions are often identified with possible worlds (where a possible world is basically a possible way everything might be). So, theories of meaning in terms of truth conditions and theories in terms of possible worlds are simply alternative ways of saying the same thing. In this sort of view, the way to explain the meaning of a particular idea or word is to explain what contribution that idea or word makes to the truth conditions of a thought or statement containing it. If the thought or sentence as transformed into a different one by replacing the one idea or word with another, what effect would that have on the truth conditions of the whole? To understand the effect a word or idea has on truth conditions is to understand what the content is of that word or idea. There are complications (Lewis, 1970), but they need not be considered here.

The second approach identifies the content of a concept or word with the way that concept or word is used, especially the way it functions cognitively, that is, the way it functions in perception, inference, planning, thinking, memory, and action. To explain the function of a word or concept is to indicate how having that idea or concept in a thought can affect the way that thoughts arise from perception, for example, or lead to action.

With respect to a concept or word with perceptual content, such as *red*, it is relevant how certain kinds of perception can lead to percepts involving the concept of red or thoughts involving that word and how those percepts and thoughts can lead to certain memories. There is probably not a direct connection between, as it were, red thoughts, that is, thoughts involving that concept and overt actions. Perhaps the concept of *danger* is more directly connected with action than with perception. Certain logical concepts and the corresponding English words — *not*, *and*, and *or* — might be explained by appealing to immediate implications between thoughts, implications that hold because of that concept or word, so that to understand *and* might be to understand how a conjunctive thought of the form *P and Q* is related to *P* and related to *Q* — how those two conjuncts immediately imply their conjunction, and how it immediately implies them.

Verificationism and procedural semantics are versions of the thesis that content has something to do with function in thought (for my own version of this thesis, see Harman, 1987).

The third kind of semantics is rather different, holding that an account of meaning or content must provide a translation into one's own language or experience. Quine (1960) offered an account of meaning of this form. For Quine, the theory of meaning is basically the theory of translation into one's "home language." In this view, to give the meaning of an expression in another language is to provide a synonymous expression in one's own language, and similarly, if one wants to give the content of somebody else's thought, one has to find a concept or idea of one's own that is equivalent to it.

The claim that content is given by translation can be combined with one or both of the other approaches to meaning. For example, it might be said that what makes one notion the correct translation of another is that the two notions function in the same way. There would still be an issue as to whether one or another kind of semantics is primary. To hold that the translational approach is primary would be to hold that the main thing semantics is or ought to be interested in is how to translate other people's words or ideas into one's own language. Alternatively, it might be said that the main goal of semantics is an understanding of function or truth conditions. Another, more likely possibility is that none of the approaches has primacy over the others.

Is semantics entirely objective according to one or another of these approaches? If the first or second approach has primacy, the answer is "yes." Semantics can be entirely objective, and a completely objective description of meaning can be given. On the view that meaning is primarily truth conditions or the view that meaning is primarily usage, meaning would seem to be the kind of thing that can be grasped via the scientific method by doing experiments and finding objective regularities. But the approach that takes the primary notion of meaning to be given by translation into one's own language supposes that there are aspects of meaning that are not completely objective, because there is an ineliminable relativity to one's own language, something that one has to be able to understand oneself. So, clearly, the third approach, holding that a theory of meaning is primarily a translation into one's own language corresponds to what is expected by advocates of das Verstehen rather than what is expected by the positivists. That's why I put Quine on the das Verstehen side rather than on the objective physicalistic side, although in other respects Quine would seem to go on the other side. In many ways, Quine advocates physicalism and natural science, but not as providing the whole story about semantics!

SEMANTIC PROBLEMS

Now I look at some objections to each of these approaches so as to try to reach a resolution of the issue.

Let me start by considering problems with the view that the theory of meaning is basically the theory of translation. (By that I mean always the theory of translation into one's own view. It's not just a theory of what constitutes a translation from one language into another language. Translation into one's own language is crucial.)

When I try to take this view seriously, the first problem that occurs to me is that there are people with ideas that go beyond anything that I can express in my own language, including my present language of thought. So, I cannot simply identify an expression's having meaning with its having a translation into my language!

In fact, a formal proof can be given of the claim that there are ideas that cannot be translated into my language. The basic idea behind the proof is that a certain notion of truth for sentences in my language can be expressed in some other language, but not in my own language on pain of my language being inconsistent (through allowing the liar paradox; Tarski, 1956).

Similarly, a person blind from birth might not have a full concept of *red*. Nevertheless, such a person could allow that sighted people had such a concept. So a person can allow for meaningful concepts that cannot be equated with any concepts that person has.

It seems then that a purely translational theory must be ruled out. Yet, there are also objections to any completely objective theory of meaning. For it would seem that someone can fully understand the conditions under which a concept or term is being used without knowing what it means. Before Mary leaves her black-and-white room, it would seem that she can have a completely objective understanding of how sighted people use the term *red* without understanding the term herself. She can't know what *red* means, because she doesn't know what it is like to see something red, having no notion of her own to translate it into. So it looks as if a purely objective account of meaning or content cannot be adequate either.

This might seem to suggest trying to defend the theory that meaning is basically translation into one's own language, seeing that the other views also run into problems. Seeing problems in any completely objective approach, we might try to modify the translational approach so as to meet the objections to it. For example, we might try to start with a basic translational account of meaning and then extend it via family resemblances, paradigms, and so on. The basic or paradigm case of meaning would be somebody else meaning something that we can understand, because we have an equivalent in our own language or conceptual framework. But we also must allow for the fact that our concepts can change over time. We acquire new concepts as we learn new subjects, such as neuroscience and quantum physics. Now suppose that someone who has not learned quantum physics hears someone else talking about quantum numbers. It may well be that the first person has no concept that is equivalent to the concept of quantum number, but nevertheless this person might have the idea of going out and learning some physics and eventually maybe understanding it. This person can imagine eventually acquiring a concept into which the other person's notion of quantum number can be translated. So we can by analogy have the idea of other people having meaningful concepts that we cannot understand right now.

Similarly, although before leaving her room Mary does not yet know what it is for something to be red, she can think about the day she will be released from the room, at which point she will acquire a concept of something's being red, this thought allowing her to extend her notion of meaning and attribute meaning to other people's current concept of red.

I am not sure this is a successful way to develop the idea that the translational approach is the primary semantic theory in order to meet objections to the translational approach. In any event, we should also consider whether there is a way to defend the more objective approach from the problems it faces.

CAN MARY KNOW ALL THE OBJECTIVE FACTS?

One possible defense rejects the argument about Mary by denying that, before she emerges from her room, she knows every objective fact. Notice that one of the objective facts is that *under normal conditions a perceived red object will look red to a normal observer*. Now it is clear that Mary can know that this last sentence is true, given what other people mean by it. Maybe in some sense she knows the fact that is expressed by that sentence. But there is another sense in which she does not know that fact, because the full appreciation of that fact is possible only for someone who has the full concept of *red*, and Mary does not have that concept. She knows a lot of things about red, but she doesn't have the same concept of red as other people. She doesn't know exactly what normal observers know when they know the stated fact. So it looks as if there is something objective, that is, something about the world, that Mary doesn't know.

Let us look at this point carefully. What doesn't Mary know? It isn't just that she doesn't know something subjective — what red things look like. She also lacks an understanding of the proposition that something is red. So, when she first sees what red things look like she really acquires two pieces of information or two understandings. She has an understanding of something about other people's experience, but she also has an understanding of something about the objective world, what it is like for something to be red.

Does this mean that the objective approach can be defended after all? What does the example of black-and-white Mary show? By itself, the example does not show that meaning cannot be a matter of objective truth conditions or use conditions. It only seemed that it could show this, because it seemed at first that Mary could know all the objective facts without knowing what it is like to see something red, so that knowledge of the objective facts would not suffice for knowing what it is like to see something red. But now we see that before she leaves her room Mary does not know all the objective facts. Not only does she not know certain subjective things—what it's like to see something red—but there are certain objective things that she doesn't know, for example, what it is for something to be red. So, black-and-white Mary does not show that an understanding of the objective facts is not enough (Harman, 1990).

As a rejoinder to this unexpected argument, it might be denied that an object's being red is an objective fact about the object. Perhaps this is merely a subjective fact, depending on the subjective reactions of human perceivers. So, black-and-white Mary's failure fully to grasp that fact does not prevent her from grasping any objective fact, it might be argued.

But this rejoinder itself faces a counterargument. It is by no means obvious that *being red* can be noncircularly analyzed in terms of *looking red,* because *looking red* appears to be a complex notion involving the notion of something's being red! Something looks red to you if your visual experience presents it (or represents it) as being red: It looks to you as if something is red (Harman, 1990).

The argument need not stop at this point, but it should be clear that there is some reason to suppose that my title should be not "Can Science Understand the Mind?" but maybe "Can Science Understand the World?" The difficulty may not be just a difficulty about understanding aspects of the mind; it may apply also to understanding objective aspects of the world. For whether something is red or not is a property of something in the world. In as much as das Verstehen is needed, or some kind of translation into one's language and experience is needed, one is going to have just as much problem understanding claims about colors of objects in the world as one is going to have understanding claims about people's experience. So, maybe we can conclude that science by itself cannot fully understand the world, but there is not something special as far as these considerations go for the mind.

But that conclusion would be too strong.

A DIFFERENT SORT OF KNOWLEDGE

Even controlling for not having a concept of the objective conditions, there are still going to be cases in which one could know what the objective conditions are but not know what the meaning is. Knowing the ways in which a concept functions and knowing what the concept is are two different things. I briefly mention an example.

A few years ago, I was trying to specify how logical notions are used (Harman, 1986b). The notions expressed by *and* and *or* seemed easy enough, but I had some trouble with *not*. I ended up with something rather complicated:

> N is a one-place sentential operator that is used in such a way that A and $N(A)$ immediately exclude each other, and each is immediately implied by anything that immediately excludes the other.

(Immediate implication and immediate exclusion are connections that one recognizes immediately as opposed to connections one recognizes by virtue of recognizing intermediate connections.) It seemed to me that this statement really does characterize one notion of negation. But there are various kinds of negation: There is intuitionistic negation and classical negation, and the rules for these are rather different. What sort of negation does this account capture? Now, this was not my first attempt at characterizing negation. I was at first inclined to think that a slightly different account was correct for classical negation, but Soames convinced me that what I had characterized was more like intuitionistic than classical negation. This brought home to me the message I mentioned before—having a characterization of the way something is used may not be by itself sufficient to tell what the relevant notion means.

I think that the moral carries over to other concepts beyond just negation. It is generally true that understanding the conditions under which a concept is used is not going to tell one by itself without some further thinking about what the concept means. One may or may not be able to figure it out, but there is a step to be figured out. Das Verstehen is needed. Dilthey, Quine, and all others are right. There are aspects of mental life that cannot be understood from a purely objective scientific point of view.

ACKNOWLEDGMENT

Preparation of this chapter was supported in part by a grant from the James S. McDonnell Foundation to Princeton University.

REFERENCES

Block, N. (1990). Inverted earth. *Philosophical Perspectives*, *4*, 53–79.

Burge, T. (1979). Individualism and the mental. *Midwest Studies in Philosophy 4*, 73–121.

Cohen, L. D., Kipnis, D., Kunkle, E. C., & Kubsansky, P. E. (1955). Case report: Observation of a person with congenital insensitivity to pain. *Journal of Abnormal and Social psychology*, *51*, 333–338.

Comte, A. (1830–42). *Cours de philosophie positive*. Paris: Bachelier.

Dennett, D. C. (1991). *Consciousness explained*. Boston: Little, Brown.

Dilthey, W. (1989). *Introduction to the human sciences* (R. Makkreel & F. Rodi, Eds.). Princeton, NJ: Princeton University Press. (Original work published 1883)

Grice, H. P. (1957). Meaning. *Philosophical Review*, *64*, 377–388.

Harman, G. (1986a). *Change in view: Principles of reasoning*. Cambridge, MA: MIT Press/Bradford Books.

Harman, G. (1986b). The meanings of logical constants. In E. Le Pore (Ed.), *Truth and interpretation: Perspectives on the philosophy of Donald Davidson* (pp. 125–134). Oxford: Blackwell.

Harman, G. (1987). (Nonsolipsistic) conceptual role semantics. In E. Le Pore (Ed.), *New directions in semantics* (pp. 55–81). London: Academic Press.

Harman, G. (1990). The intrinsic quality of experience. *Philosophical Perspectives*, *4*, 31–52.

Jackson, F. (1982). Epiphenomenal qualia. *Philosophical Quarterly*, *32*, 127–132.

Jackson, F. (1986). What Mary didn't know. *Journal of Philosophy*, *83*, 291–295.

Melzack, R., & Wall, P. D. (1983). *The challenge of pain* (rev. ed.). New York: Basic Books.

Lewis, D. (1970). General semantics. *Synthese*, *22*, 18–67.

Nagel, T. (1974). What is it like to be a bat? *Philosophical Review*, *83*, 435–450.

Newell, A. (1990). *Unified theories of cognitive*. Cambridge, MA: Harvard University Press.

Place, U. T. (1956). Is consciousness a brain process? *Journal of Psychology*, *47*, 44–50.

Pylyshyn, Z. (1984). *Computation and cognition: Toward a foundation for cognitive science*. Cambridge, MA: MIT Press.

Quine, W. V. (1960). *Word and object*. Cambridge, MA: MIT Press.

Shoemaker, S. (1982). The inverted spectrum. *Journal of Philosophy*, *79*, 357–381.

Simon, H., & Kaplan, C. A. (1989). Foundations of cognitive science. In M. I Posner (Ed.), *Foundations of cognitive science* (pp. 1–47). Cambridge, MA: MIT Press.

Skinner, B. F. S. (1974). *About behaviorism*. New York: Random House.

Smart, J. J. C. (1959). Sensations and brain processes. *Philosophical Review*, *68*, 141–156.

Tarski, A. (1956). The concept of truth in formalized languages. In A. Tarski (Ed.), *Logic, semantics, metamathematics*, (pp. 152–279). Oxford: Oxford University Press.

Watson, J. B. (1913). Psychology as a behaviorist views it. *Psychological Review*, *20*, 158–177.

Weber, M. (1978). *Economy and society* (Vols. 1–2). (G. Roth & C. Wittich, Eds.). Berkeley: University of California Press. (Original work published 1922)

8 Explaining and Interpreting: Two Ways of Using Mind

Jerome Bruner
New York University School of Law

On February 8, 1672, Isaac Newton presented a paper to the Royal Society of London in which he argued principally on the basis of experiments with prisms that the ambient white light of daylight was not elementary but composed rather of a mixture of all the hues in the spectrum. Cohen (1956) assures us that this was one of the most unadorned empirical demonstrations that Newton ever launched, requiring little by way of logical, geometrical, or mathematical reasoning of the kind made so familiar in Newton's later *Principia*. The idea came to Newton, so gossipy historians like to tell us, on the basis of observations he made with a prism bought at the Stourbridge Fair in the Spring of 1666 when he was 24, shortly before he quit his quarters in Trinity College because of the threat of the Plague.

Although his explanation of achromatic light was principally descriptive in the manner of, say, Kepler's account of planetary motion, it also contained counterintuitive but demonstrable claims concerning the constancy of different sort of rays under refraction and reflection, in contrast to the lack of such constancy for achromatic light under those same conditions.

Newton regarded his work on color (as he did much else in the 1709 *Opticks*) as simply a matter of empirical demonstration plus a little geometry about angles of incidence and reflection, and he was notably annoyed when another Fellow of the Society, one Dr. Pardies, referred to his 1672 paper in the *Philosophical Transactions* as offering Newton's color "hypothesis."

Newton's explanation of color mixing has endured right into the present, and even prompted interesting progeny ranging from last century's Young-

Helmholtz theory to yesterday's views of Edwin Land on color mixing. Not only has its explanatory power endured, but it has had an astonishing continuity of development over three centuries. It is a model history of explanation in science.

But it is only one side of my story, this exemplary scientific achievement. Eventually the relevant volume of the *Transactions* or the *Opticks* itself came into the hands of a charismatic and brilliant young preacher–theologian in the village of Northampton in the Massachusetts Bay Colony, who read it with something more than mere scientific curiosity. The event I relate took place around 1740, around the time of the so-called Great Awakening of that date when there were great social and political stirrings in the colonies, which, as Perry Miller tells us, could as well have been a rising of debtors against creditors, or of common men against the gentry, or a turning away from the authoritarian Puritanism of a century before. It may even have been exacerbated by an epidemic of sore throat that spread throughout the colonies from Virginia to New England in that year. Or perhaps it was an echo of John Wesley's evangelical, anti-Establishment preaching to the tin miners in far-off Cornwall, who gathered in zealous assemblies of 10,000 at a time to hear the outdoor sermons of that astonishing Non-Conformist, who galloped from town to town on horseback to deliver sermons to as many as three such assemblies a day. In any case, the Great Awakening was a veritable frenzy, particularly in the Connecticut Valley, and so alarming was it to the sequestered Harvard faculty, indeed, that they condemned it in terms reserved for only the severest public aberrations: it was "enthusiasm."

The Northampton preacher in question, of course, was the well-born young Yale graduate and admirer of John Locke and Isaac Newton, Jonathan Edwards, later to become President of Princeton University, if only for the 4 months preceding his death. I shall not trace all of the complexities of the political or theological scene of that day (if those two scenes can indeed be separated), but I must say enough to make clear how it came about that shortly after reading Newton's publication, Edwards delivered a sermon based upon it to his congregation. Why, after telling his parishioners about Newton's discovery, did Jonathan Edwards then tell them that Newton's unlocking of another of God's secrets gave hope to Everyman, following which he urged upon them that by the exercise of their own efforts they too could do the same?[1]

---

[1]I am indebted for this account to my late colleague Perry Miller, who read me accounts of this episode to be included in his masterly volume, *Errand Into the Wilderness* (1956) then in preparation. Although much of the history and some of the reasoning in this section can be found in Miller's volume, the story of Edwards' "Newton sermon" was omitted from the final draft of that book.

Why should Edwards have chosen to give such a sermon about Newton's discovery at that time and in that place? And why did he go to such pains, as we shall see in a moment, to justify his quirky use of Newton in this way? We are concerned in all this with how the mind of Jonathan Edwards was working, in contrast to the mind of Isaac Newton. So consider first his elaborate justification for such a sermon.

Edwards was smitten with John Locke's ideas about language and thought to be found in Book III of Locke's *Essay Concerning Human Understanding*. Indeed, he had begun making entries about it in his notebooks in his college days in New Haven. Locke, you recall, argued that words gained their meaning by referring to complex ideas, and that the ultimate transparency of words was assured by the decomposability of complex ideas into simpler ones more directly accessible to experience. Edwards, although agreeing with Locke, still felt that this was not enough to account for what words communicated. Words, he argued, excite more than ideas. They also arouse passions and convictions and impel us to actions, all of which were as important to the meanings of words as the ideas that they aroused. Armed with this rather crude pragmatic postulate, Edwards could now argue that he was furthering Locke's argument that the true function of language was the fullest possible communication, and that our task as speakers was to make this full function possible. For Edwards, given his reading of Locke, "an idea became not merely a concept but an emotion" (Miller, 1936, p. 179). It also became a related call to appropriate action.

In his sermon, then, Newton's accomplishment was not only about ideas and observations, but about the acts they implied. Therefore, go forth and unlock a few secrets of God on your own: Knowing, willing, and doing should be a unity. Nor was this his only hortatory sermon. He was possessed by his new idea — or ideology. He spent other Sunday perorations not only on delineating ideas of good and evil, but on explicating them in the practices of wicked merchants and landlords. By 1748, 2 years after his protector and uncle, the High Sheriff Colonel Stoddard, died, Edwards was summarily dismissed from his post by those very merchants and landlords who recognized all too well where his theory was leading. They were no longer amused by its incendiary candor. Neither were the divines of the Harvard faculty, who were greatly relieved to witness the downfall of such enthusiasm.

We know what Newton accomplished. What of Edwards? Perry Miller is of the view that he helped break the hold of European deductive rationalism over American religious thought; helped form the American mind with an activist epistemology fit for the New World. The trustees of Princeton must have had something of this sort in mind when they called him to the Presidency in 1756.

Now what was Edwards making of Newton? Plainly, he was not interested in elucidating Newton's explanation of the composition of light, but in interpreting it. He was seeking, we would say, a deeper human significance in Newton's work; seeking a meaning behind the meaning. His preoccupation was with how things should be, rather than with how they were, with prescription rather than description: how the mind should be used, how the world should be treated, what should prevail between God and man. Newton happened to provide a remarkable substantive instantiation for Edwards' interpretive aspirations. For all that, Edwards was obviously using his mind to make his point. And to what end? Well, in conventional terms, Edwards proved nothing, explained nothing. Yet that is too dismissive. For his interpretive line of thought, perhaps, did bring something powerful into being. By espousing the democracy of mind, by giving a rationale for epistemic self-reliance (echoed a century later by Ralph Waldo Emerson), he helped form the "American ethos." Anomalously, by his own use of mind, he changed the very social reality he was rebelling against.

To understand this accomplishment, we must go beyond empirical verifiability and beyond formal consistency of the asserting "A-and-not-A" variety. We might simply say that Jonathan Edwards was a shrewd reader of the Great Awakening, and that he used it well as the context for the text he was hawking. Newton, on the other hand, showed no interest in the public rumblings that accompanied the Plague, whose eruption drove him from Cambridge in 1667. It was only an annoying interruption of his revolutionary reflections upon the refrangibility of "different sorts of hues." Besides, explanatory standards of the kind that occupied Newton were scarcely affected by the Plague. Whereas the interpretive possibilities open to Jonathan Edwards might well have been shifted toward sympathy for self-reliance by even so trivial an epidemic as the sore throats of 1740. But I think we can put the matter more precisely than that.

For reasons both heuristic and expository, I focus more formally on the contrast between *interpretation* and *explanation* for two reasons.[2] The first is that I think the concept of interpretation may fall in principle, outside the reach of conventional computability. It would be useful to explore why that is so and what its implications may be for our ideas about "how the mind works," to revert to George Miller's grand question. The second reason is that I want to show that what is not subject to the constraints of conventional computability is not "outside" the grasp of the human sciences and may indeed be as close to its center as one can get, a matter discussed later.

---

[2]The reader will readily recognize how indebted I am in this discussion to von Wright's *Explanation and Understanding* (1971).

Let me take a first step toward our problem. I take it as a given that all cognition, whatever its nature, relies upon representation—how we lay down knowledge in a way to represent our experience of the world. I happen to think that representation is a process of construction, as it were, rather than a mere reflection of the world. But even if one thought of it as simply reflecting the world, there would still have to be some canons of selection operative. The contrast between explanation and interpretation, then, needs to be explicated in light of views about the nature of representation and about the operations we perform to utilize our representations in particular tasks. So what is involved in representation?

At the most general level, obviously, the first function of representation is world making. We construct a model of a world from our encounters, from stored memories of these, from imagination, and through applying transformational processes to these world models that enable us to go beyond the information given either in perception or memory. Our representations must, to a certain degree, be faithful to recurrent regularities in the world, or we would stumble far worse than we do. We are prodigious at predicting. We spin our representational models just as fast or as far as needed for us to keep ahead of expected conditions. Perhaps the cost of this flexible fast-forward feature is that our representations must be kept free of surplus cognitive baggage, which is probably required anyway by inherent limits on our processing capacities, though as George Miller reminded us years ago, this limit can be evaded by filling our seven slots with gold rather than dross. But that, of course, is a dividend gained only by transforming our representations "powerfully," which means with a view to wider, more generative future use.

So how do we transform knowledge to assure its wider, more flexible future use? The standard answer, of course, is that we construct theories to bridge the gap between what has been given in experience and what might be encountered under altered conditions—hypothesis spaces, experiment spaces, and production systems that tell us which acts to take in face of which exigencies. Eventually, the culture chips in with some help, providing some representational ready-mades so that we don't have to start at the loom each time. Eventually, as it were, we learn how to run our problem solving backwards in order to convert those proactive efforts into retrospective accounts or explanations, so that we can pass them on to others for their guidance.

These are roughly the causal theories and explanations that we construct in order to predict, control, and understand events about which we are concerned. For them, I am prepared to accept some version of Hempel's notion about "covering laws" and rules of subsumption by which we include a presently puzzling set of putative explananda under a more abstract set of nomic principles. Who could doubt Hume's principle that when we attribute cause within such a theory, we must assure that the terms in a causal proposition be independently determinable to avoid confusing logically redundant connections with truly causal ones? Blackbirds, we come to realize, are not black, because they are definitionally ravens.

When we try to explain causally, we conventionally require three steps. One explicates how we came by our hypotheses, a second how we selected certain of them in light of evidence (including what counts as evidence), and a third is an expressive one that revolves around justifying the results of the first two steps as being believable or acceptable. This last step has usually been swept under the rug, although in recent years it has engaged the attention of Kuhn (1970), Polanyi (1953), and others. Such a short menu obviously leaves out a lot else about theory making and explaining—such as specifying acceptable procedures required to "get into" the theory's domain, or indicating which "style" of explaining goes in which domain (like functionalism in cellular but not molecular biology, etc.). Causal theories, whatever their variant, seem to share a common bottom line: to explain things in a way that furthers prediction and/or control. The only expressive thing we demand of such theories is that they should be parsimonious, giving us "more for less," as it were. I suspect that elegance of explanation has much to do with this feature.

Aside from this demand for parsimonious elegance, scientific-causal explaining seems a curiously impersonal undertaking. Such theories are neither normative nor redemptive; they neither enjoin nor can they save or damn. Nor are they indexical: They present the view from everywhere or from nowhere in particular. They assume, moreover, that when a causal link is merely probabilistic, residual variance is the result of incomplete knowledge and is in principle asymptotic to full but later certainty.

If we confined our world making to inert objects and events—to how light refracts or balls roll down inclined planes—we could live quite happily with causal theories and causal explanations only. Yet, we do not live by inert objects and events alone. We want to know why Jonathan Edwards and John Winthrop, only a century apart, had such different views. And, as important, we want to offer interpretations of such questions that will have their impact upon our hearers by virtue of something more than their verifiability. We might even harbor the aim of changing people's way of construing the world just by virtue of the "compellingness" or "rectitude" of our interpretation. This is the world of culture. Causal explanations of nature may neutralize perspective and indexicality, whereas cultural interpretations grow out of and then become part and parcel of the explananda they are seeking to elucidate. I surely do not have to argue that one's view of cultural phenomena, how one chooses to measure them, and so on, derive from one's place and condition within one's own culture. That is banal. More serious, perhaps, is the effect one's view has on those to whom it is made known.

When H. L. A. Hart promulgated a theory of punishment in jurisprudence, or when Oliver Wendell Holmes set forth a doctrine of legal realism, the law did not remain unchanged (as light remains indifferent to the elucidation provided by Isaac Newton). The law itself changes—or at least judges and lawyers change and thereby alter the selection of precedents by which law defines itself, for precedents are the closest thing the law has to a "fixed nature." It is not simply that cultural interpretations do not achieve causal power: They simply cannot do so when their explanans become in practice part and parcel of the explananda they seek to elucidate.

I am not making the 19th-century claim that explanation is general and nomothetic, whereas interpretation is particular and idiographic.[3] Mine is a more drastic view: The mark of an interpretation is that its verisimilitude depends on its viability within the system of explananda that it seeks to elucidate. That is to say, an interpretation is not simply an explanans designed to explicate a set of explananda. It also makes implicit claims about its explananda that rest upon intentional states in being on the occasion of interpretation. In a word, interpretation can never rise above or escape from the situation of interpretation it seeks to interpret even when it is hidden behind the mask of explanation. I think this tendency to disguise the interpretive as the explanatory led W. H. Auden to make his cruel remark, "Thou shalt not commit social science." If that is indeed what he intended to condemn, I quite agree.

Let me briefly draw together and clarify some of the claims about interpretations at which I have already hinted. Interpretation of the cultural world is (a) irretrievably indexical and dependent upon the perspective and meaning-making dispositions of the participants in the transactions to be interpreted, (b) dependent on a "narrative logic" for imposing order on its explanada, and (c) capable by the form of its expression of altering or maintaining the explananda it seeks to interpret. It must seem to follow from this brief set of assertions that I reject entirely the notion of an explanatory or "causal" psychology. But I most certainly do not, and I have no intention of claiming at this point that our lives as scientists have all been in vain. I happen to believe that psychologists live in both realms: That is their strength. Yet, their good fortune does not give them license to blur the two genres, if I may use that term. Rather, what I am saying is that our efforts at explanation—indeed, our work as problem-solving researchers—can never be taken at face value or without cultural interpretation. If one would tell me that at the .0001 level women are better at relating and men

---

[3]See Harman's essay in this volume for another, more interesting view of the nomothetic idiographic distinction.

better at achieving, I would simply reply that it is a statement that cannot stand uninterpreted on its own bottom in the world of culture. Uninterpreted, it says too little, too much, and if it claims to mean something at all on its own, it is simply playing a cultural game of parading under false identity. What it asks for, then, is the use of the mind in an interpretive way. I now return to explicating that matter.

Let me reiterate that we perceive, classify, judge, and remember specific encounters with particular people in particular situations. We also have abstract beliefs about human nature in general, about social class, political power, legitimacy, and the like. Typically, classification of a particular person's social class will bias how you judge their intelligence, and your speech register when addressing them will likely change accordingly. You will talk to them accordingly, which in turn will alter their response to you. More often than not, the transaction will produce something like self-fulfilling or self-defeating prophecies. Let us say that E. E. Jones now appears and surreptitiously reveals to both parties what they are up to. Both take thought and resolve to avoid such "difficulties" in the future, and so they go forth to future encounters with others.

By informing the participants, we have in effect put them in a mini version of the Prisoner's Dilemma. How they resolve their problems will depend on how they go about resolving such social "dilemmas." Because the general finding they have learned about is of no great predictive use in particular instances, they turn to the usual form of knowledge that contains information about the particulars of people's experience with similar events: what happened to whom in what situations impelled by which intentions guided by which beliefs, and so on. They are into what our colleague Geertz calls "thick interpretation."[4] Rather than escaping, they have got in more deeply. Knowledge of a top-down population rule may, in a Faustian way, make the bottom-up task more rather rather than less difficult.

So what makes for this "thickness"? Surely not just the reverberation of cultural biases in interpersonal transactions of the kind made so familiar by Jones (1990) and Gergen (1982). There is a far more puzzling difficulty than the transactional one. It stems from the manner in which self enters into those baroque transactions to which I just alluded.[5] For by all views, self is constructed in the course of transactions with nature and culture, both of

---

[4]The reality of "thick interpretation" does not in itself constitute a justification of "interpretive anthropology." That needs justification on a somewhat different level, a matter to which I turn later.

[5]I believe it matters little at this point how one "defines" self—whether as a set of executive routines, as a phenomenological given, or as a production system in a computational routine. All the theoretical versions of self that have been formulated in the literature of psychology over the last century are subject to the dilemma I am setting forth— from James and Baldwin to Markus and Johnson-Laird.

which are likewise constructed in coordination with self-construction. We estimate our traits, our capabilities, and our options and commitments by reference to a world we have constructed, and in turn construct that world in light of those intrapsychic judgments. Both of these—self and personal world—are powerfully influenced by the cultural models made accessible to us by the language we speak and the canonical forms we inherit from those around us. I have long been convinced that it is this intractable complementarity of self and world that makes theories of personality appropriate objects for anthropological investigation. They are cultural texts in their own right—like myths and laws and property rules. Indeed, it is no surprise that in recent years many of the best critiques of theories of personality have come not only from text-oriented psychologists and anthropologists (e.g., Polkenhorne, Gergen, Geertz, Rosaldo, and Shweder) but from literary theorists concerned with the textual narrative techniques by which characters and plots in literature and autobiography are constructed (e.g., Chatman, 1978; Eakin, 1985; Geertz, 1973; Gennette, 1972; Gergen, 1982; Greimas, 1987; Gunn, 1982; Olney, 1980; Polkinghorne, 1988; Rosaldo, 1980; Shweder, 1991). The bottom line in all this, of course, is that the process of self-in-world construction is a hermeneutic or interpretive one, and that the best that we as students of mind can do to understand it is to follow suit.[6] This does not mean that the only approach to understanding selfconstruction (or self-in-world construction) need be interpretive. We would be foolish indeed, for example, to pass up the opportunity to consider that a particular person under study happened to be in the top 1% of the distribution of introversion as measured by standardized texts, or that their use of passive verb constructions in accounting life events was 3 standard deviation units up from the normal. It is only that, in the end, the full issue of their self-construction cannot be resolved without recourse to an interpretive technique of analysis.

Cultures, of course, have a certain stake in obscuring the complementary relation that exists between self and cultural world. Institutionally, we make it seem as if the nature of self were, to use the current jargon, "essential-

---

[6]But again, this does not rule out the work of explanatory psychology, but only puts it in a new perspective. Psychologists of a deterministic bent may write and research endlessly about responsibility, but their conclusions cannot be understood without reference to established doctrines within jurisprudence that let us treat the concept not only as a folk-psychological given, but as, for example, a canonical formulation in such binding documents as the Mac-Naughton Rules governing pleas of insanity or reduced responsibility. The "proofs" of a Sigmund Freud or a B. F. Skinner regarding the illusory nature of the concept are not proofs in the Newtonian sense at all, but only commentaries on the culture—not unlike those of Jonathan Edwards. When Skinner cites experiments in operant conditioning to disprove "responsibility" as legally understood, it has no more status than Jonathan Edwards citing Newton in support of his views about the "democracy of mind." The proof of the pudding in each instance is not in verification, but in the power of such claims to change a culture's world view.

ist"—stemming from inherent conditions in the world out there, the world of posivitivism. Institutionally, we do all we can to make self seem like the outcome of natural (rather than cultural) conditions. This autochthonous bias is reinforced by invoking certain "natural kind" categories such as intelligence or temperament or "masculinity." We make it seem as if self develops entirely from the inside out, that it is not a function as well of the culturally patterned procedures for "making sense" of our position in a cultural world to whose structure we also contribute. It is not surprising, then, that the bogus nature of this presumption is now so often exposed by those whose self constructions have been distorted and denigrated by the position they are forced to occupy in the culture—women, minorities, and others who are publicly judged as socially aberrant. They are the first to recognize the importance of cultural reinterpretation in removing the stigma that attaches to a self judged to be culturally marginal. In a sense, their protest is akin to what Jonathan Edwards did in altering the widespread cultural presuppositions that were still in force at the time of the Great Awakening.

Let me return for a moment to the ancient "nomothetic–idiographic" distinction—the old notion that the two differed principally by virtue of their particularity or generality . I am not prepared to accept this view. It was usually said that our representations of the cultural world, by virtue of the particularity of history and personal individuality, were more idiosyncratic, that we were able to represent nature by general rules for depicting the inanimate. If this were all there were to it, we would never be able to cross a particular street or fix a particular furnace. There must be far more to it than that. Let me try to explain.

I have had some technical toys in my lifetime whose idiosyncratic details I knew microscopically and almost, as it were, with my soul—such as a sailing vessel in whose close company I traveled for many thousands of miles under sometimes unobliging conditions. Never mind that I anthropomorphized her. I also knew a lot of very high-tech details about her and even spent more money than I should have for scientific instruments that would tell me more. The particularity of my knowledge knew virtually no limit. I knew the permissible torsional strain on her 21-strand, stainless-steel shrouds, the directional thrust that derived from the difference between the position of her center of drive and her center of hull resistance. It is a subject on which I can quickly become a bore (and sometimes do).

Yet, my knowledge of *Wester Till's* particularity was not the same as the particularity of Jonathan Edwards' knowledge of his Northampton parishioners and their condition of life. His knowledge was riven with issues of intentionality—what things stood for, what the Great Awakening "meant" to the participants, what they were prepared to believe. In his world, events were dominated by agents with putative goals and with barriers to be overcome enroute to them. The outcomes in that world were seen to hang on the negotiations between these characters — why those merchants and landlords couldn't see his point and why Colonel Stoddard's power receded with his death. Each requires the construction of a little story.

Nothing of that order stumped me about *Wester Till*. The trick there was nothing like empathy or story making. All I needed was more detailed knowledge and a technique for reducing that knowledge to some general framework that would permit me to predict and control particular events — such as how fast I could travel downwind without jumping off a wave into a broach. You could measure variables in that Northampton situation until your hypothesis generator burned out without coming to a similarly controlled prediction — any closer, say, than the local wise man might come, armed with little more than a sense of likely stories on the local scene, stories lacking in independently determinable variables and parameters.

I use the word "story" advisedly. For that seems to be how human beings use their minds when faced with cultural-personal matters. We are given every cultural encouragement to do so, to encode in narrative. For the narrative is our natural as well as our conventional way for dealing with issues involving intentional states, desires, values, negotiations, and so on. It is not surprising, then, that the study of narrative is such an ancient pursuit, or that narrative persists as the chosen instrument for representing everyday human events. Nor is it surprising that our principal means for deciding normative quarrels, as in the law, should consist of a set of procedures for deciding which among two contending narratives best meets the criteria set forth by points of law. So what can we say about narrative as a mode of representing states of the world? Let me set out a sketch.

A narrative account always implies a prior canonical or norm-governed state of affairs that has been breached or upset in some way, usually by a precipitating event or deficit. Somebody did something or something happened that runs counter to common expectancy. The precipitating event may be either something "real" or the mental state of a protagonist or protagonists — usually both, as with the alienated disenchantment of Philoctetes who has cruelly been made a castaway by the Greeks in Sophocles' play of that name and refuses to return the bow of Heracles that by prophecy is needed to assure a Greek victory over the Trojans. The narrative action comprises efforts and maneuvers intended to reconstitute that initial canonical state or to contain the breach. There are obstacles to carrying out the reconstituting action. But the reconstituting action need not achieve conclusive results: It suffices that it render the circumstances and their sequelae clearer. A story, then, is about protagonists with intentional states, acting deliberately or inadvertently toward a goal by means relevant to the setting in which the story is laid. Its parts or constituents take their meaning from the role they play in the story as a whole. The whole, moreover, inevitably implicates a dual landscape: one in the alleged "world itself," and the other constituted by the mental states of protagonists. Story, whether purportedly real or fictive, requires temporary suspension of disbelief, but because at the end it will not be fully verifiable, it must justify this suspension by exhibiting verisimilitude.

A principle of relevance governs the telling of a story. It must contain not only an account of events along the lines noted earlier, but it must also contain a justification for being told on this particular occasion. Story and justification—the what and the why of telling—are carefully distinguished by tense marking, for example, or even by loci of signing in sign language. This suggests that stories lead rather a double life. The "what" of a story has due regard for such matters as coherence as well as the Gricean conversational maxims. Yet, the "why tell" fulfills the requirement of intersubjective accommodation with one's interlocutors—as when we tell a story to excuse our lateness or our rudeness. Accordingly, a story communicates not only a tale but implies one's plight, one's cultural position, and/or one's perspective on events recounted. In consequence, stories are constructed with a recipient rhetorically in mind. This, of course, imposes indexicality on the stories we tell, which, in turn, creates an ambiguity about the stories one "tells oneself": who is telling what to whom and to what end. This rhetorical ambiguity of story telling, of course, leaves perpetually in doubt what the "real" story is, or whether there is such a thing. In consequence, when the real story must be determined, as in legal process, we resort to such elaborate but artificial procedures as oaths, uniform rules of evidence, and so on—rules that, as Geertz has demonstrated, are themselves expressions of establishment cultural values.[7]

Stories, whether in our heads or told to others, are rarely original. They are modeled on stories in the culture's tool kit. Stored stories are not so much specific tales—though plenty of such are available in all cultures—as they are generic: genres of stories. It is widely believed by anthropologists and students of culture generally that genres are ambered versions of orientations toward the culture itself—sketch maps of possible social realities. A culture's narrative store, then, serves to structure communal reality, transmit values, and instantiate action. And so the maxim about life imitating art. More to the point, it imitates culture.

Do we know about stories only what we learn from others telling them? This seems highly unlikely. Our own research suggests that we have access to some sort of mental narrative generator very early on, one primed to incorporate the forms of story on offer in the culture, but which nonetheless may be characterized by some universal architecture. Schank and Abelson

---

[7]See Geertz's (1983) Storrs lectures on this subject presented at the Yale Law School.

(1977) suggested a form of script structure for storing the recurrent regularities encountered in restaurants or postoffices or doctor's offices. That is one way of storing those canonical states, breaches of which motivate stories, but it seems somewhat impoverished and lacks a normative element. It is only about expectable events and acts and not about breaches and the troubles that ensue from them. Efforts to write generative narrative grammars have not been notably successful, for stories are too dependent on the context of telling, too susceptible to what seems like unprincipled recursion, too lacking in either a standard lexicon or in definable story parts. Perhaps we should take heart from Propp (1968), Genette (1972), Mandler (1984), and Greimas (1987), who have at least tried to derive story formation rules from the properties of a story as a whole. Their struggles with order-preserving transformations, with deletion rules and caselike grammars, may help us toward a formal grammar and something approximating computability. But for reasons already stated, I doubt this will take us all the way. For I doubt whether the hermeneutic process, given the complexities already mentioned, is reducible to computable steps. More likely, it is upon the development of an interpretive anthropology and a counterpart cultural psychology that we shall have to depend for elucidation. Both of these will be more interpretively narrative than causally explanatory in form—more like the historian's than the scientist's trade.

George Miller (1990) concluded a recent paper with a carefully documented lament. Cognitive psychology, he argues, has become so specialized that its preoccupation with fundamental cognitive processes has displaced the study of how they work together to constitute higher cognitive activity— that is, how perception directed by attention permits us to gather information that can be evaluated against memory so that we can think of how to transform things into a more highly valued state of affairs that we can imagine. He then issues a "challenge to the adventurous" to say what those higher mental processes are.

Well, I can suggest a few answers to be seen through a glass darkly. To begin with, they rarely work in isolation, these higher cognitive processes, but in transaction with a culture that, in turn, responds reciprocally to the acts that follow from our thoughts. The culture, moreover, provides us with prosthetic devices that assure this reciprocity. Through these higher mental processes, furthermore, we construct representations of self and world, not simply in the interest of predicting or explaining, but in order to transact reciprocal interpretations that make possible the existence of a culture. These processes do much of this work by forging experience and memory into narrative form, a skill in which mind early and endlessly becomes engaged. Peggy Miller estimated that the working-class White children of

Baltimore whom she studied were exposed to seven personal experience narratives an hour which, reckoning a 10-hour day of exposure, comes to a quarter of a million personal experience narratives during the first 10 years of speech comprehension. This leaves out the child's own rhetoric-ridden productions and "story" stories encountered at home and in school.

We live in so narratively saturated a world that, as Flaubert once said, we become victim to the belief that it is "how the world really is." Producing this enchantment is surely one of the mind's great accomplishments, one of the ways in which it works.

Our stories, finally, may come to change the cultural world into which they are launched—much as Jonathan Edwards used Newton's discovery and Locke's propositions to change how people used their minds. Newton's empirically impeccable laws never touched the behavior of light. Yet, Locke's empirically immune narrative assertions about human agentivity, by shaping the first 10 amendments to our Constitution, bequeathed us a rhetoric of "rights" that is now as much a part of our reality as war and taxes. It is not that Newton or Edwards had a monopoly on how the mind works or "should work." These are two different modes of using mind. And *vive la difference*.

REFERENCES

Chatman, S. (1978). *Story and discourse: Narrative structure in fiction and film*. Ithaca, NY: Cornell University Press.

Cohen, I. B. (1956). *Franklin and Newton*. Philadelphia: American Philosophical Society.

Eakin, J. P. (1985). *Fictions in autobiography*. Princeton, NJ: Princeton University Press.

Geertz, C. (1973). *The interpretation of cultures*. New York: Basic Books.

Geertz, C. (1983). *Local knowledge*. New York: Basic Books.

Genette, G. (1972). *Narrative discourse: An essay in method*. Ithaca, NY: Cornell University Press.

Gergen, K. (1982). *Toward transformation in social knowledge*. New York: Springer.

Greimas, A. (1987). *On meaning: Selected writings in semiotic theory*. Minneapolis: University of Minneapolis Press.

Gunn, J. V. (1982). *Autobiography: Toward a poetics of experience*. Philadelphia: University of Pennsylvania Press.

Jones, E. E. (1990) *Interpersonal perception*. San Francisco: Freeman.

Kuhn, T. S. (1970). *The structure of scientific revolution* (2nd ed.). Chicago: University of Chicago Press.

Mandler, J. (1984). *Stories, scripts, and scenes: Aspects of schema theory*. Hillsdale, NJ: Lawrence Erlbaum Associates.

Miller, G. (1990). On explanation. *Annals of Theoretical Psychology, 6*, 7–37.

Miller, P. (1956). *Errand into the wilderness*. Cambridge, MA: Harvard University Press.

Olney, J. (Ed.). (1980). *Autobiography: Essays theoretical and critical*. Princeton, NJ: Princeton University Press.

Polanyi, M. (1953). *Personal knowledge*. Chicago: University of Chicago Press.

Polkinghorne, D. E. (1988). *Narrative knowing and the human sciences*. Albany, NY: SUNY Press.

Propp, V. (1968). *Morphology of the folktale* (2nd ed.). Austin: University of Texas Press.

Rosaldo, M. (1980). *Knowledge and passion: Ilongot notions of self and social life*. Cambridge: Cambridge University Press.

Schank, R., & Abelson, R. (1977). *Scripts, plans, goals, and understanding*. Hillsdale, NJ: Lawrence Erlbaum Associates.

Shweder, R. (1991). *Thinking through cultures*. Cambridge, MA: Harvard University Press.

von Wright, G. H. (1971). *Explanation and understanding*. Ithaca, NY: Cornell University Press.

9 Speaking of Objects, as Such

Susan Carey
Massachusetts Institute of Technology

George Miller was the keynote speaker for the first meeting of the Society for Philosophy and Psychology held at MIT in the mid-1970s. His paper summarized Quine's speculations concerning how children learn color words and went on to argue that linguistic analysis of the color lexicon, together with data from empirical studies of language acquisition, proved Quine's speculation wrong. This address launched a successful society, which is dedicated to two interrelated principles that Miller's career exemplifies: (a) many of the issues debated in philosophy of mind, philosophy of language, and philosophy of science are empirical issues on which the disciplines in cognitive science are making scientific progress; and (b) many of the issues debated in cognitive science have a long history in philosophy, and cognitive science ignores that history at its peril.

In this chapter, I follow Miller's lead, as I have many times in my career. I examine an important proposal of Quine's, versions of which are endorsed by thinkers as diverse as the British empiricists and Piaget. Quine, Piaget, and others maintained that early representations of the world are formulated over a perceptual quality space (Quine, the empiricists) or sensorimotor representational system (Piaget). On both Quine's and Piaget's views, the baby is not capable of formulating any representations with the properties of adult concepts such as *object*, *dog*, or *table*.

Quine's proposal is that the ontology that underlies language is a cultural construction. He stated, "Our conceptual firsts are middle-sized, middle distanced objects, and our introduction to them and to everything comes midway in the cultural evolution of the race" (1960, p. 5). Before the child has mastered this cultural construction, the child's conceptual universe consists of representations of histories of sporadic encounters, a scattered portion of what goes on. Quine speculated as to the representations underlying the toddler's uses of the words *water*, *red*, and *Mama*:

> His first learning of the three words is uniformly a matter of learning how much of what goes on about his counts as the mother, or as red, or as water. It is not for the child to say in the first case, "Hello, Mama again," in the second case "Hello, another red thing," and in the third case, "Hello, more water." They are all on a par: Hello, more Mama, more red, more water. (1960, p. 92)

The child masters the notion of an object, and of particular kinds of objects, in the course of getting the hang of what Quine calls "divided reference," through the process of mastering quantifiers and words like "same":

> The contextual learning of these various particles goes on simultaneously, we may suppose, so that they are gradually adjusted to one another and a coherent pattern of usage is evolved matching that of one's elders. This is a major step in acquiring the conceptual scheme that we all know so well. For it is on achieving this step, and only then, that there can be any general talk of objects as such. (1969, pp. 9–10)

In another place, he finished the same idea with a bootstrapping metaphor, underlining the degree of conceptual change he thinks is occuring: "The child scrambles up an intellectual chimney, supporting himself against each side by pressure against the others" (1960, p. 93). Quine also stated that once the child has mastered the notion of an object, and got the trick of divided reference, he goes back and reanalyzes "Mama," so that it is now the name of a unique enduring person.

Quine's view can be schematized as follows. Imagine a portion of the bottle experience that we adults would conceptualize as a single bottle. Babies respond to bottleness or bottlehood also and can learn many things about bottlehood; for instance, he or she can come to associate bottlehood with milk or with the word *bottle*. Now imagine a portion of the bottle experience that we would conceptualize as three bottles. The infant would also expect to obtain milk (indeed, more milk) from this bottleness and could also refer to it with the word *bottle*. Note that shape is important to the identification of bottlehood, just as the shape of the individual grains is important for distinguishing rice from spaghetti from macaroni. Similarly, even if Mama is a scattered portion of what goes one, shape is important for distinguishing Mama from Rover or from Papa. That shape is important for distinguishing what scattered portion of experience constitutes bottlehood does not mean that the baby is capable of representing "a bottle," "two bottles," or "the same bottle I had yesterday."

In this discussion I do not make contact with Quine's radical philosophical views such as the indeterminacy of translation. I assume that we can characterize the adult's ontological commitments, that these include middle-sized physical objects, and that words such as *table*, *dog*, and *person* function as sortals in the adult lexicon, in Wiggins' (1980) sense. Sortals refer to kinds of individuals (i.e., divide reference), providing conditions for individuation (establishing the boundaries of entities) and for numerical identity (establishing when an individuated entity is the *same one* as the one experienced at some other time or in some counterfactual world). One way of stating Quine's hypothesis, as I construe it, is that babies and toddlers represent no sortal concepts, no concepts that provide conditions of individuation and numerical identity, no concepts that divide reference.

Piaget, like Quine, believed that that baby must construct the concept of enduring objects, although he differed from Quine as to the mechanisms he envisioned underlying this construction. Quine saw the child's mastery of the linguistic devices of noun quantification, the machinery by which natural languages such as English manage divided reference, as the process through which the child's ontology comes to match his or her elders. Piaget held that the baby constructs the concept *object* during the course of sensorimotor development by the age of 18 months or so, and that this construction is the basis for the child's mastery of natural language. Because Piaget did not frame his discussion in terms of an analysis of the logic of sortals, it is not clear when he would attribute full sortals to the child.[1]

The Quine/Piaget conjecture about the baby's representational resources is a serious empirical claim, and as I show, it is difficult to bring data to bear it. In what follows, I first consider Quine's views, contrasting his hypothesis that children come to represent sortals only upon learning the linguistic devices of noun quantification with what I call the *sortal-first* hypothesis. The sortal-first hypothesis is that babies represent sortal concepts, that toddler lexicons include words that express sortals, and that these representations underly the capacity for learning quantifiers rather than resulting from learning them.

MASTERY OF COUNT-MASS SYNTAX

Quine's hypothesis is that the child masters the logic of sortals through a bootstrapping process, scrambling up an intellectual chimney of adjusting

---

[1]For example, Piaget thought that the logical prerequisites for representing the adult concepts *all* and *some* are not acquired until after age 5.

the meanings of natural language quantifiers to each other. To address Quine's conjecture experimentally, we must first know when in the child's life the putative scrambling is going on. Even by age 3 the child is not producing all the quantifiers that constitute the sides of Quine's chimney. The very beginnings of the English count/mass distinction are mastered in the months leading up to age $2\frac{1}{2}$. Many children age 2:0 produce nouns with no determiners or plurals, but some have begun to produce plurals and a few determiners and quantifiers (usually possessives such as *my*, plus *a* and *the*). Many 2-year-olds beginning to use determiners do not distribute them differently according to the noun's count/mass status in the adult lexicon. They still omit many determiners and use others such as *the* and *my* that do not differentiate count nouns and mass nouns. By $2\frac{1}{2}$, virtually all children distinguish in some ways the syntactic contexts in which words such as *table* and *dog* appear from those in which words such as *water* and *playdoh* appear (Gordon, 1985; Soja, Carey, & Spelke, 1991). Gordon (1982) showed that between $2\frac{1}{2}$ and 3 years of age the distinction becomes marked in syntax, as the child's speech abruptly comes to reflect the arbitrary rule that determiners are obligatory for singular count nouns, but not for mass nouns (that is, one can say "I like juice," but not *"I like dog").

The developmental facts previously summarized determine the relevant ages for an empirical test of Quine's speculations. Data bearing against Quine's claims could be of several types; for example, data show children age 2 or under take proper nouns to refer to individuals of a kind or that they take count nouns to refer to kinds of individuals. But, as already mentioned, the trick is figuring out how we can know whether toddlers' *Mama* refers to entities they conceptualize as individuals or whether their *bottle* divides reference, referring to each individual of a certain kind, as opposed to *bottlehood*.

Another type of evidence could be relevant. If it can be shown that upon first learning *a* or the plural *-s*, toddlers interpret them correctly, as signaling an individuated entity of a kind or a plurality of individuals of a kind, respectively, this would tell against Quine. This is because these are the first relevant quantifiers the child learns. If he or she interprets them correctly from the beginning, the interpretation could not have been acquired through a bootstrapping process involving the entire set of quantificational devices of noun syntax. This last point is important. In the beginnings of language learning, In Quine's view, children will not interpret those few quantifiers in their lexicons as adults do. The scramble will have just begun. Data showing that children use *a* and plurals will not be itself relevant to Quine's hypothesis: It must be shown that such quantificational devices are doing the same work as they do in the adult language.

THE COMPOSITION OF THE TODDLER LEXICON

A large proportion of the baby's first words are words for middle-sized physical objects, such as *bottle, book, dog, cup,* and *banana.* Yet, that babies have words in their lexicons that refer to object kinds in the adult lexicon tells us nothing of what these words mean to the babies. Many have argued that the earliest words are often complexive (e.g., Bowerman, 1978; Dromi, 1987; Vygotsky, 1962). That is, children appear to extend words to new referents on the basis of any of the salient perceptual properties of the original experiences in which the word was heard. These complexive uses often cut across what are for adults distinct ontological categories, as when *paper* apparently refers to the act of cutting; the act of drawing, to pens and pencils and to paper (Dromi, 1987). If such complexive uses reflect unconstrained (from the point of view of adult lexical categories) projection of word meanings, Quine's views receive support. But it is important to see that such complexive uses are not *necessary* for Quine's conjecture to be correct.

Indeed, others deny that toddlers construct complexive meanings Huttenlocher and Smiley (1987), for example, presented evidence that from the beginning babies used each word for middle-sized objects appropriately: *bottle* to refer to bottles, *book* to books, and so on. Yet, even if Huttenlocher and Smiley are right, this fact does not disconfirm Quine's conjecture. In fact, Quine presupposes that the baby uses the words in contexts adults would. His point is that, even so, the baby might not be individuating the words' referents as we do. The baby could refer only to what we conceptualize as bottles when he or she uses *bottle* but could also be referring to bottlehood. He or she could be using the word to refer to a scattered portion of what goes on, determined by perceptual similarity to the portions of his or her experience when adults use *bottle.*

TODDLER SENSITIVITY TO NOUN SYNTAX

Children as young as 17 months (at least girls that young) are sensitive to the syntactic context in which a new noun is heard in their projection of noun meaning (Katz, Baker, & Macnamara, 1974; Macnamara, 1982). Specifically, if ostensively taught a new word in a count-noun context, referring to an unfamiliar doll ("See this. This is a dax. Can you touch the dax? Can you put the dax on your head . . ."), they assume that other dolls of the same type are also daxes. But if taught in a proper noun context ("See this. This is Dax. Can you touch Dax. Can you put Dax on your head . . ."), they assume that other dolls of the same type are *not* Dax, reserving *Dax* for the original doll only.

Do these data establish that young children distinguish kinds from individuals and use count nouns to achieve divided reference? Certainly not. They *do* establish that toddlers are sensitive to the syntactic distinction between nouns following determiners and those not following determiners, but this distinction could be signaling a different semantic distinction than that between individuals and kinds. For an example of Quinian interpretation: Babies could take nouns without determiners such as *Dax*, *Rover*, and *Joan*, to refer to portions of experience defined by a stricter similarity metric than that referred to by nouns with determiners. Suppose a Quinian baby, Alice, has a brother whom she hears called both *Rupert* and *a boy*. Suppose also that she relies on shape to determine Rupertness and boyness. She could have learned from other's usage of the words that to be called *Rupert*, a given portion of experience must be very similar in shape to the original portions of experience to which the term was heard to refer; whereas to be called *a boy*, *the boy*, something need look only somewhat like the original referent. A generalization of this pattern of distinction, across *Alice* and *a baby Rover*, and *a dog*, and so on, could underly the patterns of projection found by Katz et al. (1974) and subsequent replications.

This interpretation of the Katz et al. data attributes to the baby a different meaning for *a* from the adult as well as different meanings for *bottle*, *boy*, and *Rupert*. This is, of course, Quine's position. In his view, it is only in the course of learning other quantifiers, plural markers, and so on, and adjusting to all the contrasts in usage they mark (the process of scrambling up the intellectual chimney cited above) that the baby works out the meaning of *a*, *the*, *another*, *some more*, *all*, *many*, *same*, and so on.

WORDS FOR NOVEL OBJECTS AND WORDS FOR NONSOLID SUBSTANCES

In several studies, my colleagues and I attempted to address Quine's proposal by comparing children's representations of solid physical objects, such as cups, with their representations of nonsolid substances, such as sand or gels or creams. Our idea is that because adults conceptualize the former as kinds of individuals (i.e., in terms of sortals that divide reference), but do not conceptualize the latter in this way, we might be able to find evidence that infants and toddlers respect the quantificational distinction between the two as well.

In the first studies, Soja et al. (1991) compared 2-year-olds' projection of newly learned words ostensively defined by reference either to novel solid physical objects (e.g., a brass plumbing T) or novel nonsolid substances (e.g., a hair-setting gel with grapenuts embedded in it). The objects were made of unfamiliar materials, and the nonsolid substances that were presented formed into distinctive novel shapes. The child was introduced to the novel entity and provided a word for it (e.g. *blicket* for a novel object; *stad* for a novel nonsolid substance). The child was then presented two new sets of stimuli and asked to give the experimenter the blicket or the stad. For each object trial, the choices consisted of another object of the same shape made of a different material (e.g., a plastic plumbing T) or three small pieces of the original material (brass). For each substance trial, the choices consisted of a new substance formed into the original shape or three small pieces of the original substance. Figure 9.1 shows the design for one trial of each type. There were four object trials and four nonsolid substance trials. Of course, which words were assigned to which entities varied across subjects, but for expository clarity I use *blicket* as my sample object name and *stad* as my sample nonsolid substance name.

Soja et al. (1991) carried out two analyses to assess whether children's representations of the referents of the words were influenced by the status of their knowledge of count/mass syntax. First, they collected production data and assigned each child a value corresponding to the degree to which count nouns and mass nouns appeared in selective syntactic frames (e.g., "a NOUN," "NOUNs" "too much NOUN"). Scores ran from 0 to near 1.0.

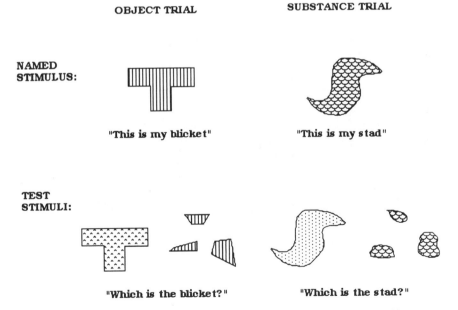

FIG. 9.1.   Object trials and substance trials in Soja, Carey, and Spelke, 1991.

Second, they introduced the new words in two different ways. In the neutral syntax condition, no syntactic information as to the count/mass status of the word was provided. The words were introduced as *my blicket, my stad* and subsequently appeared in the context *the blicket, the stad.* In the informative syntax condition, the words were introduced as *a blicket, some stad*, and further differentiated syntactically, for example, *another blicket, some more stad.*

As Figure 9.2 shows, children at age 2:0 and 2:6 used different bases for their projection of words for the two different types of entities. They projected *blicket* to the other whole object the same shape as the original referent, and they projected *stad* to the scattered portion of substance the same texture and color as the original referent. For object trials, children were sensitive to matches in shape and number; for nonsolid substance trials, children ignored matches in shape and number. Performance was more adultlike on the object trials, but performance on both types of trials was better than chance at both ages. Also apparent on Fig. 9.2, the syntactic

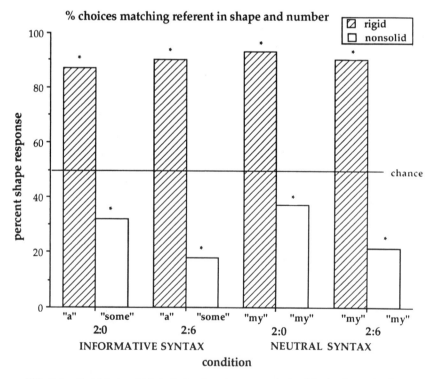

FIG. 9.2.   % trials in which test stimulus chosen matched original referent in shape and number. Soja, Carey, and Spelke, 1991.

context made no difference. The children were no more likely to interpret *blicket* as the word for a kind of individual when it was heard in a count-noun context. Similarly, hearing *stad* in a mass-noun context made them no more likely to conceptualize stad as a substance that can appear either in scattered or singly bounded portions. Further, the child's productive control of count/mass syntax did not influence the pattern of projection: Children with differentiation scores of 0 showed the same pattern as those with differentiation scores close to 1.

We conclude from these results that an entity's status as a solid physical object (or not) influences what of its properties are salient in determining what other entities are referred to by the same word. We also conclude that this distinction between objects and nonsolid substances predates mastery of count/mass syntax. These data are consistent with the sortal-first hypothesis, for they are consistent with the child's taking *blicket* to refer to each individual whole object of a kind, and *stad* to refer to a kind of substance, conceptualized as a nonindividuated entity. Yet, the data are also consistent with the following, more Quinian, interpretation of the child's representations of the blicket and the stad.

Babies, being "body-minded" (Quine, 1974), could be sensitive to the perceptual experiences that determine objecthood: boundedness, rigidity, or coherence through motion. Whenever these are detected, they could heavily weigh features like shape in their representation of these experiences. Shape would thus be a salient feature of the *blicket*, but not of the *stad*, for nonsolid substances do not maintain their shapes when manipulated. For nonsolid substances, properties such as texture and color might be salient, for these stay constant over experiences with substances. In other words, the 2-year-old could be using *blicket* to refer to blicketness and recognize blicketness by shape. The differential patterns of projection do not establish that the toddler is using *blicket* to refer to any individual whole object of a certain kind or that the toddler divides the reference of *blicket*.

One detail of the data from Fig. 9.2 favors the sortal first over the Quinian interpretation, and that is that toddlers performed more like adults on the object trials than on the substance trials. Quine's interpretation of this would have to be ad hoc, perhaps that the baby has had more object experience than substance experience. Yet, the sortal-first hypothesis predicts this assymetry. To see this, suppose the sortal-first hypothesis is true and that on first hearing the word *blicket* the child assumes that it refers to each individual object of a certain kind. The choices for testing how the child projects *blicket* included another single object and three small objects. Even if the child isn't exactly sure of which features of the blicket establishs its kind, the child can rule out that the three small objects are a blicket, for under no interpretation can they be an individual object of the same kind as the original referent. Children should then be at ceiling on the object trials, which they are. The substance trials are another story. If on first hearing *stad*, the child takes it to refer to the kind of substance of the original referent, then scattered portions have no different status from unitary portions. There is no clue from the number of piles which of the choices on the test trials is the stad. If children are not certain what properties of the original sample of stad determines the kind *stad*, they might do worse on the stad trials. And indeed, they do.

The key issue here is the role of number in determining how to project *blicket*. If the Quinian interpretation of the data is correct, the baby should project *blicket* on the basis of shape similarity, no matter whether the choice that does not match in shape consists of one object or three objects. That is, the baby should succeed on an object trial as in Figure 9.3 as well as on an object trial as in Fig. 9.1. The sortal-first interpretation predicts that performance on the object trials will fall to the level of performance on the substance trials if the cue from number is removed (Fig. 9.3). In an object trial such as that on Fig. 9.3, *blicket* is ostensively defined as before, but the choices for projection are changed: another blicket of a different material (as before), and another whole object of a different kind made of the same material as the original referent (instead of the three small objects). Now the child has no clues from the number of objects as to which is the correct choice. Performance should fall to the level of the substance trials, and indeed, this is what happens (Soja, 1987).

Apparently, the child uses the information provided by number on the object trials, but not on the substance trials. We take this as evidence that

**NAMED
STIMULUS:**

"This is my blicket"

**TEST
STIMULI:**

"Which is the blicket?"

FIG. 9.3.   Object trial in Soja, 1987.

the child conceptualizes some entities as individuals (such as kinds of objects) and conceptualizes other entities as nonindividuals (such as kinds of substances). These distinct ways of conceptualizing objects and substances predates mastery of count/mass syntax. Toddlers do not merely project *blicketness* on the basis of the shape of individual pieces of blicketness, as we determine whether some pasta is spaghetti on the basis of the shape of individual pieces. Instead, the pattern of projection suggests toddlers divide reference of *blicket* and take it to refer to any individual of a certain kind.

TODDLERS' UNDERSTANDING
OF *A NOUN, SOME NOUN*

The data reviewed in the previous section show that by age 2:0 children take *blicket* to refer to individual objects of a certain kind and *stad* to refer to nonsolid substances of a kind, and that the toddlers' representations of blickets and stads have the same quantificational structure as adults'. *Blicket* is a sortal term. These data disconfirm Quine only on the assumption that the baby did not bootstrap these representations from learning English noun quantifiers. This assumption seems warranted, given that, as a whole, toddlers at 2:0 do not produce quantifiers and the pattern of projection was independent of whether the individual subjects produced any noun quantifiers selective for count nouns. A worry, though, is that babies may have better comprehension than the production of the quantifiers.

We attempted to address that possibility by manipulating the syntactic context in which the word appeared. As mentioned previously, the syntactic environment in which the new word appeared had no effect in Soja et al.'s (1987) experiments, even at age $2 \frac{1}{2}$ when many children did produce quantifiers differentially for what are count and mass nouns in the adult lexicon. The Quinian interpretation of this fact is that quantifiers such as *a, another, some NOUN___*, and *some, more NOUN___* do not yet signal the distinction between individual and nonindividuated entities, just as the child is not projecting *blicket* and *stad* on the basis of that distinction. The sortal-first interpretation states that objects are naturally construed as individuals of a kind, and nonsolid substances are naturally construed as nonindividuated entities, even by toddlers, as shown by performance in the neutral-syntax condition. Informative syntax merely reinforces the child's natural construal of the two types of entities.

A study by Soja (1992) decided between these two interpretations and also established that our production data did not underestimate toddlers' interpretation of the quantifiers. Soja taught toddlers words for the objects and substances under a new condition: contrastive syntax. *Blicket* was introduced in a mass-noun context; *stad* in a count-noun context. That is, when shown a novel solid object, the child was told, "Here's some blicket. . . . Would you like to see some more blicket?" When shown a nonsolid substance fashioned into a distinctive shape, the child was told, "Here's a stad. . . . Would you like to see another stad?" As shown in Figure 9.4, at both ages 2 and 2 $\frac{1}{2}$, the pattern of projection was markedly different from that seen in the neutral- and informative-syntax conditions (Fig. 9.2). At both ages, the syntactic context *some NOUN__, some more NOUN__* made children slightly less likely to construe *blicket* as refering to an individual whole object of a kind. There was a slight tendency towards intrepreting it to mean something like *brass*. The syntactic context *a stad* made children significantly less likely to construe the nonsolid substance as a nonindividuated entity. Rather, they interpreted the word as meaning something like *s-shaped pile*.

Wait, you might say, doesn't this show that children at these ages do know the force of *a, another,* and so might have learned to represent sortal concepts

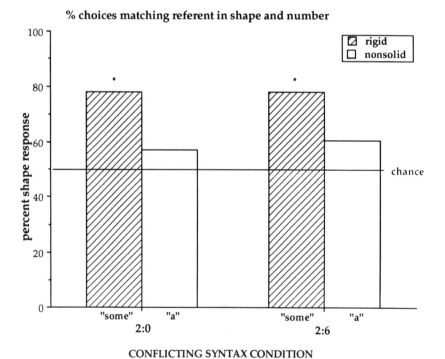

% choices matching referent in shape and number

CONFLICTING SYNTAX CONDITION

* different from chance

FIG. 9.4. % trials in which test stimulus chosen matched original referent in shape and number in Soja, 1992.

in conjunction with bootstrapping the meaning of the quantifiers? No, because of one further aspect of the data. At the younger age, this pattern was due entirely to the responses of those children who had differentiated count and mass nouns in their production. Those whose differentiation scores were low performed just like the toddlers in the informative and neutral conditions, projecting *blicket* to the other object of the same kind as the original referent and *stad* to the other substance of the same kind as the original referent. This shows that the interpretation of *blicket* as a sortal predates learning the meaning of *a, another*, and presumably underlies the latter achievement, as predicted by the sortal-first hypothesis.

These data tap the very moment children first learn the meaning of *a*. They have only begun the scramble up Quine's chimney and have not had time to adjust their interpretation of *a* to many other quantifiers. Yet, *a* signals an individuated entity of some kind. Together these data provide converging support for the sortal-first hypothesis. The child naturally construes physical objects as individuals in distinct kinds, and naturally construes nonsolid substances in terms of kinds of nonindividuated entities. These natural construals support adultlike projection of word meaning (Fig. 9.2) and support adultlike interpretation of newly learned quantifiers such as *a, some* and plurals.

PRINCIPLES OF INDIVIDUATION:
YOUNGER INFANTS

Altogether the data support the sortal-first hypothesis over Quine's conjecture, but they do not establish when the child first begins to represent sortal concepts. As already noted, it is not clear when Piaget would attribute sortal concepts to children, but it is certain that he would deny them to young infants. The argument I developed so far does not bear on Piaget's claims about the representational capacities of infants, as it concerns children age 24 months and older. Of course, a demonstration that young infants represent sortal concepts would defeat Quine's conjecture as well as Piaget's characterization of the infants' conceptual resources.

Piaget's characterization of infants' cognitive capacities was based on tasks in which the baby must solve some problem, often involving means–end analysis, and often involving planning some action. For example, Piaget's conclusions that babies do not represent objects as continuing to exist when out of view were based on the robust finding that babies under 8 or 9 months cannot remove a cover to get a hidden object. The babies' failure might be due to their failure to realize the object still exists, as Piaget thought, or equally might be due to their inability to carry out one action (remove a cover) to achieve some other goal (obtain the object). What is needed is some reflection of the baby's conceptualization of the world that relies on behaviors well within the repertoires of even neonates. Over the past 15 years or so, such a method has been developed and is now very widely used. It relies on babies' ability to control what they attend to.

The basic idea is simple. Under most circumstances, babies will look longer at what is unfamiliar or unexpected compared to what is familiar or expected. Researchers use this fact to diagnose how the baby represents some situation, especially what the baby considers surprising given his or her current state of physical knowledge. The selective-looking paradigm has been used extensively to probe babies' representations of objects, and the data from a subset of these studies can be recruited to bear on the question at hand. They establish that by 4 months of age the baby represents at least one sortal concept—the concept of a physical object. The baby has criteria for individuation and for numerical identity of objects.

Spelke and her colleagues have shown that babies establish representations of objects on the basis of criteria which individuate them—an object is a coherent, bounded, entity that maintains its coherence and boundaries as it moves through space (see Spelke, 1990, for a review). The baby predicts the motion of objects according to principles such as that one object cannot pass through the space occupied by another (Baillargeon, 1990; Spelke, Breinlinger, Macomber, & Jacobson, 1992). Most relevant to the present discussion are studies showing that babies count objects.

These studies are of two types. In the first, babies are simply presented with arrays containing a fixed number of objects, one after another. For example, two cups, followed by two shoes, two bottles, two hats, two pens, and so on. The pairs of objects are never repeated, so the arrays have nothing in common but twoness. The baby's looking is monitored and, after a while, the baby's attention to each new array decreases, relative to his or her original looking time. The baby is getting bored. After looking time has decreased to one-half its original level, the baby is presented with an array containing one object or three objects. In both cases, looking time recovers to its original level. The baby notices the difference between two objects, on the one hand, and a single object or three objects, on the other. This result, or one very like it, can be obtained with neonates.

In fact, the baby's capacity to detect similarity in number across distinct arrays serves as a methodological wedge into the problem of how babies individuate objects. The baby can be habituated, as described above to two objects and then presented with an array consisting of two distinct objects pushed up next to each other, thus sharing a common boundary. Babies dishabituate to this array, showing that they perceive it as one object rather than two. These data support the conclusion, derived from other types of data as well, that babies are not sensitive to shape or texture regularity in individuating objects; they need positive evidence of distinct boundaries, such as one object moving with respect to the other, or the objects' being separated in space.

A second source of evidence that babies count objects derives from data showing that babies can add and subtract. Wynn (1992) showed 4-month-olds events as in Figure 9.5. An object was placed on an empty stage while the baby watched, and then a screen was raised that covered the object. A hand carrying a second object was shown going behind the screen and returning empty. The screen was then lowered, revealing either one object (unexpected outcome, even though that was what the baby had last seen) or two objects (expected outcome, if the baby knows 1 + 1 = 2). Babies looked longer at the unexpected outcome.

A further experiment showed that babies expected exactly two objects, rather than simply more than one object. In this study, the expected outcome was two objects, as before, but the unexpected outcome was three objects. Again, babies were bored at seeing two there and looked longer at the unexpected outcome of three objects. Experiments of the same sort demonstrated that babies expected 3 − 1 to be 2, and 2 − 1 to be 1.

Whereas these studies were performed to explore the baby's concept of *number*, they bear on our question as well. Babies, no more than anybody, cannot count unless they have criteria that establish individuals to count. Babies clearly have criteria that establish small physical objects as countable individuals.

PRINCIPLES OF NUMERICAL IDENTITY: YOUNGER INFANTS

That babies individuate and count objects does not show that they trace identity of objects through time, that they have the representational

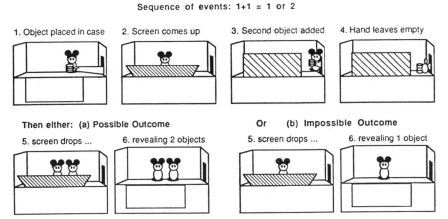

FIG. 9.5.   Addition (1 + 1 = 2) trials from Wynn, 1992.

capacity to distinguish one object seen on different occasions from two numerically distinct but physically similar objects. However, there are now two demonstrations of this capacity in infants age 4-months or younger. Spelke (1988) showed babies objects moving behind and reemerging from two separated screens, Screen A to the left of Screen B (Figure 9.6). An object emerged to the left of Screen A and returned behind it, and then an object emerged to the right of Screen B and returned behind it. At any given time, at most one object was visible, and no object ever appeared in the space between Screens A and B. Under these conditions, 4-month-olds inferred there must be two objects, as shown by the fact that when the screens were removed, revealing two objects (expected outcome), they looked less than when the screens were removed revealing one object (unexpected outcome). Baillargeon (1990) showed infants two objects at once, one on either side of a screen. The babies then used the existence of two numerically distinct objects to make sense of what would be an impossible event if only one object were involved. Together these studies show that babies use two spatiotemporal principles to individuate and trace identity of objects: One object cannot be in two places at the same time, and one object cannot go from one place to another without tracing a spatiotemporally continuous path.

In summary, infants have a concept *physical object* that functions as a sortal; they have at least one concept that divides reference.

A MAJOR CONCEPTUAL DIFFERENCE BETWEEN YOUNG INFANTS AND ADULTS

Adults use spatiotemporal information the same way as infants; indeed, adults also look longer at the unexpected events in these experiments. Adults can (and do) also ask how the magic tricks are done. But adults use another type of information in establishing individuals and tracing their identity through time: membership in kinds more specific than *physical object*.

Consider the events depicted in Figure 9.7. An adult witnessing a truck emerge from behind and reenter a screen and then witnessing an elephant emerge from behind and reenter the screen would infer that there are at least two objects behind the screen: a truck and an elephant. The adult would make this inference in the absence of any spatiotemporal evidence for two distinct objects, not having seen two at once nor any suggestion of a discontinuous path through space and time. Adults trace identity relative to sortals such as *truck* and *elephant* and know that trucks do not turn into elephants.

Xu and Carey (1992) carried out four experiments based on this design. Ten-month-old babies were shown screens from which two objects of

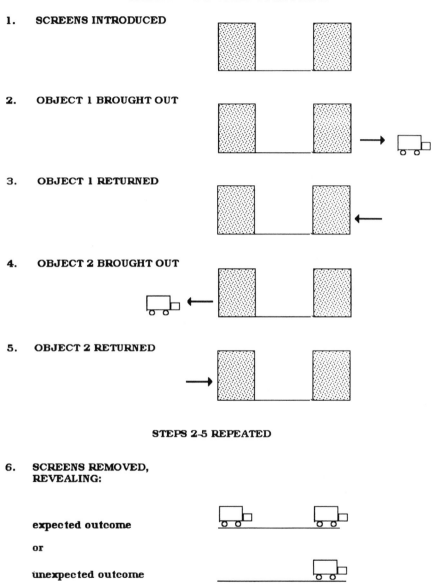

SPATIO-TEMPORAL CONDITION

1. SCREENS INTRODUCED

2. OBJECT 1 BROUGHT OUT

3. OBJECT 1 RETURNED

4. OBJECT 2 BROUGHT OUT

5. OBJECT 2 RETURNED

STEPS 2-5 REPEATED

6. SCREENS REMOVED,
    REVEALING:

    expected outcome

    or

    unexpected outcome

FIG. 9.6.   Numerical identity trials, after Spelke, 1988.

155

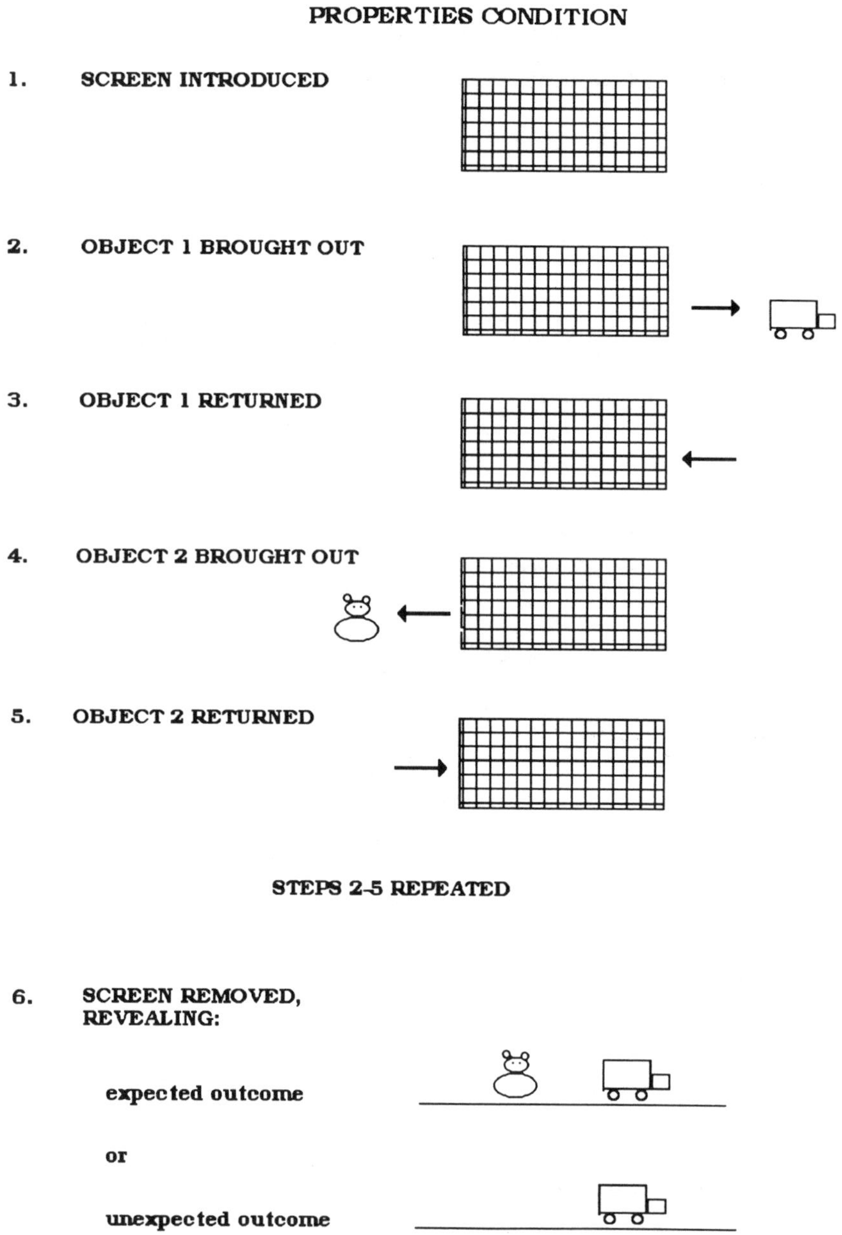

PROPERTIES CONDITION

1. **SCREEN INTRODUCED**

2. **OBJECT 1 BROUGHT OUT**

3. **OBJECT 1 RETURNED**

4. **OBJECT 2 BROUGHT OUT**

5. **OBJECT 2 RETURNED**

STEPS 2-5 REPEATED

6. **SCREEN REMOVED, REVEALING:**

   expected outcome

   or

   unexpected outcome

FIG. 9.7. Numerical identity trials, Xu and Carey, 1992.

different kinds (e.g., a cup and a toy elephant, a ball and a truck) emerged from opposite sides, one at a time. Each object was shown a total of four times. After this familiarization, the screen was removed, revealing either two objects (expected outcome) or one object (unexpected outcome). In all four studies, babies looked longer at the expected outcome. They could not use the difference between a cup and an elephant to infer that there must be two objects behind the screen.

Another group of 10-month-olds was run in a parallel version of this study based on Spelke's design (Fig. 9.6). That is, babies were shown the objects emerging from the two screens a total of four times each, and the timing of the events was the same in the one screen/two kinds studies. Babies succeeded, looking longer at the unexpected outcome of one object. Apparently, babies can use spatiotemporal information to individuate objects before they can use kind information.

We have ruled out several alternative accounts of the failure in this study. For example, it is not that babies do not notice the difference between the two objects. In one version of the study, babies were allowed to handle each object (one at a time, of course, for we didn't want to provide spatial information that there were two) before beginning the events. This made no difference to the results. Also, we compared looking time to the familiarization events when the objects were of different kinds (e.g., a cup and an elephant) to a condition when the objects emerging from each side of the screen were of the same kind (e.g., two elephants). Babies habituated much faster in the latter condition. They noticed that the elephant and the cup were different from each other; they simply could not use this information to derive the inference that there must be two numerically distinct objects behind the screen.

One way of putting these results is that very young babies represent at least one sortal concept, *physical object*, but may not represent any other sortals, even those lexicalized as basic-level count nouns in the adult lexicon. If this is true, then in one sense Quine was right. Very young infants do not have the conceptual resources to represent the meanings of words such as *bottle, ball,* and *dog*.

At 11 months, about half of the babies we test succeed at our task. It is significant that babies began to comprehend and produce object names at about 10 to 12 months of age. Again, this pattern of results is consistent with the sortal-first hypothesis. That is, babies do not seem to learn words for bottlehood; they do not learn *bottle* until they have a sortal concept *bottle* that provides conditions for individuation and numerical identity. Current studies in our lab are exploring the relations between specific words understood and success at individuation based on the kinds expressed by those words.

It is not surprising that babies use spatiotemporal information before kind information to individuate and trace the identity of objects. All physical objects trace spatiotemporally continuous paths; no physical object can be in two places at the same time. However, what property changes are possible in a persisting object depends upon the kind. An apparent change of relative location of the handle to the body of a ceramic cup signifies a different cup; an apparent change of relative location of a hand to the body of a person does not signify a different person.

In summary, these data suggest that babies have at least one innate sortal concept—*physical object*. Their object concept provides spatiotemporal conditions for individuation and numerical identity. They can use spatio-temporal information to identify individuals in their environment, and can then learn more specific sortals for kinds of these objects. Exactly how this is accomplished is the big question, of course. The present data suggest that they spend most of their first year of life on this accomplishment.

A FEW CONCLUDING REMARKS

My story is not complete. Most importantly, I have as yet no account of the mechanism by which babies begin to learn specific sortals. My goal in telling this incomplete tale is to reiterate the points George Miller made in his keynote address to the first meeting of the Society for Philosophy and Psychology. To wit, many issues philosophers attempt to address a priori are actually empirical ones. Like any empirical issues worth spending time on, they are not easily resolved. But the issues of the origins of sortal concepts and the relations between innate concepts and language are ripe for empirical progress.

REFERENCES

Baillargeon, R. (1990, August). *Young infants' physical knowledge.* Paper presented at the American Psychological Association Convention, Boston.

Bowerman, M. (1978). The acquisition of word meaning: An investigation into some current conflicts. In N. Waterson & C. Snow (Eds.), *Development of communication.* New York: Wiley.

Dromi, E. (1987). *Early lexical development.* London: Cambridge University Press.

Gordon, P. (1982). *The acquisition of syntactic categories: The case of the count/mass distinction.* Unpublished doctoral dissertation, Massachusetts Institute of Technology, Cambridge, MA.

Gordon, P. (1985). Evaluating the semantic categories hypothesis: The case of the count/mass distinction. *Cognition, 20,* 209–242.

Huttenlocher, J., & Smiley, P. (1987). Early word meanings: The case of object names. *Cognitive Psychology, 19,* 63–89.

Katz, N., Baker, E., & Macnamara, J. (1974). What's in a name? A study of how children learn common and proper names. *Child Development, 45,* 469–473.

Macnamara, J. (1982). *Names for things: A study of human learning.* Cambridge, MA: MIT Press.

Macnamara, J. (1986). *A border dispute.* Cambridge, MA: MIT Press.

Quine, W. V. O. (1960). *Word and object.* Cambridge, MA: MIT Press.

Quine, W. V. O. (1969). *Ontological relativity and other essays.* New York: Columbia University Press.

Quine, W. V. O. (1974). *The roots of reference.* New York: Columbia University Press.

Soja, N. N. (1987). *Ontological constraints on 2-year-olds' induction of word meanings.* Unpublished doctoral dissertation, Massachusetts Institute of Technology, Cambridge, MA.

Soja, N. N. (1992). Inferences about the meanings of nouns: The relationship between perception and syntax. *Cognitive Development, 7,* 29–45.

Soja, N. N., Carey, S., & Spelke, E. S. (1991). Ontological categories guide young children's inductions of word meaning: Object terms and substance terms. *Cognition, 38,* 179–211.

Spelke, E. S. (1988). The origins of physical knowledge. In L. Weiskranz (Ed.), *Thought without knowledge* (pp. 168–184). Oxford: Oxford University Press.

Spelke, E. S. (1990). Principles of object perception. *Cognitive Science, 14,* 29–56.

Spelke, E. S., Breinlinger, K., Macomber, J., & Jacobson, K. (1992). Origins of knowledge. *Psychological Review, 99,* 605–632.

Vygotsky, L. S. (1962). *Thought and language.* Cambridge, MA: MIT Press.

Wiggins, D. (1980). *Sameness and substance.* Cambridge: Harvard University Press.

Wynn, K. (1992). Addition and subtraction by human infants. *Nature, 358,* 749–750.

Xu, F., & Carey, S. (1992, October). *Principles of individuation and identity in 10-month-old infants.* Paper presented to the Boston University Language Acquisition Conference, Boston, MA.

10 How Mind Works, if There is One

Wendell R. Garner
Yale University

October 2, 1991

Professor Emeritus George Armitage Miller

Princeton University

Dear George,

It is my understanding that you requested me, among others, to tell you how Mind works. For me, that was a strange request, because you and I had that all figured out nearly 50 years ago. You must have forgotten. But it will be 50 years this coming June that you and I, two callow, apprehensive youths, were sitting on a bench in Emerson Hall, waiting for the departmental chairman to tell us how to begin being graduate students at Harvard. It was 8:00 a.m., and after a while a janitor informed us that nobody turned up before 10:00. That left us some time to get acquainted. We discovered that neither of us had a room to sleep and study in and agreed that we could probably get one room for the two of us more cheaply than each getting his own room. So we rented one room (appropriately it was on Wendell Street) and a summer of learning was on its way.

We couldn't just go to classes and study all day every day; thus, it was often late at night when we engaged in bull sessions. It was in these bull sessions that you and I figured out how Mind works, but we were so young and innocent that it never occurred to us either to record our deliberations for posterity, or at least to make notes so that 50 years later we would be able to capitalize on our youthful brilliance. But I may be remembering poorly just how advanced our thinking was.

My understanding is also that each of us is to pull back from our professional constraints and sort of wing it. That's fine, but I also remember that once upon a time a wise man said, to paraphrase, that after you reach 70 years (or is it 60?), all you can really do is plagiarize yourself. Whether that apocryphal wise man was indeed that wise, I do not know. Nevertheless, I do know that today I am going to plagiarize myself, with no apology, having reached both of the ages at which it is permissible, if not inevitable, to do so. What I am going to do is list several facts about Mind, discussing each of them in turn.

MIND DOES EXIST

Before commenting on how Mind works, I first have to be sure that Mind exists. That has never really been a question for me personally, and I suspect for most of us who have spent the greater part of our lives studying perception. I realize that 50 years ago stimulus–response psychology so dominated experimental psychology that many people truly did not believe there is a mind. But not for me or for you either. For a perception person (Garner, 1986), the response of a subject in an experiment is simply an indicant of the perception, just the means by which the experimental subject communicates to the experimenter.

The first time I made the existence of Mind as an explicit statement was in 1951, in a paper with Hake on the amount of information in absolute judgments (Garner & Hake, 1951). We used the mathematics of Shannon's information theory, but in doing so we also used the concept of a channel capacity. We were saying that there are indeed stimuli and responses, but that stimuli go through a channel to responses (Garner & Hake, 1951).

That channel is Mind, and there was no question to either Hake or myself that we were not interested in stimuli and responses as matters of concern in themselves; we were interested in that thing called a channel. Although we did not use the word *mind*, we implicitly accepted channel as that part of the organism that is Mind.

The next and strongest statement that Mind exists came in the 1956 paper with Hake and Eriksen (Garner, Hake, & Eriksen, 1956), in which we argued that one can learn about things inside the head even though only stimuli and responses are directly available to us as scientists. The basic technique for which we argued is the use of converging operations, a term that has become part of psychology's common language. One operation can tell you nothing about what goes on inside the head, but several operations can converge to let you know the properties of Mind without having to observe Mind directly. In this mode of thinking, Mind is an hypothetical construct, and the scientist who argues for its existence is behaving as a critical realist. That is the epistemologist's term for those people who do believe in a reality, but also believe that the organism observing reality has to engage in a process that allows it to know what that reality is. (The alternative positions are subjectivism, which denies reality, or direct realism, which denies the role of the organism.) Even though Mind is an hypothetical construct, it is to me a true entity, so real that it deserves to be capitalized as a proper name. That is why I say Mind with a capital M, not a mind.

It might be of some interest to know the circumstances that led us to write that article. All three of us were having difficulties with journal editors when we wanted to say something about perception being in the head. The typical editorial response was the stimulus–response one: There is no such thing as Mind. So we decided to write the article, making the argument for converging operations, and we did a good enough job that it was accepted for publication. Now when we sent articles to journal editors, we always referenced that paper. It is truly amazing that because we could cite a published paper (which we ourselves had written), our experimental papers were now accepted with no complaint. There's nothing like having something in print to make people believe there is truth there.

Actually, my most vivid memory of the refusal of so many psychologists at that time to believe that anything could exist between stimuli and responses is a result of a question I asked of a colloquium speaker at Johns Hopkins. The speaker was an eminent psychologist, and he was giving a talk on perceptual defense, in which subjects require a more intense stimulus to "perceive" a dirty or vulgar word than an emotionally neutral word. I asked whether such results couldn't simply be due to response inhibition. The speaker's reply to my question was that the response is the perception, so if there is inhibition to speak dirty words, there is perceptual inhibition by definition. A few experiences like that, plus our troubles with editors, made writing that paper very important to us.

MIND IS FUNCTION

To say that Mind is function is to denote the most important overall characteristic of Mind. By function, I mean that Mind is not a static entity that simply has one space for this thing, another for that thing, and so forth. It does things and is not just a storage bin for whatever happens to come along (Garner, 1980). But I didn't really need to tell you this. You didn't ask us to discuss what Mind is; you asked us to tell you how Mind works. That way of phrasing the question must have seemed very natural to you, and I doubt that you even considered the alternative of asking us what Mind is.

When I say that Mind is function, I mean function in the very broadest sense. Mind processes things, it encodes things, it selects what it will accept and rejects what it won't, it analyzes what has come to it, and it synthesizes things to form new entities (Garner, 1962, 1988). In addition to these things that Mind does, most of which can be subsumed under process, it can be functional in other ways as well. Certainly it can anticipate things, thus displaying expectancy. It can decide whether to pay attention to any particular thing or to things in general. In other words, it can decide at what effort level it will work, and that is function too.

The most natural antonym to function is structure—structure in the architect's sense of a constructed edifice and its parts. (Structure as the interrelation between parts I want to reserve for other purposes.) There are two types of structural components I want to mention. One is the structural unit used in information-processing approaches to cognitive psychology, that is, the stage. Stages themselves are not Mind, but they may be structural units used by Mind. However, Mind uses these structural units in a very functional way, processing things through the stages, but not in a discrete way. It may use several stages simultaneously, overflowing processing from one stage to another without waiting for processing in the earlier stages to be completed. Yet, the only important point is that Mind does not consist of the stages; it just uses them.

In the realm of memory, Mind is again function, organizing, preparing, encoding, and so on. When Mind does get something into memory, it stores it in structural units, to be drawn on at some later time as its functional needs require. I tend to think of these storage units as many little buckets of nuggets, but once again they are not Mind. Mind is function, not structure.

MIND IS TO KNOW

In 1966 (Garner, 1966), I wrote a paper entitled *To Perceive Is to Know*, but in the present context that should be expanded to all of Mind. The primary function of Mind is to know and, in a functional sense, to gain knowledge. This knowledge can be about almost anything. Mind is omnivorous, and I was delighted to discover that one of the definitions of omnivorous in my dictionary is "taking in everything, as with the mind." To perception psychologists, this knowledge is primarily about the real world. Yet, the knowledge can also be about language, about the organism that houses Mind, including what the organism does. Knowledge can also be about relations and about how to solve problems.

The acquisition of knowledge is so important to Mind that it will actively seek knowledge if no knowledge is simply coming to it. It will seek new parts of the world if it already knows about the part of the world it is presently engaged with. It will seek new problems to solve if it already has solutions to all the problems it is currently aware of. It will generate new ways to use language, or find new languages to learn if it has run out of languages that it already knows. The new languages may be new forms, such as metaphor, simile, poetry, or even mystery stories. All of this is saying that Mind is an active process, which carries out all sorts of functions. And to risk commenting in a realm about which I know little except as a father, this active seeking of knowledge starts almost at birth.

Now here is a point about this knowledge that is, I think, rather important. As most psychologists would agree these days, the knowledge that Mind seeks is of information, not energic and other physical properties (Garner, 1974, 1988), whether we are talking about perceiving the reality of the world about us, whether we are learning a language, or whether we are undertaking to write poetry. This point was made to psychologists, of course, by information theory, and the change in thinking about physical properties to information content was tremendously important. Of course, everything does have physical properties coincident with the informational properties, but Mind is only interested in the informational properties.

Now in case I stress the active role of Mind too strongly, I would like to note that Mind is really essentially lazy. It would like to loll about, preferably on a beach (either ocean or lake will do), and just let more and more knowledge come to it. But much as it likes this lazy life, its need for knowledge is so great, so demanding, that it gets up off its butt and becomes a very active agent seeking knowledge. So Mind's need for knowledge makes it an energetic, active seeker. However, its desire to loll on the beaches never quite leaves it, and at times does succeed in producing laziness. Mostly, though, Mind is an active seeker of knowledge.

MIND IS A CRITICAL REALIST

Just as Mind would like to lazily loll about on the beach, Mind would also like to be very egotistical. In extreme form, it would love to be a subjectivist, believing there is no reality outside itself. What fun that would be! Just generate ideas, accept them as reality, and the rest of us can lump it.

Unfortunately for Mind, it is also very pragmatic, and soon discovers, when trying to be subjectivistic, that it isn't acquiring any knowledge. So there comes that compelling need to acquire knowledge, at whatever cost. The attempt to turn in on itself leaves Mind with a sense of total failure, as indeed the subjectivist position would, because a subjectivist has no way of confirming its ideas and may begin to doubt them without that confirmation. As a result of this doubt, a great depression sets in for Mind. Rather than remain depressed, Mind accommodates to the facts of life and admits that there is a real world out there. So Mind is a realist, but of the critical realist variety that the scientist has to be when using converging operations.

Yet, being basically egotistical, Mind wants to have as much of the action as it can. It has available to itself several rational processes that allow it to feel that it is in control of the knowledge acquisition process. One of these rational processes is to seek information that is not immediately available to it, so that it can combine different kinds of information to decide what is the truth about the world it lives in. In doing this, Mind is using the technique of converging operations that scientists themselves use, and with this technique it can determine what reality is while still maintaining control of the knowledge acquisition it so desperately wants (Garner, 1974, 1986).

Another process is one I have already mentioned, and that is to use its functional ability to select information. It is really the converse of seeking information. In seeking new information, Mind can find a set of converging operations that lead to its idea of what reality is. But when it selects information from that available to it, it is limiting the convergence available to it, and therefore having more control over which hypothetical constructs about the real world it will accept. This latter function of selection, while allowing Mind more control over its idea of reality, can also lead to a more erroneous idea of the real world. However, Mind is egotistical and intends to control its knowledge acquisition even to the point of accepting erroneous conclusions. (Reminds us of some psychological theorists we know, doesn't it?)

Given Mind's desire to control the action, and to be as egotistical and subjectivistic as possible, it is clear that Mind simply shuns the epistemological position of direct realism. Such a position says that the world out there is in charge of knowledge, not Mind. That is intolerable to Mind, so Mind simply rejects the whole idea of direct realism. Mind is positive that the real world can be understood only with Mind's active participation in seeking and selecting information, and should Mind fail to seek and select the right information, then it's the real world out there that is out of kilter, not Mind. This amounts to saying that Mind can never accept the fact that it might be wrong. Mind is truly egotistical in every way.

MIND IS FLEXIBLE

In some ways, the world allows Mind to do its thing, to be in control of the acquisition of knowledge. But just as Mind wants to control things, so does the world of reality. This conflict means that Mind and reality are in a constant struggle to dominate how Mind is to perceive reality. Fortunately, Mind is flexible enough to cope with this conflict.

Critical realism is easily considered in terms of its two words. Realism concerns the world of reality, while critical concerns what Mind does. The real world actually has more control over what mind can and cannot do than Mind would like to believe. There are many aspects of the real world that produce mandatory functioning on the part of Mind. If we as scientists are trying to understand the role of reality and the role of Mind, we use the distinction between mandatory and optional processing as the major way of distinguishing between Mind and world reality (Garner, 1981, 1986). For example, if Mind cannot change its mode of functioning with learning or experience, then we feel sure that Mind's functions are controlled by the real world. In like manner, if all Minds, in many different organisms, function in exactly the same way, then we again attribute control of processing to the real world. Because there are many properties of the real world which do produce mandatory processing, like it or not, Mind has to accept functional control by the real world. It does so begrudgingly—trying to seem gracious in its defeat—because in its egotistical way it wants to control everything it does and not to be coerced by properties of the outside world.

On the other hand, there are many properties of the real world that do not require mandatory processing, but allow option on the part of Mind. In these cases, Mind will usually change how it functions as it gains experience or learns more about the information it is processing. Likewise, all Minds will not function in the same way, each having its own idiosyncrasies.

It is in this area that Mind is in its glory. It can, for instance, decide to process some material in a serial fashion, or it may decide that parallel processing is its thing, at least for now. It may even decide to do both serial and parallel processing at the same time, on the same information, whether the processing involves learning, problem solving, writing, or just plain perceiving (i.e., acquiring) knowledge (Garner, 1970, 1978).

So Mind is indeed flexible in two ways. First, it is flexible in functioning mandatorily if the world so demands, although usually with ill grace. But if allowed by the real world to function optionally, it takes the challenge with delight, confusing experimenters as much as possible by changing functional modes when they (the experimenters, that is) are trying to discover the one and only way that certain information is processed. It is indeed a joy for Mind, and a misery for us experimentalists, to have this flexibility and option on the part of Mind.

MIND IS CREATIVE

As I have just noted, Mind is happiest when it can function in optional ways, doing what it wants to and in the way that it wants to. But to enjoy being a free spirit does not guarantee that Mind will be very effective, first doing this and then that to suit its whims. Mind is a very effective entity, so it must somehow be good at what it is doing. That occurs because Mind is creative, and that property of Mind ensures that it will perform well when turned loose on its own.

Just as nature abhors a vacuum, Mind abhors a meaningless world, a world without structure, or, worst of all, an empty world. So Mind seeks, if what it has is not meaningful; it selects, if attending to everything that impinges on it is too difficult. The selection allows Mind to find a more orderly world, even if in fact the world is not as orderly as Mind would like. If the world is empty, then Mind is most subjectivistic, creating something out of nothing. It can form images.

Sometimes these images are simply memories. These memories may be snatched out of one of the buckets of nuggets, or Mind may combine several items out of the memory buckets and recombine them into something new. This process has every right to be called creative, because something new is created out of pieces of old things.

Of course, when Mind's organism is asleep, then Mind is really turned on to be at its creative best by dreaming. Even in dreams, there may be some constraints from the real world that Mind experienced before its host organism fell asleep, but these constraints are minimal, and Mind has almost an orgy of creativity. I suppose if Mind could have its way, it would spend most of its time dreaming or creating in other ways. As I have said, Mind is egotistical and subjectivistic, wanting to do its own thing. Dreaming comes about as close to what Mind wants as possible.

A concept that I have used to illustrate Mind's creativity is that of an inferred subset of stimuli (Garner, 1962; Garner & Clement, 1963). This idea, in simple form, is that a single stimulus cannot be redundant, at least meaningfully redundant in the information-theoretic sense, because the property of redundancy is a property of a subset of stimuli, not of a single stimulus. Yet, the single stimulus can seem more redundant (or good in the Gestalt sense), and this is where Mind's creativity comes in. For the single stimulus to be meaningful, Mind infers what its alternatives might be. The single stimulus plus these alternatives form the necessary subset. By inferring these subsets, Mind feels very good, even egotistical, as is its wont. But I add a comment on this matter: Mind certainly is creative in generating the inferred subset of alternatives, but that single stimulus out in the real world has properties that imply what Mind infers. Mind, however, will not really admit that. It wants to take full credit and glory for the entire creative process. Oh, well, I suppose it does no harm to let Mind feel cocky. It keeps Mind's morale up.

MIND IS NOT BEHAVIOR

Because acquiring knowledge is Mind's primary function, it doesn't care whether it does something with the knowledge or not. Just knowing is quite enough to keep Mind happy and, as I have just said, when knowledge is created by Mind, then Mind is at its happiest. Yet, notice that in Mind's most creative mode, forming images or having dreams, no action on the part of the organism is necessary at all. Behavior is just not part of Mind, and Mind is not the least bit unhappy about this state of affairs. Remember that Mind is egotistical, subjectivistic, and happiest when it can just ignore the world of reality and wallow in its own lazy dream state on the beaches, with its eyes shut, its ears plugged, and with its host organism so sound asleep that it will not bother it with reality.

A brief sidebar is necessary here. As I mentioned before, when we experimental psychologists do experiments with people as subjects and try to learn something about Mind, we must have a way of communicating with the subject. So we talk with the subject or require him or her to do silly things such as push buttons, or these days, respond on a computer keyboard. It is absolutely essential that we communicate with the organism whose Mind we are trying to understand, but there must be no misconception that the organism's behavior is Mind. It is only an indicant of Mind, a means of communication, without which we couldn't get very far in our scientific endeavors. We want to learn about Mind, and I suppose it is seductive to consider the behavioral message as Mind itself. Certainly back in the golden age of stimulus–response psychology, that seduction was successful. Or did people really believe that behavior is Mind by definition, thus effectively denying the existence of Mind?

I, in my turn, have no intention of denying behavior. Organisms do things, some of them quite complicated, and none of us would be what we are if our own personal organisms couldn't do things. Now is when another property of Mind comes in — its flexibility. Mind can, in its gracious mode, control or at least monitor — behavior. After all, if an organism is kind enough to house Mind, then the least Mind can offer in return is the courtesy of generating or monitoring the organism's behavior. In its egotistical way, it will do it, but will never admit to liking to have to deal with behavior. It is utterly bored at carrying out this gracious act and makes little attempt to hide its boredom.

MIND IS A PRODUCT OF EVOLUTION

Despite Mind's desire to be left alone to do its own thing without interference, as I have pointed out, Mind is also pragmatic; when necessary, it will accommodate the demands of reality. The most extreme situation occurs when the world of reality allows no functional options for Mind, thus requiring mandatory function and process on the part of Mind. How has Mind managed to cope with these undesired demands on it?

The answer, I believe, is that in the course of evolution, Mind has adjusted to the world of reality and acquired many characteristics that make it able to deal with the real world. Elsewhere, I have referred to these characteristics as *psychophysical correlatives*. That is to say, for every property of the real world there is a correlated property of Mind, so that Mind and the real world are not very far apart in how they function. But Mind has also had something to do with the nature of the real world, especially, but not exclusively, in the realm of language. I have called this *inverse evolution* (Garner, 1986). Language is a product of Mind, so both spoken and written language reflect properties of Mind. Thus, the term correlative is meant to imply a two-way, symbiotic relation. Mind has evolved to be able to cope with the world of reality, but reality has been created to be compatible with the properties of Mind.

Shepard (1981) argued this point even more strongly than I with my use of the term correlative. He spoke of *psychophysical complementarity*, in which properties of Mind complement properties of the real world, and vice versa. His complementarity idea is that the real world and Mind can function together in a way in which neither could alone. His best example is the relation between a lock and a key, in which the two must mesh so they can jointly perform a needed function which neither could perform alone.

In commenting on various metatheoretical approaches to the study of Mind, Posner (1978) once described me as adopting an evolutionary point of view. As you can tell from my comments here, I heartily accept the description. Shepard himself is very explicit on this matter, arguing that it is through biological evolution that Mind has come to mirror the real world. But I think it is important to remember the correlative or complementarity idea. The relation between Mind and reality is a two-way street. Nevertheless, evolution is how Mind has come to do so well what it does.

IN CONCLUSION

So there you have it, George. That is how Mind works, and how it got to work so well. But remember that evolving aspect of Mind. By the time you quit thinking about all this, Mind may take a great evolutionary jump. It might even become complementary (with an e) to computers. However, I think Mind is strong enough to withstand this onslaught from computers, this idea that intelligence can be artificial. It knows that only Mind is intelligent, and that it is definitely not artificial. Remembering the idea of inverse evolution, however, Mind may make computers in its own image, and thus dominate the relation between Mind and computer. That would, however, be just the latest in many accommodations and adjustments that Mind has had to make over its evolutionary history. Mind has survived and become more effective in this process, so there is no reason for pessimism.

At the beginning of this letter, I commented that we had solved the problem of Mind in our late-night sessions nearly 50 years ago. But of course in terms of today's thinking, we had not. I think we can both be impressed by the enormity of new knowledge about Mind since our embryonic days as psychologists. Perhaps we were also so constrained by the prevailing stimulus–response mode of our beginning years that we didn't really believe there was Mind either. But I don't think so. We really did think, and if we thought, then we had Mind.

Another way to say this is by misquoting a famous Frenchman: "Sum, ergo cogito."

With fond memories,

Wendell R. Garner

REFERENCES

Garner, W. R. (1962). *Uncertainty and structure as psychological concepts*. New York: Wiley.

Garner, W. R. (1966). To perceive is to know. *American Psychologist, 21*, 11–19.

Garner, W. R. (1970). The stimulus in information processing. *American Psychologist, 25*, 350–358.

Garner, W. R. (1974). *The processing of information and structure*. Potomac, MD: Lawrence Erlbaum Associates.

Garner, W. R. (1978). Aspects of a stimulus: Features, dimensions, and configurations. In E. Rosch & B. B. Lloyd (Eds.), *Cognition and categorization* (pp. 99–133). Hillsdale, NJ: Lawrence Erlbaum Associates.

Garner, W. R. (1980). Association lecture: Functional aspects of information processing. In R. S. Nickerson (Ed.), *Attention and performance VIII* (pp. 1–26). Hillsdale, NJ: Lawrence Erlbaum Associates.

Garner, W. R. (1981). The analysis of unanalyzed perceptions. In M. Kubovy & J. R. Pomerantz (Eds.), *Perceptual organization* (pp. 119–139). Hillsdale, NJ: Lawrence Erlbaum Associates.

Garner, W. R. (1986). Interactions of stimulus and organism in perception. In S. H. Hulse & B. F. Green, Jr. (Eds.), *One hundred years of psychological research in America: G. Stanley Hall and the Johns Hopkins tradition* (pp. 199–240). Baltimore, MD: Johns Hopkins Press.

Garner, W. R. (1988). The contribution of information theory to psychology. In W. Hirst (Ed.), *The making of cognitive science: Essays in honor of George A. Miller* (pp. 19–35). New York: Cambridge University Press.

Garner, W. R., & Clement, D. E. (1963). Goodness of pattern and pattern uncertainty. *Journal of Verbal Learning and Verbal Behavior, 2*, 446–452.

Garner, W. R., & Hake, H. W. (1951). The amount of information in absolute judgments. *Psychological Review, 58*, 446–459.

Garner, W. R., Hake, H. W., & Eriksen, C. W. (1956). Operationism and the concept of perception. *Psychological Review, 63*, 149–159.

Posner, M. I. (1978). *Chronometric explorations of mind*. Hillsdale, NJ: Lawrence Erlbaum Associates.

Shepard, R. N. (1981). Psychophysical complementarity. In M. Kubovy & J. R. Pomerantz (Eds.), *Perceptual organization* (pp. 279–341). Hillsdale, NJ: Lawrence Erlbaum Associates.

11 How the Mind Thinks

Philip N. Johnson-Laird
Princeton University

The function of the mind is to perceive, to think, and to control action. Cognitive science offers the following thumbnail sketch of these processes: Perception is a process that translates energy impinging on the senses into internal symbolic representations of the external world. Thinking is a process that transforms and manipulates internal representations to enable individuals to anticipate events, to make decisions, and to form intentions and plans. The control of action depends on translating internal representations into instructions for sequences of behavior. What is crucial to thinking is therefore, not the physical make-up of the thinking organ—the brain—but the organization and functioning of mental representations and processes. This doctrine—of which George Miller has been a notable champion (e.g. Miller, Galanter, & Pribram, 1960)—treats the mind as a device that constructs representations in a symbolic notation and that uses these representations in order to think. It is a member of a special class of devices—a class that can be described as computational, symbol manipulating, or information processing (the terms are interchangeable).

Not everyone accepts the idea of the mind as a computational device. Some thinkers have advanced metaphysical arguments against it. For example, Husserl (1929), who founded the philosophical movement known as *phenomenology*, denies the existence of mental representations. Other more recent theorists also reject the information-processing account of the mind (see, e.g., Edelman, 1987; Gibson, 1966). Of course, it offends many people. They find the very idea demeaning to humanity, not to say sacrilegious. I return to some of these skeptical views at the end of this chapter, but first my intention is to push the computational hypothesis for all that it is worth. The thesis that the mind is a machine is, in my view, the culmination of three great traditions: the humanist tradition that goes back to Leonardo da Vinci, who observed the human body with the eye of a mechanical engineer; the biological tradition that has delineated the biochemical machinery of life and reproduction; and the mathematical tradition that has made explicit the notion of a computational machine.

My basic hypothesis is that thinking is a computational process that leads from one mental representation to another. To explore this hypothesis, I need to answer three questions:

1.   What is computation?
2.   What is a mental representation?
3.   What is thinking?

I answer these questions in the first part of the chapter, and in the second part I show how a computational theory elucidates deductive, inductive, and creative thinking. Finally, I consider the implications of consciousness and emotions for the computational thesis.

WHAT IS COMPUTATION?

One answer to the question is: Computation is what computers do. Many people accept this answer. Although it is not very informative, they judge that at least it is true. In fact, it is misleading. Computation was analyzed by logicians long before the invention of the programmable digital computer, and the logical analyses pin down the concept of computation in a more comprehensive way. The aim of the logicians' enquiries was to determine what mathematical problems could be solved without the use of intuition, that is, in a purely mechanical way. The notion of a purely mechanical procedure, though it makes intuitive sense, has no clear definition. Different logicians proposed different ways in which to make it explicit. Remarkably, these different analyses all turned out to yield equivalent accounts of what is computable.

One way to explicate the notion of a mechanical procedure is Turing's (1936) mathematical machine. This is a hypothetical device that takes a minimum for granted, though it is the abstract ancestor of the modern computer. It is controlled by a finite set of instructions. Its data are fed into the machine on a single tape divided into squares, and each square contains a 1 or a 0. A Turing machine can carry out just three actions:

1. Read the symbol on the square on the tape that the machine is currently scanning. (It can scan only one square at any one time.)

2. Replace the symbol on the square by another symbol (either 1 or 0). Hence, the tape also functions as a memory for the results of intermediate computations and as the place where the machine puts its final results.
3. Shift the tape one square to the left or one square to the right.

Its instructions specify which action the machine carries out (and to which state it shifts) as a function of its present state and the symbol it is scanning. Turing showed that such machines could carry out all the obvious sorts of calculations, such as addition and multiplication. He also showed how to construct a "universal" machine that could simulate any particular machine. He also proved an important theorem (more on this later).

Another way to explain the notion of a mechanical computation, which again takes a minimum for granted, is the use of recursive functions. The theory analyzes computation in terms of three sorts of building blocks:

1. The zero function, which produces the same constant value, 0, for an input of any natural number.
2. The successor function, which adds 1 to any natural number, for example, the successor of 0 is 1.
3. The identity functions, which can return the identity of any member in a list; that is, one such function returns the first member of the list, another returns the second member, and so on.

There are three ways to combine these building blocks:

1. Composition: One function can call another as a subroutine; for example, the successor function is applied to the result of the zero function.
2. Recursion: The functions can be combined, in effect, to construct a for-loop, which iterates a certain operation *for* a given number of times.
3. Minimization: The functions can be combined, in effect, to construct a while-loop, which carries out a certain operation *while* a particular condition remains true.

The class of recursive functions is identical to the class of functions that can be computed by Turing machines.

According to the Church-Turing thesis, a mechanical procedure is one that can be computed by recursive functions or Turing machines (Church, 1936). The thesis cannot be proved true, because it concerns the intuitive notion of a mechanical procedure. But it could be proved false by demonstrating an effective way to compute something that lies outside the domain of Turing machines. The mathematical triumph of the theory of computability was Turing's proof that certain mathematical problems have no computable solution. For example, there can be no computable procedure that will sort problems into those that have a computable solution and those that do not. The practical triumph of the theory of computability was the design and construction of programmable computers.

It is important to distinguish what can be computed from how it is computed. Another important theorem about computability showed that a parallel machine equipped with multiple tapes or multiple processors cannot compute anything beyond the scope of a simple serial machine. How a parallel machine carries out computations is different — and may be more efficient — but what it computes remains the same. There are many ways to compute anything that can be computed — in fact, provably an infinite number of different ways. And there are also many ways in which to design computational machines. They may be serial devices, such as the familiar computers of daily life, which carry out one elementary operation at a time. They may be parallel devices, which are increasingly coming into use. So far, computers have been built according to only a handful of designs, and we can look forward to machines with architectures remote from those with which we are familiar. Of course, if the Church-Turing thesis is correct, then these machines will not be able to compute anything novel. Yet, certain phenomena depend on how a computation is carried out, for example, the time course of the computation.

The simplest computations, such as binary addition, need no memory. They merely map the input directly to the output using only a finite number of distinct states of the machine to carry out the computation. Other more complex computations, such as multiplication, cannot be carried out by such a finite-state machine. They depend on a memory for the results of intermediate computations. One has to remember (or to write down) the results of the partial products of a multiplication, and then finally sum them. Memory is the heart of computational power: The freer the access to (unlimited) memory, the more powerful the machine in terms of what it can compute. Memory, however, calls for a *representation* of information, which must be stored in some format and later retrieved for use. I turn now to the question of mental representations.

WHAT IS A MENTAL REPRESENTATION?

It is easier to give examples of mental representations than to formulate a definition, and so I begin with an example. The surfaces of objects reflect light into an observer's eye, which the lens focuses so that each cell in the retina receives light from a single point in the scene. The cells convert the energy in quanta of light into nerve impulses, that is, into an internal symbolic representation. This initial representation encodes merely the intensity of light from each point in the scene, and so it would not be of much use to the observer. Subsequent processes, however, transform this information into a representation that makes explicit the objects in the scene and their spatial relations to one another and to the observer. The ease with which this process occurs is deceptive. The observer has the subjective impression of being in direct contact with the world and is not aware of relying on a series of representations. This impression is, of course, advantageous. If you see a car bearing down on you as you cross the street, you do not pause to examine the veridicality of a representation. You get out of the way.

A perceptual representation of the world depends on a causal chain of events leading from an external state of affairs to a pattern of energy impinging on the senses, and thence to an internal state that relates to the external state. The internal state makes explicit certain aspects of the world. Thus, in the case of vision, as Marr (1982) and others argued, the perceptual system constructs a series of representations, culminating in a three-dimensional *model* of the scene. This model makes explicit the spatial relations among the objects in a way that is independent from the observer's point of view. Explicitness, here, means that the information is available to other processes without the need for further mental operations. Representations are indeed available to other processes and ultimately to procedures governing the observer's actions.

Simple organisms appear to construct only perceptual representations. More complex organisms, such as humans, can construct a variety of different sorts of representation. They have conscious access to images of various sorts—visual, auditory, kinesthetic—and they have representations of hypothetical and imaginary states of affairs, which are generated purely internally. They are useful for envisaging how the world might be and thus in anticipating events. The evidence suggests that human infants have the ability to construct such representations during their first year of life (see Spelke, 1991). The evidence also suggests that human beings understand language by constructing a propositional representation with a structure akin to the structure of sentences, and that they use this representation to construct a mental model with a structure akin to the structure of the situation that is described (see Johnson-Laird, 1983). These models are similar to those constructed perceptually, but, for most of us, they are more schematic, less complete, and less vivid.

The complex symbols of the mind are images, propositional representations, and models. Images are the phenomenal experience of perceptual aspects of models; propositional representations are constructed from linguistic expressions; models represent the structure of the world. Granted that the brain can construct an unlimited number of different representations of these sorts, but that it is a finite organism, then it must have some machinery for constructing representations out of finite resources. The complex symbols have a compositional structure, that is, their content depends on what their parts represent and on how these parts fit together.

Other sorts of more primitive mental representations may have no such structure but may be in a distributed format of the sort built up by connectionist learning procedures, such as the backwards propagation of error through a network of simple processing units (McClelland & Rumelhart, 1986). As yet, however, there is little psychological or neurophysiological evidence to corroborate the existence of distributed representations in the mind.

CONCEPTS AND MENTAL MODELS

There has been much controversy about the nature of mental models, because different theorists have different ideas about them. The fundamental principles of the present theory are:

1. Mental models are finite.
2. They are computable. No substantial case against this proposition has so far been proposed, and existing computational devices equipped with electronic cameras are able to construct internal representations of the external world.
3. Mental models have a structure that corresponds to the way in which human beings conceive the world.

What matters, therefore, is not the subjective experience of a model, but its structure: entities are represented by tokens, their properties by properties of the tokens, and the relations between them by the relations between the tokens. Thus, an assertion, such as:

The triangle is beside the circle

can be initially represented by the following sort of propositional representation:

(BESIDE TRIANGLE CIRCLE)

This representation can be used to construct a model of a specific spatial relation:

△ ○

Models of this sort are computable, as I illustrate by describing a program that constructs three-dimensional spatial models from verbal descriptions (Johnson-Laird & Byrne, 1991). The program has a lexicon in which the meaning of each word is specified in terms of constituents, which I shall refer to as *subconcepts*. It has a grammar in which each rule has a corresponding semantic principle for forming combinations of subconcepts. As the program parses a sentence, it assembles subconcepts to form a propositional representation of the sentence's meaning. This propositional representation is then used by other procedures to construct a model of a particular situation described by the sentence. Given the assertion:

The circle is on the right of the triangle

the parsing process combines the subconcepts underlying the words in the sentence to yield the following representation, which represents the meaning of the assertion:

((1   0   0) (o) (△))

The meaning of the relation *x on the right of y* is a set of subconcepts that consists of values for incrementing *y's* Cartesian coordinates in order to locate *x*:

1   0   0

The 1 indicates that *x* should be located by incrementing *y's* value on the left–right dimension while holding *y's* values on the front–back and up–down dimensions constant i.e. adding 0s to them.

What the program does with a propositional representation depends on the context of the sentence. If it is the first assertion in a description, the program uses the propositional representation to construct a complete model in a minimal spatial array:

The reader will note that an assertion about the relation between two entities with distinct properties is represented by a model in which there is a relation between two tokens with distinct properties. Depending on the current state of any existing models, the program can also use the propositional representation to add an entity to a model, to combine two previously separate models, or to make inferences.

The concept *on the right of* is part of a system based on the same underlying set of subconcepts, for example, *on the left of* is represented by the subconcepts (-1 0   0), *in front of* is represented by the subconcepts (0   1   0), and so on. The theory postulates that some such system allows human reasoners to set up spatial models and to manipulate them. It must exist prior to the mastery of any particular spatial relation, and then it can be used to acquire new high-level concepts. For example, one might acquire the relation represented by (1   0   1), roughly *diagonally up and to the right*, if it played an important part in spatial thinking and was accordingly dignified by a single spatial term. The subconceptual system also provides individuals with an idealized taxonomy. In the real world, objects do not have to be perfectly aligned, and so a judgment of the relation between them may compare their actual coordinates with alternative possibilities in the taxonomy. Hence, what a relation denotes in the world depends not just on its subconceptual analysis, but also on other concepts in the same taxonomy.

The theory of mental models extends naturally to the representation of sentential connectives, such as *and*, *if*, and *or*, and quantifiers, such as *any* and *some* (Johnson-Laird & Byrne, 1991). The theory posits that models represent as little as possible explicitly. Hence, a conditional such as *if there is a triangle, then there is a circle*, has the following two initial models:

[Δ]   o

.   .   .

The first line represents an explicit model of the situation in which the antecedent is true—the model merely lists the two items and does not specify their spatial arrangement. The square brackets around the triangle in the first model are an annotation indicating that triangles have been exhaustively represented, that is, they cannot occur in any other model (for a defense of such annotations, see Newell, 1990). The second line represents an implicit model of the alternative situation(s), that is, it has no immediately available content, but it can be fleshed out to make its content explicit. Because the triangles are exhausted, the fleshing out can correspond to a bi-conditional *if and only if there is an triangle then there is a circle*:

Δ   o

¬ Δ ¬ o

where "¬" is an annotation representing negation. Alternatively, the fleshing out can take a weaker conditional form:

Δ   ο

¬ Δ   ο

¬ Δ ¬ ο

There are similar models that represent the other sentential connectives, such as *or, only if,* and *unless.*

The representation of quantifiers is also a natural extension of the theory. An assertion, such as *Some of the athletes are bakers,* has the following single model:

a   b

a   b

a   b

. . .

In this case, each line represents a separate individual, *a* denotes a representation of an athlete and *b* denotes a representation of a baker. The number of tokens representing individuals is arbitrary. The final line represents implicit individuals, who may be of some other sort. The statement *All of the athletes are bakers* has the following initial model:

[*a*]   *b*

[*a*]   *b*

[*a*]   *b*

. . .

The square brackets represent that the athletes have been exhaustively represented (in relation to the bakers). Similar interpretations are made for other quantifiers and for assertions that contain more than one quantifier, such as *'None of the athletes is in the same room as any of the bakers'.*

The theory rejects the idea that discourse is encoded in any sort of structure that does not correspond to the way in which we conceive the world. Consider, for example, the assertion:

All philosophers have read a book

Its structure in the predicate calculus is shown in the following formula:

$\forall x$ (Philosopher(x) → $\exists Y$ (book(y) & read (x, y)))

where $\forall x$ denotes the universal quantifier *for any x;* $\exists y$ denotes the existential quantifier *there is at least some y;* → denotes *if - then* in the weaker conditional sense above; and & denotes logical conjunction. The same assertion can be represented in a partitioned semantic network (Hendrix, 1979) as shown in Figure 11.1. Neither the predicate calculus formula nor the semantic network have structures corresponding to how humans conceive such a situation. A mental model for the assertion, however, captures the structure of a typical situation:

$[p] \rightarrow b$

$[p] \rightarrow b$

$[p] \rightarrow b$

. . .

where p denotes a philosopher; b denotes a book; and the arrows denote the relation, *has read*. This model has a direct structural correspondence with a typical case of the relation that holds between the two sets. As the theory implies, people do not represent merely the meaning of an assertion, but rather they use that meaning to envisage a situation characterized by that meaning (see Garnham, 1987, for corroboratory experimental evidence).

The machinery for constructing mental models depends on conceptual knowledge. One has, for example, a concept of *on the right of* and uses this knowledge to envisage one object on the right of another, that is, to construct a mental model of the situation. In the past, cognitive scientists have supposed that the meanings of words, and other concepts, are represented in semantic networks or translated one to one into a mental language. Such proposals neither square with the experience of comprehen

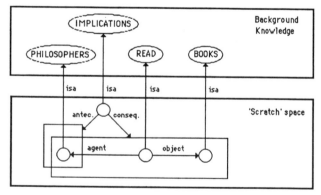

FIG. 11.1.   A partitioned semantic network representing the assertion: *All philosophers have read a book*. The isa links denote class membership. If a node occurs in both the antecedent and the consequent spaces of an implication, it represents a universally quantified assertion.

sion nor with human linguistic competence. If I describe to you a state of affairs, such as:

The circle is on the right of the triangle

then you can envisage this situation, and in certain circumstances, you can check whether the assertion is true. The mere translation of the sentence into a semantic network or into a mental language with tokens for each word:

(ON-RIGHT-OF CIRCLE TRIANGLE)

does not account for these abilities. When you envisage the situation, you do not imagine linguistic entities in a network or in a syntactic organization. If ON-RIGHT-OF were the most basic representation of the relation, then you could never verify the assertion, because neither ON-RIGHT-OF nor postulates relating it to other conceptual tokens contains information enabling you to determine what counts as satisfying the relation. That is why there must be a set of subconcepts that underlie your knowledge of *on the right of*. These subconcepts enable you to envisage the circle on the right of the triangle and to grasp the truth conditions of the assertion (though they do not specify how to verify it). They are the building blocks, as I showed earlier, for the construction of mental models.

Certain subconcepts, as Miller and I argued in our analysis of a representative sample of semantic fields (Miller & Johnson-Laird, 1976), underlie the construction of perceptual models: they include subconcepts for colors, shapes, and textures in the case of vision; other subconcepts relate to the internal milieu — bodily and emotional states; still others relate to epistemic and deontic states — subconcepts for possibility, permissibility and intentionality. Analytic concepts, such as *triangles* and *squares*, are constructed from spatial subconcepts. Concepts of natural kinds and artifacts are complex constructions that depend in part on subconcepts that specify default values; for example, a dog by default is four legged, a tiger by default is striped, and a carnation by default is red or pink. When all the defaults are used to construct a model, then the result is a model of the prototypical case, that is, an instantiation of the concept with all its default values. Yet, the subconcepts can also be used to construct models of other, more unusual, instantiations such as three-legged dogs, stripeless tigers, and green carnations. Although subconcepts are used to construct mental models, they alone probably do not determine the reference of terms. The world can present you with entities that are difficult or impossible to identify. You can construct a perceptual model of such entities, but you run into trouble identifying them. Your judgment of the extension of a concept may depend on the relative "distance" of an entity from competing concepts in the same taxonomy.

Subconcepts are part of the innate basis of thought. They are analogous to the primitives of recursive function theory out of which all computable functions can be constructed. When you grasp a concept such as *on the right of*, you neither decompose it into semantic constituents nor translate it into a token in the language of thought, but rather you access its subconcepts and combine them with others in readiness to construct a model. To have a concept fully available to you is therefore to have an automatic and unconscious access to its subconcepts, which play their part in the construction of models. Everyday concepts are thus akin to instructions in a high-level programming language, but when you use them to think, you rely on their mental compilation into subconcepts, which cannot normally be put into words in an individual's native language. Subconcepts are accordingly innate, universal, and ineffable.

This theory implies that there are three distinct sources of concepts. The first source is *evolution*. What must be genetically endowed is the basis for the acquisition of all other concepts. There is therefore an innate set of subconcepts and subconceptual combinations (analogous to composition and recursion). These subconcepts include those for physical entities, properties, and relations; those for bodily states and emotions; and those for epistemic and deontic states.

The second source of concepts is *knowledge by compilation*. It depends on an innate mechanism that assembles new concepts out of the innate subconcepts and combinations. Verbal instruction alone is no use here: there is no substitute for the construction of models of the world. Ultimately, the repeated construction of models, as in the case of *diagonally up and to the right*, compiles the relevant subconcepts to form a new concept.

The third source of concepts is knowledge by *linguistic composition*. It constructs concepts and conjectures by composing them out of existing high-level concepts. In particular, it combines the concepts corresponding to the meanings of words according to the semantic principles that relate to the grammatical rules of the language, that is, it uses a "compositional semantics" of the sort championed by Montague (1974) and his associates. Because it constructs new concepts from verbal descriptions based on existing concepts, it can come into play only after some high-level concepts have been compiled from subconcepts.

Philosophers sometimes argue that there are no good definitions and thus cast doubt on knowledge by linguistic composition as a source of new concepts. Here, however, are some concepts that can be acquired by definition (courtesy of the *Shorter Oxford English Dictionary*):

depilous: deprived or void of hair
hock-day: the second Tuesday after Easter Sunday (or, according to some, Easter week)
remise: to give up, surrender, make over to another, release (any right, property, etc.)

Definitions seldom give (or claim to give) the necessary and sufficient conditions for the extensions of concepts. Yet, an obvious fact about the English language is that the majority of words are unfamiliar (as a random sample from a good dictionary readily demonstrates). Our knowledge of their meanings must be based on definitions because we have no other sources of information about these words.

Knowledge by composition, as in the case of *depilous*, *hock-day*, and *remise*, can save time and trouble, but it is superficial. The shift from novice to expert in any conceptual domain appears to depend on a fully compiled taxonomy of concepts. Only then, according to the present theory, can concepts be immediately used to construct models or to check that they are satisfied in models constructed by perceptual or other means. Thinking similarly depends on experience that enables the individual to construct and to manipulate mental models directly.

WHAT IS THINKING?

Everyday intuition suggests that thinking is a conscious introspectible process. Someone asks you, for example, what would happen if you held up a mirror to reflect the light from the night lamp in your bathroom back into the photoelectric cell that controls the lamp. You think to yourself: the night lamp comes on when the photoelectric cell detects no ambient light, but as soon as it does detect light, it switches the night lamp off. Hence, if I hold a mirror to reflect the night lamp's light back into the photoelectric cell, it will switch the lamp off. As soon as that happens, the photoelectric cell will switch the lamp on again, the mirror than reflects light back into the cell, which switches the light off, and so on and on. In summary, the night lamp should rapidly oscillate between on and off. It probably seems that the whole process of thought is conscious. Yet, it isn't. You have no access, for example, to how your knowledge about photoelectric cells is represented, or to how you retrieve this information. No process of thought is entirely conscious, and much is profoundly unconscious, in the sense that Helmholtz had in mind when he referred to the unconscious inferences that underlie perception. The psychology of thinking would not exist as a discipline if you could discover how you think merely by introspecting.

The chapter headings of textbooks on thinking include judgment, categorization, problem solving, deductive reasoning, inductive reasoning, and decision making. These headings have grown up over the years as part of an intellectual tradition, but they are not an altogether reliable taxonomy. A better guide is to pin down the computational components of thinking that underlie these global processes (see Johnson-Laird, 1988).

Some processes of thought are goal-driven; others are not. When you try to solve the problem about the night lamp, you have a specific goal – to figure out what happens when the mirror reflects the lamplight back into the photoelectric cell. A number of computer programs, which owe their origin to Newell and Simon's general problem solver (see, e.g., Newell & Simon, 1972), work by eliciting knowledge in a goal-driven way in order to solve problems. In life, the specificity of goals varies considerably. Many problems have only the vaguest of goals, for example, to earn a living, to paint a picture, to find an interesting scientific puzzle. Such goals cannot directly control thinking in the same way that goal-driven programs work. They will either trigger too much knowledge or none at all. Perhaps the best case of thinking that is unconstrained by a goal occurs in dreams and daydreams. In one sense, a daydream may have the goal of distracting you from your current woes, but this goal is unlikely in itself to elicit specific knowledge except in the case of obsessional thoughts. In this context, psychologists talk of one idea leading to another by association. The notion is seductive, and certainly the mind may learn to associate one idea with another. You learn, for instance, that the dinner gong tends to be followed by food, and the external association between the two events is mirrored by a mental association between them. And so when you hear the gong, you will be apt to salivate in anticipation of the food. The British Empiricist philosophers based their philosophy of mind on this hypothesis. Paradoxically, the one phenomenon that it cannot explain is *association* in daydreams. The reason is simple: when an individual's mind wanders, one idea may suggest another entirely novel idea. The link cannot have been established by learning, because it leads to a thought that the individual has never entertained before. One concept, such as *light*, can lead to another, such as *dark*, by an existing association. But, how does one proposition lead to another by association? There is no existing theory of how the process occurs and surprisingly little work on the problem in psychology.

When thinking is governed by a goal, the tightest possible constraints occur if, in addition, the thought process is deterministic. Determinism is a notion that comes from the theory of computability. A machine is deterministic if given a particular input (which may be null) and a particular state of the machine, it is constrained to one and the same action. In contrast, a machine is nondeterministic if for a given input and state there is more than one possible action that it can perform, and no aspect of the machine or input determines which action it takes. A digital computer is deterministic, but it can simulate nondeterminism. If all the possible actions are equally viable, then it can choose at random from among them. If only one of the possibilities is viable, then it can search through them all until it discovers the correct one. A good example of a deterministic thought process is simple mental arithmetic. I ask you: What is 13 plus 28? If you accept the challenge, then presumably you go through a process, such as:

> 3 plus 8 equals eleven, and so the rightmost column of the result equals 1, and there is a carry of 1. 1 plus 2 equals 3, which plus the carry of 1 equals 4. And so the answer is 41.

Of course, at any step in the process, you may give up, or be interrupted by an idle thought, but the process itself is probably as deterministic as any sequence of thoughts that ever occurs. You perform mental arithmetic according to procedures that you learned in school, or, if you are a prodigy, that you devised yourself. Apart from such "algorithmic" procedures, thinking appears to be nondeterministic—an idea that, as far as I know, was first suggested by Harman (1973). This quality seems most obvious in creative thinking. If you think imaginatively, then at various points in the process alternative possibilities seem equally viable. If you could relive the process with no memory for your previous choices, then you might well choose differently the second time around.

Mental arithmetic is deterministic and goal-driven, free association is neither. Are there, you might wonder, goal-driven processes that are not deterministic? In fact, most thinking probably falls into this category. When you solve a problem, the sequence of thoughts does not seem to be controlled by a deterministic procedure. Only the simplest of open-ended problems elicit the same answer from the same individuals from one occasion to another.

There are different ways to interpret mental nondeterminism. One interpretation is that the actual choice depends on some miniscule aspect of the individual's mental or bodily state. Such factors could include the state of the digestive system, the beat of the pulse, or other events outside the domain of choice. A causal explanation of how choices are determined by such factors would amount to a deterministic theory, but we may never have such a theory. Creative processes are deterministic according to this interpretation, but, as the study of chaotic systems has revealed, a minute change in circumstances rapidly leads to major differences in outcome. Our ignorance forces us to model creativity nondeterministically. Another interpretation of nondeterminism is that the mind can make arbitrary choices. People are poor at making genuinely random choices, but departures from true randomness do not count against the existence of such a mechanism. They imply only that the mind is not equipped with a random-number generator. Nevertheless, it can make an arbitrary choice from among a set of possibilities. Still another interpretation is that quantum indeterminacies have a direct bearing on mental processes. This idea was originally proposed by the physicist, Sir Arthur Eddington, as a solution to the riddle of free will. Nothing could be less like freedom, however, than to be at the mercy of random quantum events. More recently, Penrose (1989) argued that a proper understanding of the brain's functioning calls for taking quantum events into account. However, the inability of people to generate random choices suggests that if the brain is influenced by quantum indeterminacies, it cannot fully exploit them.

So far, I have said little about the contents of thought. Much thinking concerns ideas that may be true or false (i.e., propositions), and much thinking is not propositional. A musician improvising a melody, a choreographer contriving a dance, a designer working out a motif for a fabric, are all engaged in thought, but the elements of the process are unlikely to be propositions.

The domain of propositional thinking can be subdivided according to the semantic relations that hold between one thought and the next. There are five a priori possibilities:

1. The new idea is equivalent to the old, that is, they both rule out as false the same states of affairs. This relation is deductive, and, as we shall see, most deductions in daily life exemplify it.

2. The new idea is a specialization of the old: it rules out as false fewer states of affairs than the starting point. This relation also holds deductively. For example, the following argument:

Today is Tuesday.

Therefore, Today is Tuesday or today is Wednesday.

is valid, that is, the conclusion must be true given that the premise is true. But, the conclusion throws semantic information away: it rules out fewer states of affairs than the premise. Logically untrained individuals treat such inferences as odd or improper. Specialization, however, does occur in real life, particularly when thinkers are acquiring a new concept.

3. The new idea is a generalization of the old, that is, it rules out all the states of affairs ruled out by the old idea and at least one additional state of affairs. This relation is inductive. Suppose, say, that you know that your compass is faulty or you are off course—a state of mind corresponding to the following set of models:

$$f$$

$$\neg c$$

where f denotes a model of the faulty compass; $\neg$ denotes negation; and c denotes a model of your being on course. If you check your compass and find that it is indeed faulty, you have corroborated the first model and so you might reject the second and conclude that you are on course. Such an inference is plausible, but not valid. Your initial state of mind is consistent with having a faulty compass and being off course. That is, it is consistent with the following explicit models:

$$f \quad \neg c$$

$$f \quad c$$

$$\neg f \quad \neg c$$

The fact that the compass is faulty eliminates only the third of these models, that is, it is consistent with either of the first two. And so you may, or may not, be on course. The inference therefore goes beyond the given information, eliminating a model consistent with the starting point. It increases semantic information, and that, I claim, is a useful working definition of induction (Johnson-Laird, 1993).

4. The new idea overlaps with the old; that is, they rule out certain possibilities in common, but otherwise diverge. A process of thought with such a result maintains some ideas from its starting point, but also yields certain novel ideas that are unrelated to the starting point. It abandons certain observations or ideas as erroneous and replaces them by others — the new ideas may even be difficult to reconcile with the old ones. A thought process of this sort transcends induction. It is creative.

5. The new idea is inconsistent with the old; that is, they rule out entirely disjoint states of affairs. Such a step amounts to an immediate denial of the starting point. Although denials can occur in deduction, as when one makes a hypothesis and then infers validly that it leads to a contradiction, they are unlikely to occur as a single step in thinking.

The taxonomy that I sketch here distinguishes five principal sorts of thought process:

- Calculation: goal-driven, deterministic, and not increasing semantic information;

- Deduction: goal-driven, not deterministic, and not increasing semantic information;
- Inauction: goal-driven, not deterministic, and increasing semantic information;
- Creation: not deterministic, and yielding semantic overlap with the starting point; and
- Association: not goal-driven, and not deterministic.

In the second part of this chapter, I put aside calculation and association — the clockwork and the clouds of the mind — and scrutinize the remaining sorts of thought process: deduction, induction, and creation.

DEDUCTIVE THINKING

The crew of the ill-fated Flight 007 of Korean Air Lines established two facts:

If the plane was on course, then the radar should show only water.

The radar was showing a land mass.

At this point, they should have drawn the conclusion:

The plane was not on course.

The recording of the cockpit conversation shows that instead of making this deduction, they changed the topic of conversation (Overton, 1990).

The engineers in charge at Chernobyl were carrying out an experiment in which the power to a turbine is shut off, and the energy in the rotating turbine is used to provide a brief supply of emergency electricity. They allowed the turbine to fall below the critical speed needed for the experiment, but they failed to draw the obvious conclusion that the experiment could no longer be conducted (Medvedev, 1990). They did not abort the experiment, and the resulting mishap destroyed the reactor, released 10 times the radiation of the Hiroshima bomb, and led to the deaths of many people. To understand such cognitive failures, we need to understand how the mind makes deductions.

One possibility, which has had a vogue in psychology, is that the mind contains formal rules of inference like those of a logical calculus. It searches for a formal derivation based on these rules leading from premises to conclusion. For example, the premises:

If the plane is on course, then the radar shows only water.

The plane is on course.

match the logical form of a rule known as *modus ponens*:

If *A* then *B*

A

∴ *B*

where *A* and *B* denote any propositions. This rule enables the conclusion corresponding to *B* to be derived:

∴ The radar shows only water.

The deduction is easy, according to this theory, because it is a result of the application of a single formal rule. The following premises are similar to those that presented themselves to the crew of the Korean airliner:

If the plane is on course, then the radar shows only water.

The radar does not show only water.

They match the logical form of a rule known as *modus tollens*:

If *A* then *B*

not *B*

∴ not *A*

However, no such rule exists in the mind according to the formal theories, and so the deduction is supposed to be made, if at all, some other way. For example, reasoners hypothesize that the antecedent of the conditional premise holds:

The plane is on course.

They then derive the consequent using the rule for *modus ponens*:

∴ The radar shows only water.

They have a rule that allows them to form the conjunction of any two propositions in a derivation, and so they conjoin this conclusion with the second premise:

∴   The radar shows only water, and the radar does not show only water.

This conjunction is a self-contradiction, and reasoners are supposed to be equipped with the rule for *reductio ad absurdum*, which stipulates that whenever a hypothesis leads to a contradiction, the hypothesis can be negated:

∴   The plane is not on course.

The derivation is longer and more complicated than the single step of *modus ponens*, and so *modus tollens* is more difficult.

For many years, this story about everyday deduction was accepted by all psychologists who gave the matter any thought. Its origins lie in the work of the 19th-century logician, George Boole, but its proponents include numerous students of deductive inference (e.g., Braine, 1978; Inhelder & Piaget, 1958; Osherson, 1974–6: Pollock, 1989, Rips, 1983). However, the theory of reasoning based on mental models deals with a greater variety of inferences than rule theories and pins down more accurately the strengths and weaknesses of the human deductive machine. The evidence for this claim is found elsewhere (see Johnson-Laird & Byrne, 1991; Johnson-Laird, Byrne, & Schaeken, 1992). In this chapter, I will outline the theory and allude to some of the evidence corroborating it. The model theory postulates that reasoning depends on three stages:

1. The construction of a set of models based on the premises.
2. The formulation of a putative conclusion based on these models.
3. The search for an alternative model that falsifies this conclusion.

The last of these stages is the crucial one for inference: If there is no falsifying model, then the conclusion is valid; if there is a falsifying model, then the reasoner must determine whether there is some weaker conclusion that holds in all the models of the premises; if it is uncertain whether there is a falsifying model, then the conclusion can be drawn on a tentative inductive basis.

As an example, reconsider *modus ponens* and *modus tollens*. Given the conditional premise:

If the plane is on course, then the radar shows only water

the theory postulates, as we saw earlier, that reasoners construct the following set of initial models:

[c]   w

.   .   .

in which the first model makes explicit that the plane is on course, *c*, and that the radar shows only water, *w*, and the second model is an implicit alternative. Given the premise for *modus ponens*:

The plane is on course

then, because this situation is exhaustively represented in the first model (as indicated by the square parentheses), the second model can be eliminated to leave only the first model:

[*c*]   *w*

A description of this model yields the conclusion:

∴   The radar shows only water

There is no alternative model of the premises that falsifies this conclusion, and so it is valid. In contrast, given the *modus tollens* premise:

The radar does not show only water

then the first model of the conditional must be eliminated to leave only the implicit model. Because this model has no explicit content, it seems that nothing follows from the premises. This response is the most common error that subjects make, and it is perhaps the thought that passed through the mind of the crew of Korean flight 007. To make the *modus tollens* deduction, it is necessary to flesh out the implicit model in the way that I described earlier. The weak interpretation of the conditional yields:

c w

$\neg c$ w

$\neg c \; \neg w$

and the strong bi-conditional interpretation yields:

c w

$\neg c \; \neg w$

In either case, the *modus tollens* premise (*The radar does not show only water*) eliminates all but the model:

$\neg c \; \neg w$

A description of this model yields the conclusion:

∴   The plane is not on course.

The formal-rule theory and the mental-model theory both explain the difference between *modus ponens* and *modus tollens*, and so how can we decide between the two theories? The answer hinges on three predictions that are unique to the model theory.

The first prediction is that valid deductions that require only one model to be constructed will be easier than those that require multiple models to be constructed. Byrne and I carried out many studies of deduction, and our experiments on spatial reasoning produced some crucial data (Byrne & Johnson-Laird, 1989). We examined the following sort of problem:

The cup is on the right of the saucer.

The plate is on the left of the saucer.

The fork is in front of the plate.

The spoon is in front of the cup.

What is the relation between the fork and the spoon?

We knew from earlier studies that subjects tend to imagine symmetrical arrangements. Hence, the description corresponds to a single-determinate model

plate   saucer   cup

fork   spoon

and so it should be relatively easy to answer that the fork is on the left of the spoon. When the second premise is instead:

The plate is on the left of the cup

the description is consistent with at least two distinct models:

plate   saucer   cup   saucer   plate   cup
fork   spoon   fork   spoon

The same relation holds between the fork and the spoon in both these layouts, but the model theory predicts that the task should be harder, because two models need to be constructed to make the deduction. In short, the one-model problem should be easier than the multiple-model problem.

Some theories use complex rules to make two-dimensional deductions (e.g., Hagert, 1984), and these theories make the opposite prediction to the model theory. For the one-model problem, the first task is to derive the relation between the plate and the cup, using a rule for the converse relation and a rule for transitivity:

> The cup is on the right of the saucer.   (First premise)
>
> The plate is on the left of the saucer.   (Second premise)
>
> ∴ The saucer is on the left of the cup.   (Converse of first premise)
>
> ∴ The plate is on the left of the cup   (Transitivity of *on the left*)

Now one can infer the relation between the fork and the spoon, using a two-dimensional rule of inference (or an equivalent postulate):

> ∴ The fork is on the left of the spoon.

In the case of the multiple-model problem, however, the relation between the plate and cup is stated in the second premise (The plate is on the left of the cup), so the relation does not have to be deduced. Hence, the one-model problem calls for a longer derivation than the multiple-model problem. The rule theory makes exactly the opposite prediction to the model theory.

We carried out a series of experiments to compare the predictions of the two theories (see Byrne & Johnson-Laird, 1989). They all corroborated the model theory. For example, in our final experiment, the subjects carried out four inferences of each sort, and the percentages of correct responses were: 70% for one-model problems and 46% for the multiple-model problems (a highly reliable difference). In other experiments ranging over a wide variety of domains, including syllogisms, propositional inferences, and multiply-quantified inferences, we found without exception that one-model problems are reliably easier than multiple-model problems (see Johnson-Laird & Byrne, 1991).

The second prediction of the model theory is that reasoners will make mistakes by overlooking possible models of the premises, and so their erroneous conclusions will correspond to proper subsets of the models of the premises. Indeed, given the difficulty of holding more than one model in mind, the erroneous conclusions should often correspond to just a single model of multiple-model premises. We also confirmed this prediction in all the main domains of deduction. I present a typical finding from the domain of multiply-quantified reasoning (see Johnson-Laird, Byrne, & Tabossi, 1989). The premises:

> None of the Avon letters is in the same place as any of the Bury letters.
>
> All of the Bury letters are in the same place as all of the Caton letters.

yield the following sort of model, in which the barriers demarcate separate places, and the numbers of tokens are arbitrary:

/ [*a*] [*a*] [*a*] / [*b*] [*b*] [*b*] [*c*] [*c*] [*c*] /

The *a*s denote Avon letters, the *b*s denote Bury letters, and the *c*s denote Caton letters. This model supports the conclusion:

∴ None of the Avon letters is in the same place as any of the Caton letters.

No alternative model of the premises refutes this conclusion, and so it is valid. The following similar premises:

None of the Avon letters is in the same place as any of the Bury letters.

All the Bury letters are in the same place as some of the Caton letters.

yield the following sort of initial model:

/ [*a*] [*a*] [*a*] / [*b*] [*b*] [*b*] *c* *c* /

which also supports the conclusion:

None of the Avon letters is in the same place as any of the Caton letters.

This conclusion was the most frequent error, and it was drawn by 38% of the subjects. It is invalid because it can be refuted by an alternative model of the premises:

/ [*a*] [*a*] [*a*] *c* *c* / [*b*] [*b*] [*b*] *c* *c* /

The two models together support the conclusion:

∴ Some of the Caton letters are not in the same place as any of the Avon letters.

or, equivalently:

∴ None of the Avon letters is in the same place as some of the Caton letters.

or the slightly weaker conclusion (in one of its interpretations):

∴ None of the Avon letters is in the same place as all of the Caton letters.

Only 17% of subjects drew any of these valid conclusions, which is to be expected given the difficulty of constructing multiple models. Some subjects made an error that seemed odd at first. They concluded:

All of the Avon letters are in the same place as some of the Caton letters.

In fact, this conclusion is precisely what one would expect from individuals who have considered only the second model. It is hard to see how such errors could occur regularly in formal derivations. No obvious mechanism in proofs yields erroneous conclusions that happen to correspond to single models of the premises.

The third prediction of the model theory is that knowledge can affect the *process* of inference: if reasoners reach a conclusion that fits their beliefs, they will tend not to search for alternative models of the premises; but if they reach a conclusion that conflicts with their beliefs, they should search harder for alternative models of the premises. Beliefs have long been said to influence deductive reasoning (e.g., Henle, 1962; Revlin & Leirer, 1978). But, according to formal theories, they act as a bias on the initial interpretation of premises or as a censor that checks conclusions. They could not affect the process of deduction itself, because formal rules are by definition blind to content. Jane Oakhill, Alan Garnham, and I examined the influence of beliefs on conclusions that subjects draw for themselves (see, e.g., Oakhill, Johnson-Laird, & Garnham, 1989). These studies used materials in which the putative conclusion based on an initial model of the premises was either congruent or incongruent with the subjects' beliefs. This manipulation had a striking effect on performance. For instance, when subjects were given the premises:

All of the Frenchmen are wine drinkers.

Some of the wine drinkers are gourmets.

most of them (72%) drew the conclusion:

∴ Some of the Frenchmen are gourmets.

When they were given premises with the same logical form, but a different content:

All of the Frenchmen are wine drinkers.

Some of the wine drinkers are Italians.

hardly any subjects (8%) drew the corresponding conclusion:

∴ Some of the Frenchmen are Italians.

The model theory predicted the difference on the following grounds. In the first case, subjects built an initial model of the form:

[f]   *w*   *g*

[f]   *w*   *g*

[f]   *w*

.   .   .

in which *f* denotes a Frenchman *w* denotes a wine drinker, and *g* denotes a gourmet. This model supports the conclusion:

∴ Some of the Frenchmen are gourmets.

Because this initial conclusion is congruent with the subjects' belies (as assessed by an independent panel from the same population), they do not search assiduously for an alternative model that might refute it.

In the second case, subjects build the same sort of model:

[w]   *w*   i

[f]   *w*   i

[f]   *w*

.   .   .

in which *i* denotes an Italian. This initial model supports the conclusion:

∴ Some of the Frenchmen are Italians

but this conclusion is contrary to the subjects' beliefs (as assessed by the panel), and so they were more likely to search for an alternative model, such as:

[f]   *w*

[f]   *w*

[f]   *w*

       w   i

       w   i

.   .   .

This model of the premises refutes the conclusion, and so the subjects responded, "Nothing follows." Theories based on formal rules cannot easily explain this phenomenon. They cannot refer to the believability of the initial putative conclusions, because these invalid conclusions do not occur in formal derivations from the premises. The model theory, however, predicts this case of *satisficing*: If subjects reach a conclusion that fits their beliefs, they halt their process of inference.

The theory of mental models has successfully predicted some robust phenomena of deductive reasoning. The theory rejects the idea that deduction depends on formal rules of inference. It proposes instead a computational process in which reasoners construct models of premises, draw conclusions from them, and search for alternative models that might falsify these conclusions. This theory predicts the relative difficulty of different deductions in terms of whether they call for one model or multiple models of the premises. It correctly predicts that erroneous conclusions arise, because reasoners satisfice and overlook alternative models of the premises. It also correctly predicts that reasoning can be influenced by whether or not an initial conclusion accords with general knowledge or belief.

INDUCTIVE THINKING

The distinction between deduction and induction, though clear to logicians, is less obvious in daily life. I suspect that inductive thinking is also based on models: reasoners construct a model based on observation and background knowledge, but they go beyond this information in order to generalize. For instance, when the car ferry, Herald of Free Enterprise, sailed from the Belgian port of Zeebrugge on March 6, 1987, the master of the vessel made the plausible induction that the bow doors had been closed. They had always been closed in the past, and there was no evidence to the contrary. The chief officer made the same induction, as did the bosun. But the assistant bosun, whose job it was to close the doors, was asleep in his bunk, and had failed to do so. Shortly after leaving the harbor, water rushed into the ferry, and it turned over and sank with the loss of 188 lives. A plausible induction turned out to be tragically wrong.

In everyday life, the process of induction seems to be part of the normal business of making sense of the world. When the front doorbell rings, your immediate thought is:

Someone is at the front door.

Your conclusion is plausible, but invalid, and so Polya (1957) has suggested that formal, but invalid, rules are the heuristic basis of such inferences. Because formal rules, as we have seen, do not appear to underlie deductions, it is likely that inductions have another basis. You have a model of the bell and bell-push, and the obvious cause of the ringing is that the bell-push has been pressed (by a person).

The case for models is supported by the extraordinarily imaginative ways in which ordinary individuals can interrelate events. Tony Anderson and I observed this phenomenon in some unpublished experiments. In one experiment, we chose pairs of sentences by randomly selecting them from different stories, for example:

John made his way to a shop which sold TV sets.

Celia had recently had her ears pierced.

We asked the subjects to explain what was going on. We had surmised that the task would be very difficult; to make it easier in another condition of the experiment, we gave subjects coreferential pairs of sentences:

Celia made her way to a shop which sold TV sets.

She had recently had her ears pierced.

In fact, the subjects readily volunteered explanations. For example, they said that Celia was getting reception in her earrings and wanted the TV shop to investigate, that she was wearing new earrings and wanted to see herself on closed circuit TV, that she had won a bet by having her ears pierced and was going to spend the money on a TV set, and so on. They were almost as equally ingenious with the sentences that were not coreferential.

A critical factor in thinking, as Tversky and Kahneman (1973) have shown, is the availability of relevant knowledge. Anderson and I investigated its role in induction by using such premises as:

The old man was bitten by a poisonous snake.

There was no known antidote.

Every subject inferred that that the old man died. In one condition of the experiment, the experimenter responded to every conclusion with the words, "Yes, that's possible but not in fact true." Most of the subjects were then able to envisage alternative models in which the old man survived. Of course, they eventually ran out of ideas, but they tended to think of them in the same order from one subject to another. The conclusions to the snake-bite problem, for instance, tended to occur in the following order:

1. The old man died.
2. The poison was successfully removed, for example, by sucking it out.
3. The old man was immune to the poison.

4. The poison was weak and not deadly.
5. The poison was blocked from entering the circulatory system, for example, by the man's thick clothing.

The availability of relevant knowledge has some consistency within the culture.

With premises of this sort, reasoners can never be certain that they have exhausted all possibilities. Indeed, by the end of the experiment, the subjects' confidence in their initial conclusions had fallen significantly, even in a group in which the experimenter responded, "Yes, that's possible" to each idea. Inductions occur so often in everyday life, precisely because there is seldom enough information to make valid deductions. Life is not deductively closed, and there may always be some other, as yet unforeseen, counterexample to a putative conclusion. The challenge for inductive theories based on rules is to account for the variety of imaginative connections between events in our first experiment and the correlated sequences of ideas in our second experiment. They can be explained in terms of the manipulations of models, as Bara, Carassa, and Geminiani (1984) have shown in a computer simulation.

Theorists, especially in artificial intelligence, tend to think of induction as a process that uses rules to produce linguistic generalizations. Hence, a major question has been to find the right language in which to represent inductions. There has been much debate among the proponents of different mental languages, such as semantic networks, production systems, and versions of the predicate calculus. Yet, as I suggested, to think of induction as a quasi-linguistic process may not do justice to human thinking. The purpose of induction is to make sense of the world, either by enabling individuals to predict or to categorize more efficiently or, better still, to understand phenomena. The mind builds models, and the structure of models is the basis of human conceptions of the structure of the world. The products of induction may therefore be models — either models that simulate phenomena (descriptive inductions) or else models constructed from more fundamental subconcepts (explanatory inductions). After such models have been constructed, they can, if necessary, be used to formulate verbal generalizations.

If induction depends on linguistic generalizations, then a great variety of rules of generalization are necessary (see, e.g., Michalski, 1983; Winston, 1975). The following are some typical examples of such rules:

1. *If p and q then r* is generalized as *if p then r*.
2. *If p and q then r* is generalized as *if p or q then r*.
3. *If p and q then r and if p and s then r* is generalized as *if p then r*.
4. *If p then r* is generalized as *if p or q then r*.
5. *Some A are B* is generalized as *All A are B*

There is a seemingly unlimited set of possible rules. Yet, models yield a much more parsimonious theory. Only one mental operation is necessary: the addition of information to models in order to eliminate otherwise possible states of affairs. The rules above for sentential connectives are equivalent to adding information to a model so as to eliminate it. Consider Rule 1, for example. An assertion of the form:

If p and q then r

corresponds to the follow set of initial models:

$[p \ q] \ r$

. . .

in which the conjunction of p and q is exhaustively represented in relation to r. These models can be flushed out explicitly:

$$p \quad q \quad r$$
$$p \neg q \quad r$$
$$\neg p \quad q \quad r$$
$$\neg p \neg q \quad r$$
$$p \neg q \neg r$$
$$\neg p \quad q \neg r$$
$$\neg p \neg q \neg r$$

When the model:

$$p \neg q \neg r$$

is eliminated, the resulting set is equivalent to:

if p then r

conjoined with the redundant tautology, q or not-q. The operation of eliminating a model — by adding information that contradicts it — suffices for any generalization depending on sentential connectives, because generalization is nothing more than the elimination of possible states of affairs.

Information can be added to models in order to generalize from a finite number of observations to a universal claim (see rule 5 above). You observe the following causal relation between a set of viruses and a set of symptoms:

v   *s*

v   *s*

v ⟶ *s*

in which the arrow denotes a causal relation between a virus and a symptom, and nothing is known about the relation, if any, between the other viruses and symptoms. You can describe this model in the following terms:

A virus causes a symptom.

The addition of further causal relations transforms the model into the following one:

v ⇌ *s*

v   ↘ *s*

v ⟶ *s*

You can describe a model of this sort as follows:

All of the symptoms are caused by a virus.

Hence, the effect is still equivalent to the linguistic operation of replacing an existential quantifier ("a") by a universal quantifier ("all"). The addition of a further causal link, however, yields a still stronger model:

v ⇌ *s*

v   ↘ *s*

v ⟶ *s*

which you can describe in the following terms:

A virus causes all of the symptoms.

In the predicate calculus, the linguistic effect of the operation is to move an existential quantifier from inside to outside the scope of a universal quantifier:

$\forall s\, \exists v$ (*v* causes *s*) is generalized as $\exists v\, \forall s$ (*v* causes *s*)

The model theory has led us to a linguistic rule of generalization that does not appear to be used by any of the artificial intelligence (AI) inductive programs.

The operation of adding information to models enables us to generalize from the weakest possible model to the strongest possible one. Hence, the addition of information to models suffices for all possible generalizations in those everyday domains that can be described by the predicate calculus. It replaces the need for a battery of linguistic operations.

An advantage of models is that they embody knowledge in a way that naturally constrains inductive search. They maintain semantic information, they ensure internal consistency, and they are parsimonious, because each entity is represented only once. They can focus attention on the critical parts of the phenomena. Models also elucidate the clues about induction that have emerged from the psychological laboratory. Because of the limited processing capacity of working memory, models represent only certain information explicitly and the rest implicitly. One consequence is that people fall into error, and the evidence shows they make the same sorts of error in induction as they do in deduction. Thus, in deduction, they concentrate on what is explicit in their models, and so they often fail to make such deductions as *modus tollens*. In induction, they likewise focus on what is explicit in their models and so seldom seek anything other than evidence that might corroborate their inductive conjectures. They eschew negative instances and encounter them only when they arise indirectly as a result of following up alternative hypotheses (see, e.g., Klayman & Ha, 1987, Wason, 1960). In deduction, people are markedly influenced by the way in which a problem is framed: what a model represents explicitly depends on what is explicitly asserted, and so individuals often have difficulty in grasping that two assertions have the same truth conditions; for example, *Only the bakers are athletes* and *All the athletes are bakers* (see Johnson-Laird & Byrne, 1991). In induction, there are equally marked effects of how a problem is framed (see Hogarth, 1982). In deduction, disjunctive alternatives cause difficulties. They call for multiple models, and reasoners have difficulty with them. Disjunctive information also appears to hinder decision making. For example, subjects, say they will choose a vacation if they pass an exam; they also say they will choose it if they fail the exam. Yet, they do not choose the vacation when the outcome of the exam is unknown (see Shafir & Tversky, 1991; Tversky & Shafir, 1991). Finally, knowledge appears to play exactly the same part in both deduction and induction. It biases the process to yield more credible conclusions.

The price of tractable induction is imperfection. Psychologists often concentrate on the minor imperfections in induction that yield clues to the nature of its mechanism. They overlook its catastrophes—the fads of pseudoscience, the follies of superstition, and the disastrous inferences that lead to such events as the sinking of the Herald of Free Enterprise. The origin of these errors is in the human inductive machine: its failure to examine alternatives, its too exclusive focus on what is represented explicitly, and its bias towards satisficing on the basis of belief.

CREATIVE THINKING

To show that creative processes are computable, we need to characterize what is meant by creativity. I propose the following working definition:

1. A creative process combines or transforms existing elements to produce a result that is novel for the individual and perhaps for society as a whole. It is not merely perceived or remembered.
2. The creative result satisfies preexisting criteria.
3. Creativity is not a deterministic or rote procedure. It allows for freedom of choice.

This account admits mundane examples, such as the spontaneous discourse of daily life, but it does not exclude the most exalted works of the imagination, such as artistic masterpieces or revolutionary scientific theories.

Of course, new ideas cannot be constructed out of nothing: Mental elements must exist to provide the raw materials for even the most original works of art or science. According to the model theory, these elements, like all elements of thought, ultimately depend on innate subconcepts and methods of subconceptual combination. People who merely regurgitate existing ideas from memory or perception are hardly creative. The results must be new — at least for the individual creator. Society reserves the highest awards for those who are first, but uniqueness is a matter of history, not psychology. What we need to understand are the mental processes underlying the creation of novel ideas, and so, if we exclude cases of indirect influence or downright plagiarism, we can put to one side the issue of uniqueness.

If no criteria or constraints governed the creative process, then its results could be produced by purely arbitrary means. Some modern works of art have been generated in this way, but even in these cases artists usually exercise some judgment in selecting which results to preserve. Creation therefore depends on criteria, though no one has a conscious access to all of the relevant criteria. The cumulative effect of the possibilities they allow is an unlimited number of potential creations, just as the rules of language permit an unlimited number of different sentences. If the criteria allowed only one possibility at each step in the process, an artist or scientist could produce only as many works of the imagination as the number of different beginnings. Once started, the results of the process would be wholly determined. That, I submit, is an implausible basis for a theory of creation. Creativity, like most other forms of thought, is not deterministic.

If creativity is computable, then a consequence of the preceding working definition is that there are three broad classes of creative procedures. The first class mimics the evolution of species according to the neo-Darwinian synthesis of genetics and natural selection. There are two stages: a generative stage in which ideas are formed in an entirely arbitrary way (out of existing components) followed by an evaluative stage in which the results are assessed according to criteria. Whatever survives the evaluation, which may be little or nothing, is the result of the process. Arbitrary processes rapidly cease to be productive if they apply only to a static set of basic concepts. The complete genetic specification of a human being was not assembled from a single shuffling of an unorganized set of genes—an evolutionary step that is no more likely than that of a monkey typing randomly composing the works of Shakespeare. Evolution is the archetypal recursive process: it applies to its own successful results. The existing elements characterize viable species, and new species derive from those that have passed a fitness test. The process has been mimicked by the "genetic algorithms" developed by Holland and his colleagues (see, e.g., Booker, Goldberg, & Holland, 1990), which have produced novel solutions to such problems as the design of more compact computer chips.

The mechanism for constructing new ideas could be entirely random and the results filtered through a set of constraints. The whole process could be repeated recursively in multiple stages as in a genetic program. The mechanism is inefficient, but it is the only one available if the generative process cannot itself be guided by criteria—a condition that is the basis of the modern evolutionary synthesis of genetics and natural selection. Yet, in the creation of ideas, criteria could be used to constrain the generative process directly. The great advantage of such a system is its efficiency: if the only ideas that are ever produced lie within the criteria, then the system can save time by avoiding hopelessly implausible conjectures. The most efficient procedure would use all available criteria to guide the generation of new ideas. It would be feasible only for those domains where an individual has mastered a set of criteria that suffice to guarantee the viability of the results. If all available criteria are used to generate an idea, by definition none is left for its evaluation. Granted that creation is not deterministic, there will be certain points in which criteria allow more than one possibility, and so the only way to choose from among them will be nondeterministic, for example, by making an arbitrary decision. The process can then occur in just two stages (possibly interleaved) with no need for recursion: (a) the generation of ideas according to criteria, and (b) an arbitrary selection, where necessary, from among them. I have nicknamed such algorithms "neo-Lamarckian" because criteria that have been acquired from experience govern the generative stage—by analogy with Lamarck's theory of evolution. I have also written some computer programs for the improvization of melodies that work according to this neo-Lamarckian architecture (Johnson-Laird, 1991). Competent improvisers seldom make mistakes. They extemporize original melodies, which are musically acceptable, and so the generative process must be constrained by a tacit knowledge of the genre's criteria.

Most forms of creation appear to be neither neo-Darwinian nor neo-Lamarckian. Ideas are generated under the guidance of some criteria, but their initial form leaves something to be desired—that is to say, the individual applies further criteria to their evaluation and decides that more work needs to be done, and so the ideas are revised, recombined, and so on. The procedure resembles the genetic algorithm in that it is recursive—it is applied repeatedly to its own output, but it differs in that criteria are used in both the generative and evaluative phases of the program.

Many creative individuals do indeed work extensively on the results of their earlier efforts—revising and revising and revising. They are clearly using a multistage procedure. But, why? If they are applying criteria at each stage, why don't they apply all of these criteria immediately in the very first generative stage? Why the need for a time-consuming division of labor over several stages? It seems odd to waste time formulating an inadequate product if one has the ability to perceive its inadequacy and to set matters right.

One reason for a multistage procedure is the limited processing capacity of working memory. In the case of writing, for instance, an author's goal is to express the right ideas with the right words. The limitations of working memory make it difficult to carry out both these tasks at the same time. In their initial drafts, writers tend to focus on getting the ideas sorted out. Later, they concentrate on improving the prose. For example, in an earlier draft of this chapter, I wrote: "Light falls on the surfaces of objects in the world and is reflected into an observer's eyes. The human eye focuses the light so that the light from each point in the scene falls onto a single cell in the light-sensitive array of cells in the retina at the back of the eye ball." The ideas were right, but their expression was clumsy. After some revision, the final version read as follows: "The surfaces of objects reflect light into an observer's eye, which the lens focuses so that each cell in the retina receives light from a single point in the scene." This version is certainly more succinct. Why didn't I write the passage in these words originally? Presumably because my first efforts were concerned with getting my ideas down on paper, and this task took up all of my cognitive capacity.

Another reason for the inability to marshall criteria is probably to be found in mental architecture. The mind seems to depend on a hierarchy of processors that compute in parallel and that communicate data one to another, but that have no access to each other's internal operations and representations (see, e.g., Fodor, 1983, Johnson-Laird, 1983, and Minsky, 1985, for various versions of this "modular" hypothesis). It isolates mental representations and procedures so that they can be used by one ability, but not others. For example, most people who can read music are unable to write down melodies they can sing. They lack a conscious grasp of the intervals from one pitch to another that occur in the melody. Only after extensive training in musical dictation are they finally able to write down melodies. The difficulty of the task arises, because the internal representations that underlie singing are not available to conscious judgment.

Likewise, some criteria are available to critical processes, but not to generative processes, and vice versa. Some criteria can be communicated verbally, discussed, refined, and debated, but their conscious availability is far from enabling them to control the generation of ideas. At the core of creativity are unconscious procedures composed from the subconcepts that I described earlier. When one learns to create, one has to master these unconscious roots of creativity. One has to assemble a set of subconceptual procedures. Conscious verbal instruction alone is useless. The process is similar to the compilation of high-level functions into low-level machine instructions. It takes work. In mastering new scientific concepts, there is no substitute for working with the concepts. In artistic creativity, there is no substitute for a period of apprenticeship. One learns by imitating successful creators and by trying to create for oneself in a particular domain. One must enter an almost interminable circle of trying, assessing one's failure, and trying once again. Only in this way can one build up the set of subconcepts and principles that govern the generative process: Only in this way can one "internalize" the criteria of genre or paradigm. It follows that there is no general recipe for enhancing one's creativity across all domains. Those nostrums and exercises that purport to increase one's creative ability have no effect on internalizing the criteria of a particular domain: No robust evidence exists to bear out their alleged efficacy. One learns to create by creating, but one must make his or her attempts in the particular artistic genre or scientific paradigm in which one wishs to excel.

Theories based on semantic networks or production systems postulate that scientific thinking consists in the manipulation of languagelike expressions. But, thinking, as I argued, is the manipulation of models rather than linguistic formulae. Operations on formulae perhaps occur when a mathematician searches for a formal proof within a calculus, but otherwise the basis of thought appears to be our understanding of problems and ideas, and this understanding depends on the construction of mental models. Indeed, many scientific discoveries appear to derive from images or models of phenomena. The classic cases include Snell's law of the reflection of light, Kekulé's discovery of the structure of benzene, and, according to Wise

(1979), Maxwell's development of the field theory of electromagnetism. As Wise pointed out, models generate problems, and their answers may in turn call for a reorganization of the models themselves. A model may accordingly be misleading, and a theorist may be forced to transcend the customary conception of events. Galileo's discovery of the law of inertia, for example, called for an idealization of actual movements, which are affected by friction, and for putting to one side the customary Aristotelian model of falling objects.

The intuitions of scientists bear out the claim that thinking is based on models rather than expressions in a mental language. Of all the quotations on this point, the remarks of Einstein in a letter to Hadamard(1945) are the most apt. He said, "The words of the language, as they are written or spoken, do not seem to play any role in my mechanism of thought. The psychical entities which seem to serve as elements in thought are certain signs and more or less clear images which can be 'voluntarily' reproduced and combined." The role of imagery in scientific discovery thus seems indubitable (see also Miller, 1984) and calls for procedures that can construct and manipulate models of phenomena rather than quasilinguistic strings of symbols.

The heuristic procedures for manipulating models in ways that yield novel concepts are largely unknown. Yet, we can be reasonably certain about several aspects of the process. It is unlikely to be based on a neo-Darwinian or genetic algorithm. Conceptual innovation would be all but impossible if thinkers had to begin with truly arbitrary possibilities. Likewise, it is not based on a neo-Lamarckian procedure: the constraints of knowledge on the play of ideas are not such as to guarantee success in a single manipulation. Hence, the most likely algorithm is a multistage one. Granted a multistage algorithm, the initial models must be based on existing knowledge: One cannot construct a model without some existing concepts, and the experimental manipulations of models are likely to be partially constrained by knowledge. Once again, we see how important knowledge is to the process of creation: there are unlikely to be recipes that enhance creativity over all domains. Unfortunately, a common effect of expertise is to close off intellectual horizons. Hence, one needs a delicate balance between the necessary mastery of subconcepts and the freedom to manipulate the resulting models.

Finally, the construction of a new model, as a result of repeated mental experimentation and evaluation in relation to the world, may lead to an explanation. Success, if it is achieved, depends on many iterations of the process. It takes further work, however, to derive an explicit theory from such a model. Repeated construction of models can lead to the compilation of new concepts from the set of subconcepts. But the conscious grasp of the nature of these concepts is not immediate. Scientists only gradually discover the full import of their ideas (see, e.g., Gruber, 1974, on Darwin's intellectual development).

CONSCIOUSNESS, EMOTIONS, AND COMPUTABILITY

Thinking, I have argued, is a computable process, but many skeptics reject the idea. Some find it morally repugnant, just as some find the evolution of species by natural selection offensive. Moral intuitions, or any other intuitions, are not a reliable guide to matters of fact. There are, however, at least three more substantial arguments:

1. Computer programs have no grasp of meaning: They do not understand anything. Thinking depends on understanding. Therefore, thinking is not a computational process (Searle, 1980). Existing computers certainly have little grasp of the truth conditions of assertions. For understanding, they require much richer causal connections with the world than are currently available. They need to be able to perceive the world and to construct the same sorts of models as the human perceptual system. They also need to be able to act on the world with the same flexibility and exquisiteness of control as the human motor system. The transduction of energy from the world into an initial representation is a physical process, not a computational one, but it can be carried out by electronic cameras. The process of constructing models of the world from such representations appears to be computable. This step is central to understanding. Hence, no case exists against the potential for computational machines (equipped with sensory and motor peripherals) to build models of the world, and therefore, to begin to understand language.

2. Computers think logically: people do not. Therefore, thinking is not a computational process (person on top of Clapham omnibus). In fact, it is easy to program a computer to think illogically. The programs that implement the model theory of reasoning generate invalid conclusions based on proper subsets of the models of premises; they also generate the valid conclusions based on all the models of the premises. Hence, the argument is based on a false premise: the theory of computability in no way constrains computational machines to think logically.

3. Computers only do what they have been programmed to do, so they are not creative. Thinking is creative. Therefore, thinking is not a computational process (cf. Poincaré, 1929). This argument begs the question. It makes no case for the proposition that machines that follow a program cannot be creative. Computer programs have yet to make a reputation for themselves as innovators. However, one obvious reason for their lack of creativity is our ignorance. We lack explicit knowledge of the subconceptual criteria of artistic genres and scientific paradigms. The cognitive skills underlying profound innovation may not be computable, but the question is open.

Suppose one grants that thinking is a computable process, is it really the case that the brain is a computational machine? Certainly, it is quite unlike any existing computer. It is a vast parallel system in which millions of nerve cells, which are each processors, are wired up in a highly complex way. The cells communicate with one another, and those adjacent to one another have similar functions so that different regions of the brain specialize in different functions. The brain runs continuously and does not need to be programmed; whereas computers can be switched on and off, and they do need to be programmed. However, there is nothing intrinsic in the design of computational devices that calls for them to be programmed, that is, for there to be a principled distinction between hardware and software. The distinction between the two is, in fact, a useful convenience (which derives from Turing's universal machine). Nowadays, there are many computational devices, such as chips controlling electronic cameras, that do not need to be programmed. Indeed, the distinction between hardware and software grows increasingly difficult to make. Likewise, the switching on and off of computational machines depends on their source of energy and whether it can be interrupted without destructive effects. The class of computational machines accordingly includes autonomous devices with built-in-programs, parallel processors, and the capacity to run continuously. Even with its unique architecture, the brain could still be a computational device.

Yet, many skeptics deny this claim. The striking feature of these denials, especially those proceeding from neurophysiological convictions (e.g., Edelman, & Crick, cited in Horgan, 1992), is that they fail to consider the Church–Turing thesis. They do not even try to show that the brain uses procedures that are not computable. But, if it does, and these procedures are effective, that is, they do not rely on mysterious or magical principles, then such a demonstration would falsify the Church-Turing thesis. It would show that the concept of computability that is made explicit in recursive functions or Turing machines does not exhaust all that is truly computable. Of course, one can argue that the brain functions in an intrinsically unknowable way, and so, as Descartes argued, cognitive science is impossible. I do not suppose that this claim is one that the skeptics have in mind.

Yet, is it really the case that consciousness, emotions and bodily sensations are computable processes? Consciousness depends on computational architecture (Johnson-Laird, 1983). It owes its origin to the emergence of a high-level operating system from the network of parallel processors, which sets goals for the other processors, receives high-level information from them, and monitors their performance. Self-awareness depends on access to a model of the self—a model that is incomplete, and perhaps inaccurate. This model can be used in a special mode of processing, which occurs when the operating system calls for the construction of a model of its own operations. This "self-reflective" procedure can be applied to its own output so that the system can construct a model of its own use of such models, and so on, in a series of ever-ascending levels of representation, though the limited capacity of working memory severely constrains the process. For example, normal perception provides the operating system with a model of the world. The operating system can replace this model by a model of itself processing these contents: it perceives itself perceiving the world. It can also call for a model of this experience, and so become aware of perceiving itself perceiving the world. This self-reflective procedure resembles recursion, but the operating system must be able to move freely from one level to another in order to exploit knowledge at the different levels.

Humans can be conscious of their emotional feelings and bodily sensations. Oatley and I proposed a theory according to which these feelings are an independent means of guiding behavior (Oatley & Johnson-Laird, 1987). They prepare the organism for a general course of action appropriate to the situation. They are more flexible than innate releasing mechanisms, but they are evolutionarily older than the complex inferential processes considered in this chapter. Their consequences are rapid and effective, because they propagate within the parallel hierarchy independently from the propositional messages to which thinking depends. Hence, humans can experience emotions without knowing what caused them: the subjective experience of feelings does not require any sort of propositional knowledge.

Emotions and bodily sensations raise an intriguing possibility that would curtail the computational account of the brain. Through them, the brain may exercise direct physical effects on its computational units. Certain neurotransmitters, for example, may speed up, retard, or modify, specific neural events. Imagine a large parallel machine made up of many processing units; now suppose that there is a separate system that enables the physical mode of processing of individual units to be speeded up, retarded, or altered in still other ways. This system is, in turn, influenced by computations carried out by the machine. Such a machine would be partly computational and partly physical, that is, its performance would depend on interactions between the computational procedures that it was running and the system governing the physical performance of the processing units. The human brain may be such a system, and mental phenomena may depend on both the computational and the physical aspects of its performance.

CONCLUSIONS

How does the mind work? George Miller told me not so long ago that all his life he had wanted to know the answer to this question, and that he hoped that his friends contributing to this volume would be able to tell him. This chapter addresses a special case of George's question: How does the mind *think*? I have suggested that its thought processes are computable, and that when thinking has a propositional content, it depends on the mind's capacity to construct models of the world. Deduction depends on searching for alternative models that would falsify putative conclusions; induction depends on adding information to models; creation depends on constructing models based on novel combinations of subconcepts. The theory is best supported in the case of deduction, but I argue that nothing in principle makes induction, or even creation, essentially noncomputable. Computer programs already exist that are able to carry out these processes in domains with well-understood criteria.

Thinking can be carried out by machines, both those made out of flesh and blood and those based on silicon. Emotional experiences, however, may not be purely computational phenomena: feelings may have direct causal effects on the machine. There is an irony in this claim. Computers, it is said, have no feelings; yet, all social mammals from rats to humans appear to experience them. And animals, according to Descartes, are mere machines. Emotions remind us that mere machines carry out physical processes too.

The mind has been likened to many machines. First, it was said to work like a clay tablet, then like clockwork, and then like a steam engine—on which, Huxley averred, consciousness was the whistle (it made a lot of noise, but did not provide the essential motive force). It has been likened to a telephone exchange in which incoming calls speak of the stimuli impinging on the organism, and outgoing calls arrange for appropriate actions. Most recently, it has been likened to a computer. What underlies all these analogies is the belief that mentality is not beyond scientific explanation. We understand (we think) the workings of clocks, engines, telephone exchanges, and computers. If the mind truly resembles them, then we have a good chance of understanding it too. The computer is sometimes said to be merely the latest "machine metaphor" in the sequence—a metaphor that will be supplanted in due course by some other, more fashionable, idea. Yet, as I have argued, we should distinguish the computer from the theory of computational devices. Only if the Church-Turing thesis is undermined are we ever likely to need a new metaphor for how the mind thinks.

REFERENCES

Bara, B. G., Carassa, A. G., & Geminiani, G. C. (1984). Inference processes in everyday reasoning. In D. Plander (Ed.), *Artificial intelligence and information-control systems of robots*. Amsterdam: Elsevier.

Booker, L. B., Goldberg, D. E., & Holland, J. H. (1990). Classifier systems and genetic algorithms. In J. G. Carbonell (Ed.), *Machine learning: Paradigms and methods*. Cambridge, MA: MIT Press.

Braine, M. D. S. (1978). On the relation between the natural logic of reasoning and standard logic. *Psychological Review, 85*, 1–21.

Byrne, R. M. J., & Johnson-Laird, P. N. (1989). Spatial reasoning. *Journal of Memory and Language, 28*, 564–575.

Church, A. (1936). An unsolvable problem in elementary number theory. *American Journal of Mathematics, 58*, 345-363.

Edelman, G. M. (1987). *Neural Darwinism: The theory of neuronal group selection.* New York: Basic Books.

Fodor, J. A. (1983). *The modularity of mind: An essay on faculty psychology.* Cambridge, MA: Bradford Books/MIT Press.

Garnham, A. (1987). *Mental models as representations of discourse and text.* Chichester, UK: Ellis Horwood.

Gibson, J. J. (1966). *The senses considered as perceptual systems.* Boston: Houghton Mifflin.

Gruber, H. E. (1974). *Darwin on man: A psychological study of scientific creativity.* London: Wildwood House.

Hadamard, J. (1945). *The psychology of invention in the mathematical field.* Princeton, NJ: Princeton University Press.

Hagert, G. (1984). Modeling mental models: Experiments in cognitive modeling of spatial reasoning. In T. O'Shea (Ed.), *Advances in artificial intelligence.* Amsterdam: North-Holland.

Harman, G. (1973). *Thought.* Princeton, NJ: Princeton University Press.

Henle, M. (1962). The relation between logic and thinking. *Psychological Review, 69*, 366-378.

Hendrix, G. G. (1979). Encoding knowledge in partitioned networks. In N. V. Findler (Ed.), *Associative networks: Representation and use of knowledge by computers.* New York: Academic Press.

Hogarth, R. (Ed.). (1982). *New directions for methodology of social and behavioral science. No. 11: Question framing and response consistency.* San Francisco: Jossey-Bass.

Horgan, J. (1992, February). Profile: Francis H. C. Crick, the Mephistopheles of neurobiology. *Scientific American*, pp. 32-33.

Husserl, E. (1929). Phenomenology. *Encyclopedia Britannica* (14th ed.).

Inhelder, B., & Piaget, J. (1958). *The growth of logical thinking from childhood to adolescence.* London: Routledge & Kegan Paul.

Johnson-Laird, P. N. (1983). *Mental models.* Cambridge, MA: Harvard University Press and Cambridge: Cambridge University Press.

Johnson-Laird, P. N. (1988). *The computer and the mind.* Cambridge, MA: Harvard University Press.

Johnson-Laird, P. N. (1991). Jazz improvisation. In P. Howell, R. West, & I. Cross (Eds.), *Representing musical structure.* London: Academic Press.

Johnson-Laird, P. N. (1993). *Human and machine thinking.* Hillsdale, NJ: Lawrence Erlbaum Associates.

Johnson-Laird, P. N., & Byrne, R. M. J. (1991). *Deduction.* Hillsdale, NJ: Lawrence Erlbaum Associates.

Johnson-Laird, P. N., Byrne, R. M. J., & Schaeken, W. (1992). Propositional reasoning by model. *Psychological Review, 99*, 418-439.

Johnson-Laird, P. N., Byrne, R. M. J., & Tabossi, P. (1989). Reasoning by model: The case of multiple quantification. *Psychological Review, 96*, 658-673.

Klayman, J., & Ha, Y-W. (1987). Confirmation, disconfirmation, and information in hypothesis testing. *Psychological Review, 94*, 211-228.

Marr, D. (1982) *Vision: A computational investigation into the human representation and processing of visual information.* San Francisco: W. H. Freeman.

McClelland, J. L., & Rumelhart, D. E. (1986). *Parallel distributed processing. Explorations in the microstructure of cognition: Vol. 2. Psychological and biological models.* Cambridge, MA: MIT Press.

Medvedev, Z. A. (1990). *The legacy of Chernobyl.* New York: Norton.

Michalski, R. S. (1983). A theory and methodology of inductive learning. In R. S. Michalski, J. G. Carbonell, & T. M. Mitchell (Eds.), *Machine learning: An artificial intelligence approach.* Los Altos, CA: Morgan Kaufmann.

Miller, A. (1984). *Imagery in scientific thought: Creating 20th-century physics*. Boston, MA: Birkhauser.

Miller, G. A., Galanter, E., & Pribram, K. (1960). *Plans and the structure of behavior*. New York: Holt, Rinehart, & Winston.

Miller, G. A., & Johnson-Laird, P. N. (1976). *Language and perception*. Cambridge, MA: Harvard University Press.

Minsky, M. (1985). *The society of mind*. New York: Simon & Schuster.

Montague, R. (1974). *Formal philosophy: Selected papers*. New Haven, CT: Yale University Press.

Newell, A. (1990). *Unified theories of cognition*. Cambridge, MA: Harvard University Press.

Newell, A., & Simon, H. A. (1972). *Human problem solving*. Englewood Cliffs, NJ: Prentice-Hall.

Oakhill, J. V., Johnson-Laird, P. N., & Garnham, A. (1989). Believability and syllogistic reasoning. *Cognition, 31*, 117–140.

Oatley, K., & Johnson-Laird, P. N. (1987). Towards a cognitive theory of emotion. *Cognition and Emotion, 1*, 29–50.

Osherson, D. N. (1974–76). (*Logical abilities in children* (Vols. 1–4). Hillsdale, NJ: Lawrence Erlbaum Associates.

Overton, W. F. (1990). Competence and procedures: Constraints on the development of logical reasoning. In W. F. Overton (Ed.), *Reasoning, necessity, and logic: Developmental perspectives*. Hillsdale, NJ: Lawrence Erlbaum Associates.

Penrose, R. (1989). *The emperor's new mind: Concerning computers, minds, and the laws of physics*. Oxford, UK: Oxford University Press.

Pioncaré, H. (1929). *The foundations of science: Science and hypothesis. The value of science, science and method*. New York: The Science Press.

Pollock, J. (1989). *How to build a person: A prolegomenon*. Cambridge, MA: MIT Press/Bradford Books.

Polya, G. (1957). *How to solve it* (2nd ed.). New York: Doubleday.

Revlin, R., & Leirer, O. (1978). The effects of personal biases on syllogistic reasoning. In R. Revlin & R. E. Mayer (Eds.), *Human reasoning*. New York: Wiley.

Rips, L. J. (1983). Cognitive processes in propositional reasoning. *Psychological Review, 90*, 38–71.

Searle, J. R. (1980). Minds, brains, and programs. *Behavioral and Brain Sciences, 3*, 417–424.

Shafir, R., & Tversky, A. (1991). *Thinking through uncertainty: Nonconsequential reasoning and choice*. Unpublished manuscript, Department of Psychology, Princeton University, NJ.

Spelke, E. S. (1991). Physical knowledge in infancy: Reflections on Piaget's theory. In S. Carey & R. Gelman (Eds.), *The epigenesis of mind: Essays on biology and cognition*. Hillsdale, NJ: Lawrence Erlbaum Associates.

Turing, A. M. (1936). On computable numbers, with an application to the Entscheidungsproblem. *Proceedings of the London Mathematical Society* (Series 2), *42*, 230–265 (corrections, *43*, 544–546).

Tversky, A., & Kahneman, D. (1973). Availability: A heuristic for judging frequency and probability. *Cognitive Psychology, 4*, 207–232.

Tversky, A., & Shafir, E. (1991). *The disjunction effect under uncertainty*. Unpublished manuscript, Department of Psychology, Stanford University, CA.

Wason, P. C. (1960). On the failure to eliminate hypotheses in a conceptual task. *Quarterly Journal of Experimental Psychology, 12*, 129–140.

Winston, P. H. (1975). Learning structural descriptions from examples. In P. H. Winston (Ed.), *The psychology of computer vision*. New York: McGraw-Hill.

Wise, M. N. (1979). The mutual embrace of electricity and magnetism. *Science, 203*, 1310–1318.

On the Physical Basis, Linguistic Representation, and Conscious Experience of Colors

12

Roger N. Shepard
Stanford University

From our two respective subfields within cognitive science—language and perception—George Miller and I have each been pursuing what, at an appropriately general level of description, may be essentially the same goal. In his landmark work with Johnson-Laird, *Language and Perception*, the goal was succinctly characterized as the achievement of "a theoretical synthesis of the external and the internal" (Miller & Johnson-Laird, 1976, p. 8). This characterization fits my own search for an understanding of the properties of internal representation in terms of the properties of the external world in which the biological systems that do the representing have evolved (Shepard, 1978, 1981, 1987).

In honoring George, and in endeavoring to honor his request that each of us step back from our current research to share our thoughts about how the mind works, I focus on what has long seemed a particularly vexing problem confronting attempts to understand the internal and its relation to the external—namely, the problem of the mental representation of colors. As Miller and Johnson-Laird observed, "The importance of vision is obvious; as someone has remarked, we are all children of the sun" (1976, p. 18). Yet, whereas three of the four fundamental types of sensory attributes distinguished by Miller and Johnson-Laird (1976, p. 15), namely, *intensity*, *extension*, and *duration*, are comparable across many sensory modalities (including vision, hearing, touch, and kinesthesia) and can readily be correlated with quantifiable physical dimensions, the fourth type of attribute, *quality*, takes on, in the visual modality alone, the unique character that we call color, which does not seem to have any direct or simple physical correlate. In terms of a distinction that goes back to Locke and even to

Aristotle, whereas intensity, extension, and duration are *primary qualities*, color is the prime example of a *secondary quality*. In short, colors present perhaps the clearest challenge to any attempt to understand the relation between the internal and the external, or between the mental and the physical.

Noting that "The physical world can be characterized in terms of spatial coordinates, time, mass, velocity," Miller and Johnson-Laird asked, "What is a corresponding characterization of the world of experience?" (1976, p. 11). Then, in introducing the terms of their formal analysis, they went on to say:

> Expressions like Red(spot) and Small(spot) will be used to make formal statements about something. About what? Two answers seem possible. Either they are statements about the physical object, the spot itself that gives rise to the perception, or they are statements about some perceptual representation that the physical spot has produced. . . . The pitfalls in either answer are well known to philosophers, of course, for they are central issues in the continuing debate about the perceptual bases of empirical knowledge. (Miller & Johnson-Laird, 1976, p. 30)

At the same time, the evidence, reviewed by Miller and Johnson-Laird (1976, pp. 346–350), for cross-cultural regularities in the ways that languages assign names to colors also suggests a universal biological and (perhaps ultimately, as I argue), a physical basis for the human representation of colors. We can well understand, then, why Miller and Johnson-Laird devoted some 40 pages of their book to the problem of the representation of colors. In addition, I have three reasons of my own for taking this opportunity to consider further the problem of the representation of colors.

First, I have recently been advancing a conjecture as to the ultimate source of the now generally accepted three-dimensional, opponent-process organization of human color representation. Such an organization, long ago proposed by Hering (1887) and further developed by Hurvich and Jameson (1957) on the basis of psychophysical and neurophysiological considerations, is the organization taken as the basis of the "minimal contrastive schema" that, according to Miller and Johnson-Laird (1976, p. 344), underlies the ways in which color terms are assigned to colors in all human languages. I suggest that this organization is not merely an arbitrary design feature of the human visual system, but is an adaptive accommodation to pervasive and enduring features of the external world in which we have evolved (Shepard, 1990, 1992a).

Second, Cooper and I have just published our first full account of our own earlier empirical investigation into the representation of colors in blind, colorblind, and normally sighted subjects (Shepard & Cooper, 1992). In addition to providing further corroboration for Miller and Johnson-Laird's (1976) minimal contrastive schema, these results have a suggestive bearing on the long-standing philosophical issues, referred to by Miller and Johnson-Laird, concerning empiricism versus nativism in the mental representation of colors.

Third (and as a consequence of these recent reconsiderations of the domain of colors), I have found myself puzzling once again (as I have from time to time since first encountering the writings of the British empiricists over 40 years ago) about the philosophical problem of *qualia*: How can we understand, from an objective, scientific standpoint, the seemingly ineffable and immeasurable subjective qualities of experienced sounds, smells, tastes, feels, pains, and, especially, colors? Experienced only subjectively, qualia seem not only inaccessible to the measuring instruments of physics, but also wholly unlike the particles or waves described by the equations of physics. Yet, as Miller and Johnson-Laird remarked, " 'Red,' 'loud,' 'sour,' 'fragrant' are English words; similar words are found in other languages." Hence, "We cannot neglect these linguistic symbols," simply because questions remain about their referents (1976, p. 16). Further, "The trouble with physical specifications of the stimulus as a language for talking about color is that it does not describe what people *see* when they are exposed to those stimuli. . . . Lay terminology for color reflects the perception of it; the physical specification does not" (Miller & Johnson-Laird, 1976, p. 336).

Coincidentally, on this occasion of honoring George Miller, the philosopher Block, in presenting a paper on the problem of phenomenal experience, referred extensively to the domain of colors. He also drew distinctions between different senses of the word *consciousness* that had long seemed to me, too, to be wanting in many discussions of the problem of consciousness by philosophers, psychologists, and neuroscientists, alike. I was thus emboldened, in my own discussion of the representation of colors here, to venture onto what is for me relatively foreign philosophical terrain. If nothing else, I hope my efforts in this direction will at least serve to remind us of the territory left vacant by the absence in this volume of Block's own paper, which had previously been committed for publication elsewhere.

What follows is organized into four sections:

1. The first is a brief outline of those physical and biological facts that I take to be both generally accepted by contemporary vision scientists and most relevant for understanding the human perceptual and linguistic representation of colors.

2. The second (following Shepard, 1992a) suggests how the seemingly arbitrary biological facts may be explained as adaptive accommodations to nonarbitrary physical facts of the world in which we have evolved.

3. The third (following Shepard & Cooper, 1992) reviews data on normally sighted, colorblind, and totally blind humans that bear on the possible (perceptual, linguistic, or innate) sources of our knowledge of colors.

4. The final section sets forth what I see as the still unresolved philosophical issues concerning the conscious experience of colors, including the seeming inaccessibility of such qualia to objective science—whether physical, biological, or psychological.

PHYSICAL AND BIOLOGICAL FACTS BELIEVED TO UNDERLIE THE REPRESENTATION OF COLORS

The following are the most essential and relevant facts of human color vision. I group these under two subheadings, according to whether they have traditionally been attributed to physical laws or to the biological "brute facts" of humans and other highly visual animals that happen to populate Earth.

Facts Attributed to Physics (P)

P1. The spectral characteristics of surfaces and the composition of light itself both have potentially unlimited numbers of degrees of freedom. In general, a complete characterization of the spectral composition of light would specify the amount of that light (e.g., in terms of number of quanta per unit time) that is of each particular wavelength within the continuum of visible wavelengths, between roughly 400 and 700 nanometers (nm). Similarly, a complete characterization of any surface would specify, for each wavelength, the proportion of incident light at that wavelength that would be scattered back, rather than being absorbed, by that surface.

P2. The spectral characteristics of a surface and of its illumination are irreversibly merged in the light it scatters back to our eyes. Regardless of the number of quantities used to characterize the light scattered from any point on a surface, those quantities cannot in themselves support a determination of the intrinsic spectral characteristics of the surface at that point. The spectral composition of the light scattered back depends just as much on the spectral composition of the illumination as on the spectral reflectance properties of the surface itself—being, for each wavelength, the product of the amount striking the surface and the reflectance of the surface at that wavelength.

Facts Attributed to Biology (B)

B1. The visual system nevertheless achieve an essentially color-constant representation of each surface under natural conditions. A given surface is perceived by humans and other highly visual animals to have the same inherent color despite the wide variations in the spectral composition of illumination associated with such natural factors as the height of the sun, atmospheric conditions, and shadows. (In view of Fact P2, then, biological mechanisms of color vision cannot base their estimate of the intrinsic characteristics of a surface solely on the light reflected from that surface.)

B2. The human eye initially analyzes light into just three chromatic components. On the basis of the responses of three distinct types of retinal photoreceptors (or *cones*), having peak sensitivities in relatively long-, middle-, or short-wavelength regions of the visible spectrum, the human eye analyzes the light received from any direction in space into just three chromatic components: red, green, and blue. The resulting compression from an indefinitely large number of degrees of freedom of light (Fact P 1) to just three dimensions of representation has the consequence that (*metameric*) stimuli exist that can be distinguished by physical measurement, but that appear identical to color-normal human observers.

B3. The human visual system transforms the receptor outputs into three (light–dark, red–green, and blue–yellow) opponent-process values. Through neural computation, the visual system combines the outputs of the three (long-, middle-, and short-wavelength) types of photoreceptors to yield a representation of the light from each direction in space in terms of the relative balances, in this light, between light and dark, red and green, and blue and yellow components — the opponent-process representation proposed by Hering (1887/1964) and by Hurvich and Jameson (1957).

B4. The visual system also transforms the physically rectilinear continuum of wavelengths into a perceptually circular continuum of hues. For color-normal human observers, the two spectral colors that are most widely separated in physical wavelength — red and violet — are represented as more similar to each other than either is to a spectral color of intermediate wavelength, for example, green. The perceptual representation of spectral hues accordingly corresponds not to a straight line, but to a circle (*Newton's color circle*).

B5. The entire set of possible surface colors correspondingly forms, for color-normal human observers, a roughly spherical color space. Facts B2 and B3 entail that human observers can match the color appearance of any given surface by adjusting the contributions of just three component colors, using a suitable color-mixing apparatus. Because such color mixing corresponds to interpolating between spectral hues around the color circle and between these and the achromatic shades of gray, represented as ranging from white to black along a central axis through this circle, the colors that are distinguishable to a color-normal human observer all fall within what can be characterized roughly as a spherical globe (or equally roughly, as two cones fitted base to base). The equator (or circumference of the cones' common base) then corresponds to Newton's circle of hues, the central axis corresponds to the dimension of lightness, and radial distance out from the central axis corresponds to the dimension of saturation.

B6. Within this three-dimensional continuum, six colors—red, yellow, green, blue, black, and white—have a perceptually privileged, "landmark" status. The three-dimensional color space, though continuous, is not homogeneous and isotropic. Whereas most colors are readily perceived as mixtures of other colors (orange as a mixture of red and yellow, purple as a mixture of red and blue, pink as a mixture of red and white, etc.), six colors stand out as perceptually pure and not reducible to mixtures of any others. These privileged colors—termed *focal colors* by Berlin and Kay (1969) and Rosch (Heider, 1971, 1972; Rosch, 1975) and *landmark colors* by Miller and Johnson-Laird (1976)—are the colors defining the ends of the dimensions that arise through the neural transformation to an opponent-process representation (Fact B3)—namely, red and green, blue and yellow, and black and white. Thus, the two orthogonal chromatic dimensions red versus green and blue versus yellow—take primacy over all other possible orthogonal chromatic dimensions, such as orange versus turquoise and violet versus chartreuse. As a consequence, "Anyone with normal color vision will be able to recognize these [six landmaker colors] and to estimate how much each of them contributes to any particular sample whose color he is asked to identify" (Miller & Johnson-Laird, 1976, p. 344).

B7. Some humans represent only two dimensions of color variation, whereas some other animals may represent even more than three dimensions. Depending on the presence or absence of specific, relatively recently identified genes, the normally three-dimensional color space is effectively collapsed for some individuals (called *dichromats*) into a two-dimensional color space (most commonly, in humans, along the red–green dimension). Morever, some animals (including some fish, crustacia, and birds) found to have more than three classes of spectrally selective photoreceptors, may have color spaces of four or more dimensions.

Although these "seven plus (or minus) two" facts (B1–B7 and P1–P2) appear to be generally accepted by contemporary vision researchers (as well as by Miller and Johnson-Laird), they leave just as many questions unanswered:

1. How does the visual system achieve the disentanglement of illumination and reflectance necessary for color constancy?

2. Why do humans normally have just three classes of color receptors and, hence, just three dimensions of color representation?

3. Why are these representational dimensions anchored specifically to the black–white, red–green, and blue–yellow opposite points in an essentially spherical color space?

4. Why is the rectilinear continuum of physical wavelength curved into a circular continuum of perceived hues?

5. Are colors more properly said to exist in the surface of the object beheld or only in the "eye" of the beholder?

6. How are the colors conceived, imagined, or otherwise mentally represented in the physical absence of the colors themselves—particularly in individuals whose previous direct exposure to colors has been restricted, through some variety of colorblindness, or entirely lacking, through congenital total blindness?

7. How do the qualitative experiences of colors differ, from those of normal trichromats, in human dichromats (colorblind individuals having only two dimensions of color representation) or, especially, in any animals enjoying four or more dimensions of color representation?

8. How can even two normal trichromats be sure that their experiences of colors are the same, rather than, say, one's experience of red being like the other's experience of green, and vice versa (the so-called "inverted spectrum" puzzle)?

9. How might answers to any of these questions bear on the long-standing philosophical issues, noted by Miller and Johnson-Laird (1976, p. 30), of empiricism versus nativism?

ADDITIONAL PHYSICAL FACTS THAT MAY UNDERLIE THE BIOLOGICAL FACTS THAT UNDERLIE THE REPRESENTATION OF COLORS

There may be an intimate connection between the answers to the first five of the preceding questions—namely, those concerning color constancy, number of dimensions, choice of particular dimensions, circularity of hue, and (external versus internal) locus of colors. I suggest that the visual systems of humans (and many other highly visual diurnal species) may collapse the potentially higher-dimensional space of colors into our particular three-dimensional color space, with its preferred opponent-process dimensions and its circular embedding of hue, because this is the most effective way of attaining a color-constant representation of biologically significant objects in the terrestrial environment (Shepard, 1992a; see also Shepard, 1987, [p. 255], 1989 [p. 111–113], 1990, 1992b).

Three dimensions evidently are not sufficient to capture the full spectral reflectance characteristics of natural surfaces, which according to Maloney (1986) have somewhere between five and eight degrees of freedom. Moreover, if the retina had to accommodate photoreceptors of as many as five to eight spectrally distinct types, cones of some types would have to be more sparsely distributed across the retina—entailing a corresponding degradation in their spatial resolution. From this, I have conjectured that natural selection favored the achievement of color constancy and spatial resolution over spectral completeness in the representation of surface properties.

In order to achieve constancy, the critical dimensionality is not, I claim, the degrees of freedom of surface reflectance, but the degrees of freedom of natural illumination. During our biological evolution, the source of all significant illumination has been the essentially invariant sun, in this sense we are indeed "all children of the sun." Spectral analyses of the normal variations of daylight with times of day and atmospheric conditions have shown, however, that the light from this invariant source is subject to wide terrestrial transformations with essentially three degrees of freedom (see Judd, McAdam, & Wyszecki, 1964, and subsequent studies cited in Maloney & Wandell, 1986).

These three degrees of freedom appear to have the following physical bases (see Judd, et al., 1964; Shepard, 1992a): First, there is a light–dark variation that depends on the relative amounts of light reaching a surface directly from the sun plus clear sky versus the amounts reaching a surface only indirectly and partially by scattering from spectrally nonselective clouds, cliffs, walls, or the moon. Second, there is a red–green variation that depends on both the presence of water vapor, which selectively absorbs the long (i.e., red) wavelengths, and the angular proximity of the sun to the horizon, where the greater concentration of atmospherically suspended particles selectively filters out more of the shorter (i.e. nonred) wavelengths (with, in both cases, the complementary band of nonred wavelengths being centered around green). Third, there is a yellow–blue variation that depends on the amount of direct sunlight relative to the shortest wavelength (blue) portion scattered by the air molecules of the clear sky itself.

Now, if the naturally occurring transformations of illumination have just three degrees of freedom, the visual system must analyze its optical input into three chromatic components to compensate for those transformations and, thus, to achieve constancy in the representation of surface colors (Shepard, 1990, 1992a). This is true regardless of the particular computational scheme the system uses to estimate the necessary compensatory transformation—that is, whether something like Land's "retinex" scheme (Land & McCann, 1971), Maloney and Wandell's (1986) improved scheme (which is more color-constant—see Brainard & Wandell, 1986), or still more elaborate schemes that take account of additional sources of information provided, for example, by a direct view of the source of illumination or the clear sky, by surface orientation and shadows (see, e.g., Pentland, 1989), or by specular reflections from shiny surfaces (see, e.g., Tominaga & Wandell, 1989).

Perhaps the simplest way of putting my suggestion is this: In addition to variations in the overall quantity of terrestrial light, the principal variations in the quality of that light tend, naturally, to be at the edges of the terrestrial "window" admitting that light—that is, variations limiting the longest (red) wavelengths and the shortest (blue and violet) wavelengths. Yet the spectral complement of the red end of the admitted spectrum is a band centered on green, and the spectral complement of the blue/violet end of that spectrum is a band centered on yellow.

It may be no accident, then, that the light–dark, red–green, and blue–yellow opponent processes proposed on quite different psychophysical and neurophysiological grounds (as by Hering, 1887/1964; Hurvich & Jameson, 1957) correspond to these dimensions of terrestrial transformation of natural illumination. If so, Miller and Johnson-Laird's (1976) minimal contrastive schema may have an ultimately nonarbitrary source in the world in which we have evolved.

Just as constancy requires that our perception of an object's color be based not only on the light scattered from that particular object but also on the relations between that light and light from other locations, linguistic terms may be grounded in the relations among colors (cf. Shepard, 1978; Shepard & Chipman, 1970). As Miller and Johnson-Laird remarked, "To say that x is red means that x is closer to red than it is to any other focal color—to green, yellow, blue, black, or white. At the linguistic level of analysis, red may seem to be a simple property of surfaces, but when we analyze the operations required to use or to verify it, we see that we are dealing with a complex system of perceptual relations" (Miller & Johnson-Laird, 1976, p. 346).

The circular structure of hues may ultimately derive, also, from the need to compensate for the terrestrial transformations of solar light. If red and green are to be represented as opposites, and blue and yellow are to be represented as opposites, like diametrically opposite points on a circle, the two opposite colors in each pair must (as opposite corners of an inscribed square) be represented as further from each other than from either color in the other pair. Thus (for color-normal individuals) red is further from green than from blue, and blue is further from yellow than from red—entailing the convergence between the red and blue/violet ends of the continuum of visible wavelengths that gives rise to Newton's color circle.

In short, the way in which our visual systems and, hence, our languages represent colors may be neither arbitrary nor a direct reflection of any structure in the reflectance properties of the surfaces of objects in our environment. Rather, it may be primarily determined by the need to compensate for the natural transformations of terrestrial lighting in order that our (perhaps incomplete) perceptual representation of the inherent surface properties of each object is the same, regardless of that lighting.

Taken together, the accepted physical and biological facts thus preclude a simple answer to the question of whether color resides in the external surface or in the eye of the beholder. That a surface appears the same despite natural variations in illumination (B1), as required for biological adaptation, implies that the color that is experienced under natural conditions is determined by properties that inhere in the surface. (To this extent I concur with Hilbert's, 1987, "realist" interpretation of color.) At the same time, the facts of dimensional reduction (P1, B2, B7, including the evidence, reviewed by Maloney, 1986, that the spectral reflectances of surfaces have more than three degrees of freedom) imply that the perceptual representation of the color does not fully capture the chromatic properties inherent in the surface. Moreover, if my conjecture is correct, the subset of chromatic properties that *is* represented is determined not by the properties of the particular surface viewed, but, ultimately, by the enduring structure of the terrestrially induced transformations of the invariant light of the sun.

As a consequence, adaptation to the variations of natural illumination does not ensure color constancy under conditions that depart from those that have prevailed during our terrestrial evolution. Under a mercury vapor lamp, which deviates from the three degrees of freedom of natural illumination, we may fail to recognize our own car (Shepard, 1990), and a familiar face may appear strange or even ghastly. In general, then, the subjective experience of the color, though referred to an external surface, is surely in the observer. Under natural conditions this subjective experience partially captures objective properties of the external surface, but under unnatural conditions it may be contaminated by objective properties of the ambient light.

Of course, if some species represent colors in fewer or (as some evidence suggests) in more than three dimensions, compensation for the three principal degrees of freedom of terrestrial daylight cannot be the only factor that has shaped chromatic processing. In niches that are primarily nocturnal, underground, undersea, or just densely canopied, lighting may be so restricted in overall quantity or range of wavelengths that the small increment in constancy achievable by adding another class of photoreceptors to a simpler dichromatic or even monochromatic (e.g., rod-based) system may not offset the concomitant reduction in sensitivity or spatial acuity. In well-illuminated environments, on the other hand, the advantages of representing more of the five to eight dimensions of the spectral reflectances of potential foods, predators, or mates may sometimes favor the emergence of classes of photoreceptors beyond the three classes required merely for constancy. Thus, the evolutionary "arms races" that have produced elaborate plumage, markings, or colorations in some species might also have produced a sensitivity to richer or more subtle dimensions of surface coloration.

PERCEPTUAL, IMAGINAL, AND LINGUISTIC REPRESENTATION OF COLORS IN THE BLIND, COLOR-BLIND, AND NORMALLY SIGHTED

In our experimental investigation of how individuals represent colors that they are not actually perceiving, Cooper and I were particularly interested in comparing the cases in which the colors were not being perceived: (a) because the individual, although normally sighted, was not at the moment physically presented with those colors, and (b) because the individual, as a consequence of congenital blindness, had never perceived any colors (Shepard & Cooper, 1975, 1992). We were also interested in the intermediate case in which the individual's previous exposure to colors, although not entirely lacking, was restricted, by some variety of so-called colorblindness, to only some of the normally experienced dimensions of color variation.

We asked individuals of each type (blind, colorblind, or normally sighted) to rank order, with respect to similarity in color, all 36 pairs of colors drawn from 9 saturated hues corresponding most closely to the 9 English color terms *red, orange, gold, yellow, green, turquoise, blue, violet,* and *purple.* We asked the subjects to do so under each of two conditions: (a) when only the names of the two colors in each pair were presented, and (b) except in the case of the subjects having no color vision, when the corresponding colors themselves were actually displayed.

We analyzed the resulting data by applying nonmetric multidimensional scaling (Kruskal, 1964; Shepard, 1962a, 1962b) to the 9 x 9 matrix of average ranks for each type of individual (blind, colorblind, or normally sighted) under each of the two conditions of presentation (names or colors). The result for each matrix was the two-dimensional configuration of nine points for which the distances between the points most closely approximated a monotonic relation to the similarity data. (Incidentally, it is fitting to note here that in the development and testing of multidimensional scaling and related methods, my Bell Laboratories colleagues and I availed ourselves of George Miller's extraordinarily rich sets of psycholinguistic data [especially, Miller, 1969; Miller & Nicely, 1955] more than the data of any other single researcher — see Shepard, 1988.)

Figure 12.1 summarizes the results of principal interest here. On the left are the four solutions based on the data from 14 subjects with normal color vision (at the far left) and from 11 subjects with color deficiency of either the deutan or protan type (in the middle) — both for the names-only condition (above) and for the colors-only condition (below). Newton's color circle not only emerged for the color-normal subjects in both conditions, but also for the color-deficient subjects in the names-only condition. Despite their perceptual deficiency, the latter subjects evidently had acquired an essentially normal conception of the relations among the nine colors. In the colors-only condition, however, the color circle collapsed, as expected for these dichromats, bringing the red and green sides of the circle together.

In addition to testing the 11 subjects with the most common (dichromatic) types of color deficiency, we were also able to test one woman who (owing to the extremely rare circumstance of being born with retinal rods only and no cones) had purely monochromatic vision and, hence, total colorblindness. Her similarity rankings, obtained only for the names-only condition, yielded the somewhat degenerate color circle shown in the upper-right corner of Fig. 12.1. Suggestively, the nine hues collapsed, for her, into four clusters (red, green, orange = gold = yellow, and turquoise = blue = violet = purple), which appear to correspond to the four polar opposites of red-versus-green and yellow-versus-blue opponent-process dimensions and, hence, of Miller and Johnson-Laird's (1976) minimal contrastive scheme.

Out of the six totally blind subjects we tested (in the names-only condition), three produced similarity rankings that were highly variable and unlike the rankings that were consistently produced by the sighted subjects. The corresponding scaling solutions (not shown here) bore little if any resemblance to Newton's color circle. The remaining three blind subjects produced rankings that were somewhat similar to those obtained for the colorblind subjects under the color condition. Although the corresponding scaling solution for these three blind subjects preserved some vestige of the color circle, the red and green sides of the circle were again collapsed together, retaining primarily what might be described as a contrast between the "warm" and "cool" colors (lower-right corner of Fig. 12.1).

Incidentally, this indication that, among chromatic distinctions, the distinction between warm and cool colors is the most resistant to loss is

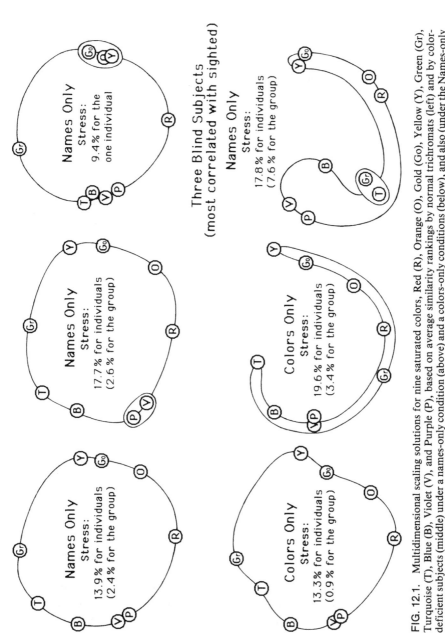

FIG. 12.1. Multidimensional scaling solutions for nine saturated colors, Red (R), Orange (O), Gold (Go), Yellow (Y), Green (Gr), Turquoise (T), Blue (B), Violet (V), and Purple (P), based on average similarity rankings by normal trichromats (left) and by color-deficient subjects (middle) under a names-only condition (above) and a colors-only conditions (below), and also (under the Names-only condition) by a single monochromat (upper right) and by the three of six blind subjects who correlated most highly with the sighted subjects (lower right). (Adapted with permission from "Representation of Colors in the Blind, Color-Blind, and Normally sighted," by R. N. Shepard & L. A. Cooper, 1992,*Psychological Science, 3,* Fig. 2. Copyright 1992 by the American Psychological Society.)

229

consistent with other indications of the primacy of this particular chromatic contrast:

1. The only two color terms (*mili* and *mola*) in the language of a New Guinea "stone-age" culture (the Dani) were found by E. R. Heider (now Rosch) and Olivier to distinguish colors that tend to be both dark and cold from those that tend to be both light and warm (Heider & Olivier, 1972).

2. Evidence reportedly exists of a physiological correlate of the warm--cool dimension of colors (Hardin, 1984).

3. Such a dimension corresponds, as I note here, to variations at the variable longest and shortest wavelength ends of the terrestrial "window" admitting solar illumination.

In a follow-up experiment using the same nine color terms originally used in our study (as first reported in Shepard & Cooper, 1975), Marmor (1978) obtained names-only similarity rankings from a larger sample of blind subjects, including 16 who were blind since shortly after birth, and 16 who became blind later in life. The results for her early-blind subjects were essentially like ours (for a detailed comparison, see Shepard & Cooper, 1992, p. 6) — though out of her larger sample of early blind subjects, a few yielded multidimensional scaling solutions that somewhat more closely resembled Newton's color circle. Not surprisingly, the results for her later-blind subjects were intermediate between those for our normally sighted subjects and those for the early-blind subjects in both studies.

The solutions obtained for all subjects who had had no color vision since birth — including Marmor's 16 early-blind subjects, our 6 early-blind subjects, and our single rod monochromat — fell outside the range of the circular solutions that (since Shepard, 1962b, and, for the names-only condition, since Fillenbaum & Rapport, 1971) have been uniformly recovered from normally sighted subjects (see Shepard & Cooper, 1992, p. 6). Still, our results (as shown in three solutions to the right and top of Fig. 12.1) and Marmor's results alike indicate that individuals whose color vision has been either deficient or absent since birth can acquire some idea of the relations among colors as those colors are experienced by the normally sighted.

Of course, the perception and representation of colors depends not only on the normal complement of color-sensitive retinal receptors. It depends also on the neural networks that have evolved to capture what has been the most color constant and biologically significant in the light scattered to those receptors from external objects. Individuals who, because they lack some types of retinal receptors, have never directly experienced the full range of colors may still achieve some understanding of the relations among such colors by virtue of the inborn opponent-process color system that I have taken to underlie the hue circle (Shepard, 1992a), and that Miller and Johnson-Laird (1976, pp. 344–346) have taken to underlie the minimal contrastive scheme essential for our linguistic representation of colors.

If so, a blind or a colorblind person's understanding of color need not be merely conceptual, however. Suggestively, one of our protan subjects told us that his mental images of red and green were much more vivid and different from each other than any color sensations he experiences when actually looking at red or green objects. Suggestively, too, the spinning black-and-white Benham disk pattern, which produces illusory sensations of red, yellow, green, and blue hues in normal observers, has reportedly led colorblind observers to say such things as "That line is definitely colored, but I don't know what to call it," and "Those lines are greener than grass" (White, Lockhead, & Evans, 1977, p. 523).

Yet, despite a lifetime of linguistic exposure, individuals who have been totally blind since birth do not seem to develop the remarkably consistent representation that is characteristic of all normally sighted individuals. Although the neural circuitry for the three-dimensional representation of colors is presumably innate, in the absence of sensory grounding in the external world, the linguistic interpretation of any activations that might subsequently arise in that circuitry (for example, through dreaming or spontaneous imagery) may be severely reduced.

THE PROBLEM OF CHARACTERIZING THE CONSCIOUS EXPERIENCE OF COLORS AND OTHER QUALIA

I conclude that although the visual system has been evolutionarily grounded in the external world in such a way that a perceived surface color is referred to an external object, the color experience itself remains in the beholder. But what is the nature of this color experience? Is it the kind of thing that can be attributed to the beholder's physical brain, or is it attributable only to a nonphysical mind?

The subjective nature of conscious experience poses a problem for any attempt to provide psychological science with an objective explanation of all mental phenomena. For, if consciousness is an irreducibly subjective, nonphysical, and inherently private phenomenon, perhaps merely an *epiphenomenon*, how can it be in any way captured by the objective methods and physical recording instruments of a public science? (For a similar point, see Block, 1991.) Again, "The trouble with physical specifications of the stimulus as a language for talking about color is that it does not describe what people *see* when they are exposed to those stimuli" (Miller & Johnson-Laird, 1976, p. 336). Moreover, if conscious experience, as a purely subjective epiphenomenon, has no objective consequences in the physical world, how could it have been differentially favored by a biological process of natural selection in that physical world?

Discussion of such questions have often been at cross purposes, because the word *consciousness* is used in very different senses. For my purpose of considering the nature of experienced qualia, two of these senses are easily distinguished. Consciousness in the scientifically less problematic sense, what I call *objective* consciousness, need not presuppose any nonphysical mental phenomenon (or epiphenomenon). Consciousness in this sense refers merely to the kind of behavioral responsiveness of a physical organism to his or her physical surroundings that leads external observers to agree that the individual in question (whether a person or animal) is alive, awake, alert, and attending (as opposed to dead, asleep, comatose, or otherwise oblivious). Consciousness in the second and scientifically more problematic sense, what I call *subjective* consciousness, refers to the privately experienced sensations, percepts, feelings, or thoughts of an individual himself or herself as when, in my own case, I am experiencing what I take to be events in the external world, whether these events really are taking place in that world or only in a vivid dream. Indeed, that these two senses are different is evident from the fact that however intensely the dreamer may be subjectively conscious of the surroundings and events in his or her ongoing dream, external observers may objectively deem the dreamer to be unconscious. Block, in his already mentioned presentation, referred to consciousness in this second subjective sense as *phenomenal consciousness* or *consciousness$_p$* (see also Block, 1991, in press).

In many discussions of the problem of consciousness, the word *consciousness* seems to refer to something more like *self-consciousness*. These discussions are concerned not with a simple, first-order awareness — whether of sensations, images, objects, qualities, events, or thoughts — but with some kind of second-order awareness of oneself as a conscious agent distinct from the nonself or of the fact of one's first-order awareness. In contrast to simpler and more direct consciousness in the first two senses, second-order awareness may have emerged only relatively recently in primate evolution. Some (e.g., Jaynes, 1976) have identified this kind of consciousness with an internal soliloquy and, hence, consider it to be dependent on language, although nonlinguistic self-representation appears to be possible in principle (e.g., see Minsky, 1965). In any case, self-consciousness appears to be both understandable as a product of natural selection and susceptible to empirical investigation (e.g., see Gallup, 1977; Oakley, 1985; Oatley, 1980). Nevertheless, it seems largely irrelevant to the vexing problem of the subjective nature of qualia, including colors.

It is this second, subjective or phenomenal sense of consciousness *simpliciter* that I see as presenting the special challenge for scientific explanation. There is no doubt that consciousness in the first, objective sense serves important adaptive functions—as in the identification of external objects through their inherent surface reflectance characteristics (e.g., Hardin, 1990; Lythgoe, 1979). Moreover, the recognition and discrimination of surface colors can be empirically investigated using many objective psychophysical, behavioral, and electrophysiological methods (supplemented, perhaps, by data analysis methods such as multidimensional scaling). Yet, how can we bridge the "explanatory gap" (Levine, 1983; Nagel, 1986) between qualia and any materialist theory? How can the appearances or "raw feels" of subjective experience, including colors, be understood in terms of psychological function, biological evolution, or physical fact?

True, whether an individual should or should not be declared conscious of any particular stimulus even in the objective sense becomes debatable when there is a breakdown in the usual agreement between different indicators of consciousness—indicators as diverse as verbal reports, manual responses, and electrophysiologically recorded cortical potentials. A breakdown may occur, for example, in hypnotically induced states of "dissociation" (see, e.g., Orne, 1959) and, more clearly, in certain kinds of brain damage leading to "disconnection syndromes" or to "blind sight" (e.g., Gazzaniga, 1970; Geschwind, 1965; Sperry, 1968; Weiskrantz, 1986). In such cases, researchers may have to choose between the two alternatives: (a) defining objective consciousness in terms of one particular indicator (such as a verbal report), or (b) abandoning the idea that consciousness is a unitary function within an individual and allowing, instead, that different parts or modules of an individual's brain may be independently conscious of different things (a view that is more consistent with my own thinking about brain function—Shepard, 1984, pp. 438–439).

What scientific consensus, if any, is eventually reached concerning such a choice will presumably depend on which way of talking proves to be most enlightening, internally consistent, and in accordance with ordinary language—in our attempts to understand everything that emerges from field observations, clinical observations, behavioral experiments, neurophysiological findings on normal and brain-damaged human and animal subjects, introspection, and even from Gedanken experiments on humans, other animals, computers, or robots. Indeed, because the subjective sense of consciousness has a relation to the objective sense that is in some ways one of "complementarity" (Shepard, 1981, p. 280; see also Nagel, 1986, p. 27), thought experiments concerning potentially objective phenomena can help at least to sharpen our thinking about the nature of inherently subjective phenomena.

How should one talk, for example, about the perceptual experience of the ferrets in whom Sur, Garraghty, and Roe (1988) had at birth induced a developmental diversion in the ascending projections of the retinal cells, with the result that when those ferrets matured, visual inputs activated the auditory instead of the visual cortex? Did those ferrets then experience qualia of the kind ordinarily corresponding to the type of stimulus externally presented (e.g., patterns of light in time and space) or to the type of stimulus that would normally have driven the cortical cells now activated (e.g., patterns of sound in time and pitch)?

Colors, among the things that are consciously experienced in the subjective sense, present us with perhaps the simplest and most compelling challenge. In their vividness, simplicity, "unanalyzability" (Shepard, 1964, p. 80), and seeming irreducibility to physical descriptions (in terms of space, time, energy, particles, or waves), colors have long served par excellence as the example of inherently subjective phenomena. Persons without training in science or philosophy (and reportedly even young children; see Dennett, 1990, p. 389) may debate such questions as: "How could you describe the sensations of red or blue to a person who has been totally blind from birth?" or "When you experience the color red are you having the same experience as I am having when I experience the color red? Or could it be that your experience of red is like my experience of green, only we have both learned to use the word *red* for whatever visual experience each of us has when looking at blood, a ripe tomato, or a sunset?" (This is often referred to as the "inverted spectrum" puzzle—e.g., see Block, 1978; Dennett, 1990; Lockwood, 1989; Lycan, 1973; Shoemaker, 1982; Smart, 1963, p. 67— though it might more fittingly be called the "inverted hue-circle" puzzle.) The problem of inner experience or subjective consciousness has long been debated by philosophers in connection with the epistomological issues concerning private "sense data" and "the existence of other minds." Yet, because the problem has seemed wholly inaccessible to scientific resolution, many philosophers and empirical scientists alike have come to reject the problem as meaningless.

I, too, accept the impossibility of verifying that the conscious experience that you call red is the same as or different from the conscious experience that I call red—or, indeed, of verifying that you have, in the subjective sense, any conscious experience at all (the problem of the existence of other minds). Still, I cannot dismiss the issue as meaningless. Moreover, the claim that conscious experience is a merely nonphysical epiphenomenon having no causal influence on physical processes in the brain or, hence, on observable behavior seems untenable.

If there is no causal influence of conscious experience on brain processes, how does anyone come to make the claim, for example, that the experience of red is something entirely different from any physical process that might go on in one's physical body, or to ask "How can I know whether your experience of red is the same as my experience of red?" The very act of giving voice to such questions (or typing them out, as I have just done) is an objectively recordable physical event that can be traced back from muscle contractions, to preceding neural firings in the motor cortex of the brain, and to still earlier neural firings in other regions of the brain, presumably including the visual cortex. None of the physical processes in this neuronal "gray matter" would itself be distinguished as in any sense redder than others by an external observer — including as invasive an observer as a neurosurgeon. Indeed, the conscious experience of red does not seem to be identifiable with any physical event, as physical events are ever described, so to speak, from the outside — that is, as we might describe such physical events occurring in a world in which life had never evolved ($physical_2$ in the sense of Feigl, 1958; Meehl, 1966).

Consider the hypothetical case of a brain scientist who, owing to a rare retinal defect, had (like the female rod monochromat tested by Shepard & Cooper, 1992) no chromatically sensitive cones and, hence, had always seen the world only achromatically (as in a "black-and-white" movie). Suppose this scientist, using whatever advanced techniques we may imagine, investigates every aspect of the physical processes that underlie visual perception in his or her own brain as well as in the brains of other individuals having either normal or anomalous color vision.

Suppose, now, that a medical breakthrough suddenly makes possible the correction of our scientist's retinal defect, and that the first visual stimulus that his or her eyes confront on removal of the eye bandages is a well-illuminated expanse of highly saturated red (or blue) paper. Will the understanding acquired by our previously colorblind scientist concerning the physical mechanisms underlying the perception, discrimination, recognition, and naming of colors provide him or her with any clue as to whether the color now vividly experienced for the first time is red or blue? It seems not. It seems that the subjective experience of the color is an entirely different kind of thing from any event or process, whether in the brain or in the external world, as it could be described in purely physical terms. If such a subjective experience is a manifestation of objective brain activity at all, it seems to be a manifestation that can only be experienced, so to speak, from the inside.

If our hypothetical scientist's cortical circuits for representing colors had developed normally, despite his or her retinal defect, our scientist, though colorblind with respect to external stimuli, might nevertheless (like the protanope described by Shepard & Cooper, 1992) have spontaneously experienced red or blue qualia in imagination or in dreams. But such internally generated qualia, having by hypothesis no correlation with objective and public events in the outside world, would not in themselves give our scientist a basis for knowing which of these qualia would postoperatively be found to be elicited by such external stimuli as blood, tomatoes, sunsets, long-wavelength light, or which should accordingly be described by the word *red*.

The hypothetical case of an initially color-normal individual whose color vision is, through some similar scientific breakthrough, suddenly upgraded from trichromatic to, say, tetrachromatic makes the same point. (Again, such four-dimensional color representation is possible because the light that surfaces scatter back to our eyes may have more than three degrees of freedom.) After receiving grafts of different receptive cones in the retina and of extra interpretive circuits in the cortex, suppose our science-fictional individual becomes able to discriminate colors that differ along four independent dimensions. Although the rest of us can match any target color by adjusting just three components in a variable color mixture (corresponding, say, to balances between white and black, red and green, and blue and yellow), the two resulting colors, though now identical to our eyes, may remain as different in appearance for the visually augmented observer as, say, orange and turquoise would be for us. In order to obtain a match, our visually augmented individual would require a fourth degree of freedom of adjustment to vary the balance between what we call orange and turquoise.

The new primary colors anchoring the ends of this new fourth dimension of color might be given new names, perhaps (like our own *orange*, *violet*, or *gold*) taken from certain fruits, flowers, or metals that best exemplify those colors. Alternatively, old color names, such as *orange* or *turquoise* might still be used for the new primaries — but with the understanding that the corresponding colors, unlike the old orange or turquoise, are neither obtainable as nor perceived to be composed of mixtures of other primaries (such as red and yellow, or blue and green).

Indeed, for the first time, we could now vary the amount of orange that our chromatically augmented person perceives in a color, while holding both the amount of red and the amount of yellow constant. How would this new, independently variable primary color between red and yellow differ in appearance from the orange that was previously experienced by mixing red and yellow? As in the preceding case of the hypothetical achromatic visual scientist, it seems that one could have no idea — until one's own visual system had actually been augmented in the way described. Even then, what in the world (from the physical wavelengths striking the retina to the patterns of firing in the added neural tissue) could possibly determine what the new qualia would be like, or whether they would be the same for other, similarly augmented individuals?

The conscious experience of an event, object, or property (such as a color) seems not itself to be a physical event, object, or property having the usual, objectively investigatable or communicable characteristics of physical things (whether neural firings in the physical brain or surface reflectances in the physical world). Nevertheless, such an experience does seem to have a causal influence on those physical processes in the brain that issue in the physical events of giving vocal or written expression to the existence of these experiences — as well as to the philosophical perplexities that they engender.

Moreover, these perplexities are not irrelevant for those concerned with the biological evolution of mind. Many have advocated the "functionalist" position that conscious experience is an emergent by-product of the evolution of a complex physical system (the brain) for analyzing and differentially responding to external objects and events. Yet, this suggestion smacks of epiphenomenalism, which (as I already noted) fails to explain why people ever came to talk about conscious experience, about the subjective qualities of colors, or about epiphenomenalism in the first place. Moreover, why should a nonphysical consciousness necessarily arise as a by-product of physical information processing, however complex that information processing may be? Surely, one can imagine a robot that outwardly manifests discriminative and adaptive reactions to its surrounding — without supposing that any states of the silicon-switching mechanisms that we have built into it are inwardly accompanied by nonphysical flashes of red or green, or of joy or pain.

If inner experience can influence overt behavior — as it seems to when people talk about the the subjective quality of the color red or when philosophers advocate epiphenomenalism, psychophysical parallelism, interactionism, or discuss the epistemological problem of the existence of other minds — then the objective consequences of subjective experience could in principle have adaptive consequences. If so, conscious experience could be differentially favored through natural selection. But what exactly would the adaptive consequences of conscious experience be — over and above those that could just as well be brought about by physical mechanisms of information processing alone, as in the robot that, by supposition, need not have anything corresponding to our inner experiences of red or green, joy or pain?

Consider a community of robots that are all well adapted to the terrestrial world and capable of communicating with each other about objects and their properties in this world. Like us, such robots must be able to distinguish objects on the basis of their inherent surface reflectances, despite illumination-dependent variations in the light that those surfaces reflect to the robots' visual sensors. Thus, each robot's visual systems must give rise to an invariant internal representation of the color of any presented object. Such an internal representation can be described in purely physical terms of, for example, a change in conducting state, electric charge, or polarity of a transistor, capacitor, or magnetic element. Of course, the robot itself need have no knowledge (i.e., internal representation) of what physical events in its internal circuitry represent particular external objects or colors—any more than our own ancestors had a knowledge of what physical events in their brains represented such external objects or colors. Natural selection has favored a veridical internal representation of the external objects and surfaces with respect to which our ancestors had to behave appropriately. A representation of the internal patterns of firings of neurons that physically represented those objects and colors in their brains would have served no adaptive function. Thus, even philosophers and scientists who thought long and hard about the mind could fail (as Aristotle reportedly did) to arrive at a correct notion, even about which organ of the body was the seat of thinking and conscious experience.

The physical event in the brain of one robot that represents, say, the occurrence of a red object in the environment need not, in fact, have the same physical embodiment as in the brain of a second robot. The internal event representing the presence of the red object could be the build-up of a charge in a certain capacitor somewhere on the left of the first robot's computer; whereas it could be the reversal of polarity in a certain magnetic element somewhere on the right of the second robot's computer. For both robots to recognize that the red object is present, to respond appropriately to that object, or to utter such a sentence as "There's that red thing again," all that is required is that the physical event that internally represents the red object in each robot's computer have a regular causal dependence on the (illuminated) presence of that red object in the robot's visual field. The particular physical embodiment of that event appears to be entirely irrelevant. In seeming contrast to the view of the Gestalt psychologists (e.g., Koffka, 1935; Köhler, 1929), a direct *isomorphism* between the brain event and a corresponding conscious experience is not required.

Subjective experience might nevertheless puzzle the robots, much as it has puzzled some human philosophers, because the causal connection between external events and their corresponding internal representational events is not perfect. The internal representational event may fail to occur, even though its corresponding external object is present—as when the inward-going causal chain is interrupted by closure of eyelids, sleep, blindness, or merely a lapse of attention. Conversely, the internal representational event may occur, even though the corresponding external object is absent—as when the internal event fires off spontaneously, causing what (in humans) we call dreams, memory images, or hallucinations. Moreover, even when the internal event is elicited by a related external stimulus, it may be an internal event that differs from the one that is normally elicited in that individual by that stimulus. This is illustrated by various visual illusions— including the striking misperceptions of the color of an object that can arise in the psychological laboratory when a hidden projector is arranged to illuminate just that object with light that is chromatically very different from the light illuminating the rest of the scene. Noting such discrepancies, sufficiently advanced robots might, like us, come to agree with one another that despite initial impressions, they do not have direct and immediate access to the external objects themselves. Rather, as Helmholtz (1856–1866/1962) proposed, they (unconsciously) infer the properties of such external objects on the basis of internal representational events (percepts) that may be only imperfectly correlated with—and, hence, ontologically distinct from—the properties of those external objects.

The language that the robots normally use to communicate with each other about external objects and properties in their shared physical environment would naturally enable them to communicate about their internal representations as well. If the word *red* has acquired an associative connection with the perceptual representation that is normally activated by the external presence of an object that reflects primarily long wavelengths, the word *red* may be elicited by an activation of that internal representation of a red object, even when that representation fires off spontaneously, in the absence of the corresponding external object. Thus, one robot might report to another that (in a dream, vivid memory image, or hallucination) it "experienced" a red object.

But how might such robots come to talk about the nature or ontological status of such subjective experiences? By hypothesis, the robots agree that internal representations are distinct from the external events to which they correspond. Thus, the experienced red is not itself a physical property (such as a spectral reflectance distribution) in the external world. But, also by hypothesis, each robot may know nothing about the physical nature of the internal event representing that object or property (such as the color red) in its own physical body or that of any other robot.

Internal representational events and, especially, those that can be communicated between individuals through a shared language could have been subject to natural selection and learning only on the basis of their causal connections to a shared, objective external world. This is why the meaning of the word *red*, to the extent that it can be shared between individuals (including robots), can only be based on the external objects (or surfaces) that normally elicit the corresponding internal representation. Only the causal relations between events, including internal events, and not the physical forms of their embodiments is relevant for this purpose. When an individual (whether a person or a robot) who has been persuaded that no red object is actually present nevertheless says, "I am having the visual experience (or afterimage, or hallucination, or vivid memory image) of a red object," the statement can be interpreted as informing us only that the process that is going on in the speaker's brain, whatever its physical embodiment may be, has much in common with the process that has normally gone on when the speaker has looked at an actual red object.

Thus, the assessment of likenesses or similarities between internal events does not presuppose that this interlocutor has any knowledge about the physical basis of those internal events (Place, 1956; Smart, 1959).

Although I have long taken this analysis to be correct as far as it goes (see Shepard & Chipman, 1970), it leaves unanswered the question of the inherent nature of qualia themselves. True, a person or a robot who reports a red or blue sensation, or who reports on the degree of similarity between two such sensations, must be describable as doing so on the basis of which events occurred within its physical brain or computer. Moreover, the individual in question must be describable as doing this without requiring that the individual have any representation of the physical nature of these alternative events, which are not themselves either red or blue. Yet, I accept that my own physical actions of typing out the preceding sentences must have a complete causal explanation solely in terms of physical processes in my physical brain.

In short, we still seem to be left with a dilemma: No analysis of the purely physical processes in a brain (or in a computer) seems capable of capturing the particular quality of the subjective experience corresponding to those processes. Yet, some such analysis should surely be able to give a causal account of how an individual comes to perform the physical act of typing out a sentence such as the preceding. Perhaps we shall have to reconcile ourselves to accepting that although both the existence of conscious experiences and the similarity relations among their qualia have physical embodiments with physical causes and effects, the conscious experiences or qualia themselves are neither characterizable as physical events nor communicable between physical systems.

The problem of consciousness is thrust upon us with special force by the so-called "split-brain" patient (see, for example, Gazzaniga, 1970; Sperry, 1968), in whom the bundle of nerve fibers (*corpus collosum*) that normally interconnects the two cerebral hemispheres has been surgically cut (e.g., in order to treat incapacitating epilepsy). Such a person may be able to indicate with his left hand whether two colors briefly presented to his left visual field are the same or different and yet may verbally report that he did not see either of these colors. (Similar "disconnexion phenomena" can sometimes arise without surgical intervention—see, e.g., Geschwind, 1965.)

If we take verbal report as the crucial indicator of consciousness, we would have to say that the split-brain patient was not conscious of the presented colors, and that the manual response, even though consistently correct, was made unconsciously. An implication of this alternative that I, for one, find difficult to embrace is that an individual who, as the result of damage to the language area of the brain, can no longer speak or write would also have to be declared no longer conscious—even though every other behavioral and physiological indication is that this individual continues to discriminate colors and to seek pleasant and to avoid unpleasant situations, exactly as before losing the power of speech—and even though, following eventual recovery of speech, the individual reports having been conscious of those colors and situations all along. Similarly, we presumably would not maintain that just because a young child or a favorite pet is mute, it feels no pain and, despite its desparate struggles and anguished facial expressions, requires no anesthesia during a normally painful operation.

The alternative is to say that both hemispheres of the split-brain patient were separately conscious, but that (owing to the well-known lateral crossover of pathways and localization of speech centers in the left hemisphere) only the right hemisphere had neuronal input from the left visual field and neuronal output to the left hand, whereas only the left hemisphere was capable of articulating its own conscious experience through speech. The implication of this alternative, when pursued to its logical conclusion, may be just as difficult for many to embrace. This is the implication that every neuronal activity, however elementary and wherever located (whether in the brain, spinal cord, retina, or little finger; whether in a human adult, fetus, housefly, or flatworm) is accompanied by its own flash of conscious experience. Indeed, unless some compelling reason can be given as to why one particular type of physical event—such as the depolarization of a neuron—should be accompanied by such a flash of conscious experience, whereas another, physically and chemically similar type of physical event should not, the only universally consistent alternatives may be solipsism, on the one hand, and a kind of panpsychism (or, perhaps better, pan-qualia-ism, cf. Feigl, 1960, p. 40), on the other.

Whether or not such issues have any relevance for scientific theory, they do seem to have relevance for moral philosophy and, hence, for scientific practice. For example, it strikes me as difficult to simultaneously defend the two following claims:

1. It is justified to carry out invasive experiments on primates that would never be permitted on human subjects, because primates are fundamentally different from humans—for example, because they are not conscious (and not because they simply do not have the political power to refuse to serve as subjects).

2. The reason we need to use primates rather than other animals (such as rats) for such invasive experiments concerning the mechanisms of perception and cognition is that only primates are similar enough to humans so that the results can be generalized to the case of humans (who, for the most part, do have the power to refuse).

CONCLUSION

I close with the conclusion that I have tentatively reached concerning each of the three issues I have considered in my attempt to explore the question of "how the mind works." These have been the issues of the physical basis, the linguistic representation, and the conscious experience of colors:

1. The physical basis of perceived colors is to be found in the minimum-dimensional representation of the (higher-dimensional) spectral reflectance properties of surfaces necessary to achieve invariance of color representation, despite the long-prevailing three degrees of freedom of terrestrial illumination.

2. The linguistic representation of colors is based on a "minimal contrastive schema" (as described by Miller & Johnson-Laird, 1976), whose structure is, accordingly, determined neither arbitrarily nor solely by the spectral reflectance properties of surfaces but, perhaps primarily, by the pervasive and enduring structure of the terrestrial transformations of solar light.

3. The conscious experience of colors presumably corresponds to causal processes that (a) achieve (under natural illumination) invariant representations of (some of) the light-reflecting characteristics of external surfaces, and (b) can (in principle) be objectively investigated in the physical brain of the experiencer by an external agent. Yet, although the relations of similarity among such subjective qualia seem to be linguistically shareable between individuals and objectively representable in multidimensional-scaling solutions, the qualia themselves remain ultimately unknowable to anyone except the experiencer.

ACKNOWLEDGMENT

Preparation of this chapter was supported by National Science Foundation Grant BNS 90-21684.

REFERENCES

Berlin, B., & Kay, P. (1969). *Basic color terms: Their universality and evolution.* Berkeley, CA: University of California Press.

Block, N. (1978). Troubles with functionalism. In C. W. Savage (Ed.), *Minnesota studies in the philosophy of science* (Vol. IX, pp. 261–325). Minneapolis: University of Minnesota, Press.

Block, N. (1991). Evidence against epiphenomenalism (Commentary on Velmans). *Behavioral and Brain Sciences, 14* 670-672.

Block, N. (in press). Consciousness ignored (a review of Dennett's *Consciousness Explained*). *Journal of Philosophy.*

Brainard, D. H., & Wandell, B. A. (1986). Analysis of the retinex theory of color vision. *Journal of the Optical Society of America, 3*, 1651–1661.

Dennett, D. C. (1990). *Consciousness explained.* Boston: Little, Brown.

Feigl, H. (1958). The "mental" and the "physical." In H. Feigl, G. Maxwell, & M. Scriven (Eds.), *Minnesota studies in the philosophy of science* (Vol. II, pp. 370–497). Minneapolis: University of Minnesota Press.

Feigl, H. (1960). Mind-body, not a pseudoproblem. In S. Hook (Ed.), *Dimensions of mind: A symposium* (pp. 33–44). New York: New York University Press.

Fillenbaum, S., & Rapoport, A. (1971). *Structure in the subjective lexicon.* New York: Academic Press.

Gallup, G. G. (1977). Self-recognition in primates: A comparative approach to the bi-directional properties of consciousness. *American Psychologist, 32*, 329–338.

Gazzaniga, M. (1970). *The bisected brain.* New York: Appleton-Century-Croft.

Geschwind, N. (1965). Disconnexion syndromes in animals and man. *Brain, 88* (Part III), 585–644.

Hardin, C. L. (1984). A new look at color. *American Philosophical Quarterly, 21*, 125–133.

Hardin, C. L. (1990). Why color? *Proceedings of the SPIE/SPSE Symposium on Electronic Imaging: Science and Technology,* (pp. 293–300).

Heider, E. R. (1971). Focal color areas and the development of color names. *Developmental Psychology, 4*, 447–455.

Heider, E. R. (1972). Universals in color naming and memory. *Journal of Experimental Psychology, 93*, 10–20.

Heider, E. R., & Olivier, D. C. (1972). The structure of the color space in naming and memory for two languages. *Cognitive Psychology, 3*, 337–354.

Helmholtz, H. von. (1962). *Treatise on physiological optics* (Vol. II) (trans. by J. P. C. Southall, 3rd German ed.). New York: Dover. (Original work published circa 1856–1866)

Hering, E. (1964). *Outlines of a theory of the light sense* (L. M. Hurvich & D. Jameson, Trans.). Cambridge, MA: Harvard University Press. (Original work published 1887)

Hilbert, D. R. (1987). *Color and color perception: A study in anthropocentric realism.* Stanford, CA: Center for the Study of Language and Information.

Hurvich, L. M., & Jameson, D. (1957). An opponent-process theory of color vision. *Psychological Review, 64*, 384–404.

Jaynes, J. (1976). *The origins of consciousness in the breakdown of the bicameral mind.* Boston: Houghton Mifflin.

Judd, D. B., McAdam, D. L., & Wyszecki, G. (1964). Spectral distribution of typical daylight as a function of correlated color temperature. *Journal of the Optical Society of America, 54*, 1031–1040.

Koffka, K. (1935). *Principles of Gestalt psychology.* New York: Harcourt Brace.

Köhler, W. (1929). *Gestalt psychology.* New York: Liveright.

Kruskal, J. B (1964). Multidimensional scaling by optimizing goodness of fit to a nonmetric hypothesis. *Psychometrika, 29*, 1–27.

Land, E. H., & McCann, J. J. (1971). Lightness and retinex theory. *Journal of the Optical Society of America, 61*, 1–11.

Levine, J. (1983). Materialism and qualia: The explanatory gap. *Pacific Philosophical Quarterly, 64*, 354–361.

Lockwood, M. (1989). *Mind, brain and the quantum: The compound "I".* Oxford: Basil Blackwell.

Lycan, W. (1973). Inverted spectrum. *Ratio, 15*, 315–319.

Lythgoe, J. N. (1979). *The ecology of vision.* New York: Oxford University Press.

Maloney, L. T. (1986). Evaluation of linear models of surface spectral reflectance with small numbers of parameters. *Journal of the Optical Society of America A, 3*, 1673–1683.

Maloney, L. T., & Wandell, B. A. (1986). Color constancy: A method for recovering surface spectral reflectance. *Journal of the Optical Society of America A, 3*, 29–33.

Marmor, G. S. (1978). Age at onset of blindness and the development of the semantics of color names. *Journal of Experimental Child Psychology, 25*, 267–278.

Meehl, P. E. (1966). The compleat autocerebroscopist. In P. K. Feyerabend & G. Maxwell (Eds.), *Mind, matter, method: Essays in philosophy and science in honor of Herbert Feigl* (pp. 103-181). Minneapolis: University of Minnesota Press.

Miller, G. A. (1969). A psychological method to investigate verbal concepts. *Journal of Mathematical Psychology, 6,* 169-191.

Miller, G. A., & Johnson-Laird, P. N. (1976). *Language and perception.* Cambridge, MA: Harvard University Press.

Miller, G. A., & Nicely, P. (1955). An analysis of perceptual confusion among some English consonants. *Journal of the Acoustical Society of America, 27,* 338-352.

Minsky, M. (1965). Matter, mind, and models. In W. A. Kalenich (Ed.), *Information processing 1965* (Proceedings of the IFIP Congress 65) (pp. 45-49). Washington, DC: Spartan Press.

Nagel, T. (1986). *The view from nowhere.* New York: Oxford University Press.

Oakley, D. A. (1985). Animal awareness, consciousness and self-image. In D. A. Oakley (Ed.), *Brain and mind* (pp. 132-151). New York: Methuen.

Oatley, K. (1980). Representing ourselves: Mental schemata, computational metaphors, and the nature of consciousness. In G. Underwood & R. Stevens (Eds.), *Aspects of consciousness* (Vol. 2, pp. 85-117). New York: Academic Press.

Orne, M. T. (1959). The nature of hypnosis: Artifact and essence. *Journal of Abnormal and Social Psychology, 58,* 277-299.

Pentland, A. (1989). A possible neural mechanism for computing shape from shading. *Neural Computation, 1,* 208-217.

Place, U. T. (1956). Is consciousness a brain process? *British Journal of Psychology, 47,* 44-50.

Rosch, E. (1975). The natural mental codes for color categories. *Journal of Experimental Psychology: Human Perception and Performance, 1,* 303-322.

Shepard, R. N. (1962a). The analysis of proximities: Multidimensional scaling with an unknown distance function. I. *Psychometrika, 27,* 125-140.

Shepard, R. N. (1962b). The analysis of proximities: Multidimensional scaling with an unknown distance function. II. *Psychometrika, 27,* 219-246.

Shepard, R. N. (1964). Attention and the metric structure of the stimulus space. *Journal of Mathematical Psychology, 1,* 54-87.

Shepard, R. N. (1978). On the status of "direct" psychophysical measurement. In C. W. Savage (Ed.), *Minnesota studies in the philosophy of science* (Vol. IX, pp. 441-490). Minneapolis: University of Minnesota Press.

Shepard, R. N. (1981). Psychophysical complementarity. In M. Kubovy & J. Pomerantz (Eds.), *Perceptual organization* (pp. 279-341). Hillsdale, NJ: Lawrence Erlbaum Associates.

Shepard, R. N. (1984). Ecological constraints on internal representation: Resonant kinematics of perceiving, imagining, thinking, and dreaming. *Psychological Review, 91,* 417-447.

Shepard, R. N. (1987). Evolution of a mesh between principles of the mind and regularities of the world. In J. Dupré (Ed.), *The latest on the best: Essays on evolution and optimality* (pp. 251-275). Cambridge, MA: MIT Press/ Bradford Books.

Shepard, R. N. (1988). George Miller's data and the development of methods for representing cognitive structures. In W. Hirsh (Ed.), *The making of cognitive science: Essays in honor of George A. Miller* (pp. 45-70). Cambridge: Cambridge University Press.

Shepard, R. N. (1989). Internal representation of universal regularities: A challenge for connectionism. In L. Nadel, L. A. Cooper, P. Culicover, & R. M. Harnish (Eds.), *Neural connections, mental computation* (pp. 104-134). Cambridge, MA: MIT Press/Bradford Books.

Shepard, R. N. (1990). A possible evolutionary basis for trichromacy. *Proceedings of the SPIE/SPSE Symposium on Electronic Imaging: Science and Technology, 1250. Perceiving, Measuring, and Using Color,* (pp. 301-309).

Shepard, R. N. (1992a). The perceptual organization of colors: An adaptation to the regularities of the terrestrial world? In J. Barkow, L. Cosmides, & J. Tooby (Eds.), *The adapted mind: Evolutionary psychology and the generation of culture* (pp. 495–532). New York: Oxford University Press.

Shepard, R. N. (1992b). What in the world determines the structure of color space? (Commentary on Thompson, Palacios, & Varela). *Behavioral and Brain Sciences. 15,* 50–51.

Shepard, R. N., & Chipman, S. (1970). Second-order isomorphism of internal representations: Shapes of states. *Cognitive Psychology, 1,* 1–17.

Shepard, R. N., & Cooper, L. A. (1975, September). *Representation of colors in normal, blind, and color blind subjects.* Paper presented at the Applications of Multidimensional Scaling Symposium, Division 5, American Psychological Association and the Psychometric Society, Chicago, IL.

Shepard, R. N., & Cooper, L. A. (1992). Representation of colors in the blind, color-blind, and normally sighted. *Psychological Science, 3,* 97–104.

Shoemaker, S. (1982). The inverted spectrum. *The Journal of Philosophy, 79,* 357–381.

Smart, J. J. C. (1959). Sensations and brain processes. *Philosophical Review, 68,* 141–156.

Smart, J. J. C. (1963). *Philosophy and scientific realism.* London: Routledge & Kegan Paul.

Sperry, R. W. (1968). Hemisphere deconnection and unity in conscious awareness. *American Psychologist, 23,* 723–733.

Sur, M., Garraghty, P. E., & Roe, A. W. (1988). Experimentally induced visual projection into auditory thalamus and cortex. *Science, 242,* 1437–1441.

Tominaga, S., & Wandell, B. (1989). Standard surface-reflectance model and illuminant estimation. *Journal of the Optical Society of America A, 6,* 576–584.

Weiskrantz, L. (1986). *Blindsight: A case study and implications.* New York: Oxford University Press.

White, C. W., Lockhead, G. R., & Evans, N. J. (1977). Multidimensional scaling of subjective colors by color-blind observers. *Perception & Psychophysics, 21,* 522–526.

13 Remembering the Future

Michael Cole
Laboratory of Comparative Human Cognition

Expectation refers to the future, and memory to the past. On the other hand, the tension in an act belongs to the present: through it the future is transformed into the past. Hence, an act may contain something that refers to what has not yet come to pass.

—St. Augustine[1]

Taxed with the assignment of telling George Miller something interesting about how the mind works, I chose to discuss a knot of ideas that have grown up in the course of my attempts to understand the role of culture in human psychological processes. I further restrict my choice of topics to matters that I have been thinking about since I left Rockefeller University, where we shared research facilities and students, so that my thoughts might just come as interesting news.

At the time that George and I parted institutional ways, I was still a cross-cultural, experimental psychologist, with some anthropological leanings. Over the past decade I have come to focus less on international, cross-cultural differences and more on the universal features of culture in shaping human thought. As far as I know, George is not familiar with this work, little of which has been published. So, it is the universal features of culture-in-mind that I discuss in this chapter.

I begin with an epigram from St. Augustine to signal as clearly as possible that I make no pretense that my thoughts on time and cognition are

---

[1] Upon finishing this chapter I encountered an essay by Valsiner entitled "Making of the Future," which contains many interesting suggestions for expanding on the basic ideas I am proposing. Valsiner's essay also contains a number of marvelous quotations from Greek and later European philosophers.

original. I am certain they have been discovered countless times before. Yet, I have found my personal course of rediscovery very satisfying, and I offer the following remarks in the hope that they will prove stimulating to George's further education and to mine.

PAST, PRESENT, AND FUTURE

We are all accustomed to the notion of remembering as the summoning up of past experiences in the process of dealing with the present. The study of memory, conventionally understood, has been one of psychology's most productive growth industries since the 1960s, thanks in no small part to George Miller's contributions.

Nor is concern with the question of time and cognition alien to George's work. Speaking of tasks confronting American psychologists during and after World War II, Miller commented:

> It's the purpose or goal of a machine to get a gun aimed at some particular point, for example. It [the gun] has a goal in the old teleological sense that scientists had ruled out on the grounds that the future cannot control the present. But in the servo-system the *future position* of that gun controls the *present motion* of the gun in a very real, perfectly intelligible sense. (Interview with J. Miller, 1983, p. 24),

It was, I argue, the goal not of the gun, but of the gunner and servo-mechanism designer to aim a gun at a particular point. In particular, I hope to demonstrate the way in which the designer's goal influences the fine structure of the gunner's actions through the servo mechanism is but an esoteric example of the general properties of mediation through artifacts, or what Vygtostky (1929) referred to as "the cultural mode of thinking."

In an earlier era, when learning theories were in the ascendency and before American psychologists were helping to create smart tools for wartime use, Edwin Boring, one of Miller's former colleagues at Harvard, pointed out quite clearly that our common-sense ideas about events occuring in the present are really based on the memory of the past. Appropriately enough, Boring's message returned lately through the popularity of the work of Edelman (1989), a Rockefeller colleague not known for having a high opinion of psychologists. Edelman's book, *The Remembered Present*, begins with the quotation of a passage published by Boring in 1933:

> To be aware of a conscious datum is to be sure that it has passed. The nearest actual approach to immediate introspection is early retrospection. The experience described, if there be any such, is always just past; the description

is present. However, if I ask myself how I know the description is present, I find myself describing the processes that made up the description; the original describing is past. . . . Experience itself is at the end of the introspective rainbow. The rainbow may have an end and the end may be somewhere; yet I seem never to get to it. (Boring, 1933/1963, p. 228)

Edelman summarized a vast array of evidence from the neurosciences to substantiate his theory about what sort of organism human beings must be if the phenomenal present is "really" the past. I am less concerned with the technical adequacy of Edelman's neurological model than I am with the fact that remembering the present, if somewhat odd, is nonetheless broadly recognized.

What then of memory for the future? Whether we look to the ideas of St. Augustine on the future as expectation, Miller, Galanter, and Pribram (1960) on plans, or Bernstein (1967) on the organization of living movement, one message repeats itself: The present is a dynamic, evolving, trajectory which not only integrates current sensory input with prior experience, but also "calculates" an "imagined future" which then "feeds back" to complete the fundamental, transformational cognitive cycle. Ingvar (1985), whose article on "memory of the future" triggered the idea for this chapter, summarized evidence that plans, ambitions, and "sets" are normally remembered in great detail, just as memories of the past can be reconstructed. In addition, he summarized the neuropsychological evidence that memory for the future is selectively lost owing to lesions of the prefrontal and frontal cortices. Ingvar referred to these structures as the "neuronal substrate of the future"(p. 130).

Of course, in one sense we all take for granted the existence of a memory of the future. I can speak coherently, for example, of my memory of what I will be doing (plan to do) this weekend. Research on the selective disturbance of planning functions as a result of prefrontal and frontal lobe lesions has been well known for a long time (Luria, 1970). Previously I did not think of such phenomena as memory for the future. It was only when I recently happened upon a reference to Ingvar's article, while ruminating about cultural mechanisms of cognitive development, that memory for the future began to seem like a necessary property of human thought.

To understand why memory for the future is a particularly interesting idea, I need to back up to sketch a few of my ideas about culture and the role of culture in creating and recreating human beings.

CULTURE AS THE SPECIFIC MEDIUM
OF HUMAN LIFE

My notions of culture have undergone a good many changes over the years as my personal experience and reading warred with each other in search for coherence. Early on, I found myself sympathetic with Boas' combination of configurationism and cultural relativity, which served as a foundation for my thinking about cultural context. These ideas then became fused with those of Luria (1979) and Vygotsky (1978) on the mediated nature of human thought. Such a fusion could not help but be incoherent at some point, because Luria and Vygotsky were not cultural-relativist anthropologists; they were psychologists who focused on the morphological development of culturally organized behavior in face-to-face interactions, and they adhered to a 19th-century notion of historical progress. In dealing with the incoherence of crossing a synchronic, configurational anthropological theory of thinking with a diachronic, structural/functional psychological theory of a very different sort, I stumbled into talking about *cultural psychology* (Cole, 1988, 1990).[2]

A summary of my version of cultural psychology begins with the work of the Soviet cultural-historical psychologists, Luria (1928), Vygtosky (1929), and Leontiev (1930). Central to their formulations is the notion that human beings live in an environment transformed by the artifacts of prior generations, extending back to the beginning of the species (Geertz, 1973; Ilyenkov, 1977; Sahlins, 1976, Wartofsky, 1979). The basic function of these artifacts is to coordinate human beings with the physical world and each other. Cultural artifacts are simultaneously ideal (conceptual) and material. They are ideal in that they contain, in coded form, the interactions of which they were previously a part and which they mediate in the present. They are material because they exist only insofar as they are embodied in material artifacts.[3] This principle applies with equal force whether one is considering language/speech or the more usually noted forms of artifacts

---

[2]Elsewhere I have surveyed a group of ideas about cultural psychology with affinity to my own (Cole, 1991). For example, Shweder (1990) focuses on the context- and content-specificity of human thought as well as the centrality of mediation by meaningful symbols. Bruner's (1990) vision of cultural psychology also emphasizes the premise that human experience and action are shaped by our intentional states. A fundamental tenet of Bruner's approach to cultural psychology is that it locates the emergence and functioning of psychological processes in the social-symbolically mediated everyday encounters of people in the lived events of their everyday lives. These events are organized in large part, Bruner argues, by a "folk psychology," understood as "a system by which people organize their experience in, knowledge about, and transactions with the social world" (p. 35). In my terms, what Bruner refers to as a folk psychology is treated as a central mediational structure, parts of which are recruited in each situation people find themselves in.

[3]Readers familiar with contemporary sociological theories of action will readily recognize a close affinity between the views about mediation derived from the writings of the cultural-historical school that I am expressing and those of Giddens (1984). For example, Giddens wrote "According to the notion of the duality of structure, the structural properties of social systems are both medium and outcome of the practices they recursively organize . . . Structure is not to be equated with constraint but is always both constraining and enabling" (p. 25).

which constitute material culture.[4] The American anthropologist White explained, "An axe has a subjective component; it would be meaningless without a concept and an attitude. On the other hand, a concept or attitude would be meaningless without overt expression, in behavior or speech (which is a form of behavior). Every cultural element, every cultural trait, therefore, has a subjective and an objective aspect (1959, p. 236).

The special characteristics of human mental life are precisely those characteristics of an organism that can inhabit, transform, and recreate an artifact-mediated world. As Soviet philosopher Ilyenkov put it, "the world of things created by man for man, and therefore, things whose forms are reified forms of human activity . . . is the condition for the existence of human consciousness" (1977, p. 94). The special nature of this consciousness follows from the dual material/ideal nature of the systems of artifacts that constitute the cultural environment. Human beings live in a "double world," simultaneously "natural" and "artificial."

The characteristics of human psychological processes that accompany this view of human nature as created in "culture as historically accumulated systems of artifacts" were described in particularly powerful language by White, who wrote:

> Man differs from the apes, and indeed all other living creatures so far as we know, in that he is capable of symbolic behavior. With words man creates a new world, a world of ideas and philosophies. In this world man lives just as truly as in the physical world of his senses. . . . This world comes to have a continuity and a permanence that the external world of the senses can never have. It is not made up of present only but of a past and a future as well. Temporally, it is not a succession of disconnected episodes, but a continuum extending to infinity in both directions, from eternity to eternity. (1942, p. 372).[5]

Among other properties White here attributes to culture, his emphasis on the way it creates an (artificial) continuity between past and future merits special attention, as I show later.

With this skimpy background about some of the basic systems intuitions underlying the notion of culture I am employing, let me turn to two different ways in which remembering the future is fundamental to human thought and action.

---

[4]D'Andrade (1986, p. 22) made this point when he told us that "material culture — tables and chairs, buildings and cities — is the reification of human ideas in a solid medium."

[5]Although it would be an error, in view of recent decades of work on protocultural features among primates (Parker & Gibson, 1990), to overstate the discontinuities between homo sapiens and other species, I concur with Hinde (1987) in believing that these phenomena do not imply culture in the way in which human beings have culture.

THE FUTURE IN THE WORD

In the first publication in English by a member of the cultural-historical school of psychology, Luria wrote that the key feature of human, mediated thought processes is that "instead of applying directly its natural function to the solution of a particular task, the child puts between that function and the task a certain auxiliary means . . . by the medium of which the child manages to perform the task" (1928, p. 495). Insofar as we consider the class of mediating artifacts called words, in what sense is the future contained within them? I try to answer this question in several overlapping examples. What these different examples have in common is that the activities described are mediated by systems of artifacts, paramount among which is language. In thinking about these examples, it is necessary to keep firmly in mind the fundamental nature of artifacts: Artifacts are elements of the physical world that have been appropriated and transformed in the course of prior human experience. Every word can be considered a crystalized structure that has mediated many interactions successfully in the past (or it would not exist) and carries within its shape coded traces of the structure of those previously successful occasions.

A word such as *love*, for example, is more than a description of a (vague) set of emotions; it is a bundle of semantic/pragmatic potential which points to future feelings and behaviors. To say that I love my wife, my children, or my work is to specify a broad range of obligations, inclinations, or behaviors. It enables others to predict that I will be glad to get home Sunday noon, that I not only worry about my children's fate, but would sacrifice my own well-being on their behalf, and that early Sunday evening I am more likely to be found at my computer terminal than my television set.

Burke, who proposed similar ideas many decades ago, beautifully captured the way in which words, trailing their pasts, imply their futures as well. In *Literature as Equipment for Living* (1941/1973), he discussed the ways in which proverbs are tools for "consolation or vengeance, for admonition or exhortation, for foretelling" (p. 293). Proverbs, Burke wrote (p. 296), are *"strategies* for dealing with *situations."* Consulting the *Oxford Concise Dictionary*, he reported that a *strategy* is defined as "movement of an army or armies in a campaign, art of so moving or disposing troops or ships as to impose upon an enemy the place and time and conditions preferred by oneself" (p. 297). When used to describe rhetorical strategies that posit particular future states as the "given" content of an argument, rather than particular spatial positions of adversaries, the scholars of ancient Rome and early modern Italy referred to this process using the word *prolepsis*, meaning "the representation of a future act or development as being presently existing" (*Webster's Dictionary*).

In recent years we have seen some interesting suggestions about the role

of prolepsis in the organization of human psychological functions. Rommetveit (1974) pointed out that ordinary human discourse is at times
proleptic "in the sense that the temporarily shared social world is in part
based upon premises tacitly induced by the speaker" (p. 87). Through
prolepsis, "what is said serves . . . to induce presuppositions and trigger
anticipatory comprehension, and what is made known will hence necessarily
transcend what is said" (p. 88).

Stone and Wertsch (1984) used prolepsis in this manner to characterize
the way in which teachers seek to induce children's understanding of how to
complete cognitive tasks with which they are having difficulty; in effect, the
teachers presuppose (a least hypothetically) that the children understand
what it is they are trying to teach as a precondition for creating that
understanding.

Recognizing a variety of ways in which instantiation of the future as
present reality enters into the process of constructing and comprehending
meaning, I illustrate how, according to a cultural-mediational theory of
mind, the interlocking systems of artifacts that constitute every human
culture, or the "cultural tool kit," to use a metaphor proposed by Wittgenstein (1972), can be considered simultaneously to be systems of strategies
for dealing with the future that their past history presupposes.

SOCIAL ORGANIZATION OF THE FUTURE
IN THE PRESENT

Although the example of language acquisition could be pursued a great deal
further, I switch gears and discuss a ubiquitous form of prolepsis which
arises from the disjunction in cultural history of parents and children, or the
younger and older generation, broadly considered. In addition, I argue that
the mechanisms of cultural development bear both interesting similarities
and differences to biological development.

With respect to biological development, we know that the genetic code
assembled when sperm and egg unite at conception provides the constraints
within which the biological process of development takes place. As cells in
the zygote proliferate and distinctive new structures come into being, this
genetic code represents the "final cause" or "end in the beginning," which
makes the emergence of new forms and functional relationships possible.
For example, about 5 weeks after conception the hands begin to emerge as
limb buds. Cell proliferation occurs very rapidly, and as cells multiply, the
limb buds elongate in the shape of a paddle. Then five protrusions appear
on the edge of the paddle which will become a five-fingered hand, with
muscles, bone, tendons, nerve cells situated in a pattern appropriate to a

human hand. None of this could have happened if the genetic code had not provided the necessary constraints "ahead of time."

Cultural constraints are not contained in biological form, but are rather embodied in the material/ideal, patterned, artifacts that mediate the life of the community. In the case of both biological and cultural constraints, of course, the final cause or *telos* is only an "if all other things equal" final cause. The actual process of development is one of probabilistic, not predetermined, epigenesis (Gottlieb, 1973).

There is no secret about the sense in which cultural constraints exist in children's futures; they are born into a culturally structured world. Many years ago, Dollard (1935) suggested that we think of the encounter of a new human being with this distinctive form of environment in the following terms:

> Accept two units for our consideration: first, the group which exists before the individual; and second, a new organism envisioned as approaching this functioning collectivity. The organism is seen at this moment as clean of cultural influence and the group is seen as functioning without the aid of the organism in question. We will suppose that the organism is nearing the group through its intra-uterine development and that it is finally precipitated into group life by the act of birth. Let us ask ourselves at this point what we can say systematically about what this organism will be like when it comes of age, sex granted. All of the facts we can predict about it, granted the continuity of the group, will define the culture into which it comes. Such facts can include the kind of clothes it will wear, the language it will speak, its theoretical ideas, its characteristic occupation, in some cases who its husband or wife is bound to be, how it can be insulted, what it will regard as wealth, what its theory of personality growth will be, etc. (pp. 14–15)

Dollard's thought experiment clearly indicates the sense in which cultural constraints are in the child's future, but it does not explain how the palpable *cultural* constraints in place in adulthood are transformed "backwards" into palpable *material/physical* constraints at birth.

The answer, again, I believe, is prolepsis. To give an idea of the process of prolepsis at work as an intergenerational process, I chose examples from several points in the lifespan (birth, early infancy, early childhood, and adulthood).

THE FIRST FACE-TO-FACE MEETING

During the process of birth, the realignment of biological, behavioral, and social factors affecting development brings about perhaps the most revolutionary stagelike change in all of development. The moment of birth is also especially interesting, because (modern medical procedures for determining the fetus' gender aside) it is an early and fundamental moment when the child's phylogenetic and cultural histories begin to intertwine owing to the cultural mediation of the child's experience.

Rather than concentrate on the potential consequences of cultural variations in birthing practices (see, for example, Richardson & Guttmacher, 1967), I focus on the way that birth provides evidence of the process of prolepsis. In addition, this example illustrates one way in which the ideal side of culture is transformed into the material cultural organization of the child's environment as well as the special nature of sociality characteristic of culture-using creatures. The example (taken from the work of pediatrician Macfarlane, 1978) also clearly demonstrates White's point that culture provides a specifically human form of temporal continuity.

Figure 13.1 presents in schematic form five different time scales operating simultaneously at the moment when parents see their newborn for the first time. The vertical ellipse represents the events immediately surrounding birth, which occurs at the point marked by the vertical line. At the top of the figure is what might be called "physical time," or the history of the universe that long precedes the appearance of life on earth.

The bottom four time lines correspond to the "developmental domains" (Wertsch, 1985) that, according to the cultural framework espoused here, simultaneously serve as major constraints for human development. The second line represents phylogenetic time, the history of life on earth, a part of which constitutes the biological history of the newborn individual. The third line represents cultural-historical time, the residue of which is the child's cultural heritage. The fourth line represents ontogeny, the history of a single human being which is the usual object of psychologists' interest.

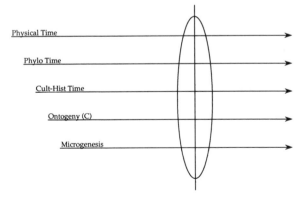

FIG. 13.1. The five time scales, or "genetic domains" relevant to understanding the role of culture in human development emphasized by cultural-historical psychologists. The vertical line indicates the moment when parents first see their child and discover its sex.

The fifth line represents the moment-to-moment time of lived human experience, the event called "being born" (from the perspective of the child) or "having a baby" (from the perspective of the parents) in this case. Four kinds of genesis are involved—phylogenesis, culturogenesis, ontogenesis, and microgenesis—each lower level embedded in the level that precedes it.

Macfarlane's example forces us to keep in mind that not one but *two* ontogenies must be represented in place of the single ontogeny in Fig. 13.1. That is, at a minimum one needs a mother and a child interacting in a social context for the process of birth to occur and for development to proceed. These two ontogenies are coordinated in time by the simultaneous structuration provided by phylogeny and cultural history.

When we consider the behaviors of the adults as they first catch sight of their newborn child and categorize it as male or female, we see the way in which the mother and child's ontogenies are coordinated under constraints provided by a combination of phylogeny, cultural history, and the mother's ontogenetic experience. The parents almost immediately start to talk about and to the child. Their comments arise in part from phylogenetically determined features (the anatomical differences between males and females) and in part from cultural features they have encountered in their own lives (what they know to be typical of boys and girls in their culture). Typical comments include "I shall be worried to death when she's 18" or "It can't play rugby" (said of girls). Putting aside our negative response to the sexism in these remarks, we see that the adults interpret the phylogenetic-biological characteristics of the child in terms of their own past (cultural) experience. In the experience of English men and women living in the 1950s, it could be considered "common knowledge" that girls do not play rugby, and that when they enter adolescence they will be the object of boys' sexual attention, putting them at various kinds of risk. Using this information derived from their cultural past and assuming cultural continuity (e.g., that the world will be very much for their daughter as it has been for them), parents project a probable future for the child. This process is depicted in Figure 13.2 by following the arrows from the mother→(remembered) cultural past of the mother→(imagined) cultural future of the baby→present adult treatment of the baby.

Two features of this system of transformations are essential to understanding the contribution of culture in constituting development:

1. Most obviously, we see an example of prolepsis. The parents literally represent the future in the present.
2. Perhaps less obviously, we see the way in which the parents' (purely ideal) recall of their past and imagination of their child's future becomes a fundamentally important *material* constraint organizing the child's life experiences in the present.

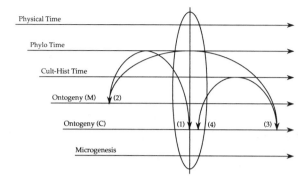

FIG. 13.2.   Actual face to face interactions remind us that two ontogenies must be considered in evaluating how culture influences the development of gender-specific characteristics of the child in later life. The sequence of events occurs as follows:
1. Mother sees that baby is a girl.
2. Mother consults her own past (cultural) experience for what she knows about female children.
3. Mother imagines future of the child in light of her own past experience (she is unlikely to become a rugby player).
4. Mother behaves toward baby in the present in terms of how she imagines the future of the baby to be in the future.
In this way, the imagined/ideational activity of the mother is converted into material changes in the baby's present.

This rather abstract, nonlinear process of transformation gives rise to the well-known phenomenon that even adults totally ignorant of the real gender of a newborn will treat the baby quite differently depending on its symbolic/cultural "gender." Adults literally create different material forms of interaction based on conceptions of the world provided by their cultural experience. For example, they bounce "boy" infants (those wearing blue diapers) and attribute "manly" virtues to them whereas they treat "girl" infants (those wearing pink diapers) in a gentle manner and attribute beauty and sweet temperaments to them (Rubin, Provezano, & Luria, 1974).

Macfarlane's example also demonstrated an important distinction between the social and the cultural, which are generally conflated in "two-factor" theories of development. *Culture* in this case refers to remembered forms of activity deemed gender-appropriate for the child as an adolescent and for the parents raising a female child; *social* refers to the people whose behavior is conforming to, and implementing, the given cultural pattern. In addition, this example motivates the special emphasis placed on the *social* origins of higher psychological functions by cultural-historical psychologists (Cole, 1988; Rogoff; 1989, Valsiner, 1988; Vygotsky, 1934/1987; Wertsch, 1985). As Macfarlane's transcripts clearly demonstrate, human nature is social in a sense different from the sociability of other species. *Only* a culture-using human being can "reach into" the cultural past, project it into the (ideal/conceptual) future, and then "carry" that ideal/conceptual future "back" into the present to create the sociocultural environment of the newcomer.

This example gives us a way to think systematically about the qualitative change in human behavior associated with the acquisition of language that occurs continuously throughout infancy. Vygotsky (1934/1987) and Luria (1948/1970) pointed out that as children master the lexicon of their native language/culture, there is a change in the interfunctional organization of their entire personalities; the cultural -historical and phylogenetic lines of development now interact from, so to speak, the inside. The process of prolepsis simultaneously undergoes a quantum increase in complexity, as the child's cultural-historical context interacts with those of the older generation.

Finally, this analysis of parental comments on first seeing their child helps us to understand ways in which culture contributes to both continuity and discontinuity in individual development. In thinking about their babies' futures, these parents assume that the "way things have always been is the way things will always be," calling to mind White's telling image that, temporally, the culturally constituted mind "is not a succession of disconnected episodes, but a continuum extending to infinity in both directions, from eternity to eternity" (see page 251). In this manner, the medium of culture allows people to "project" the past into the future, thereby creating a stable interpretive frame which is one of the important elements of psychological continuity.

This assumption, of course, is wrong whenever there are conditions of cultural change following the birth of the child. The invention of new ways to exploit energy or new media of representation, or simple changes in custom , may sufficiently disrupt the existing cultural order to be a source of significant developmental discontinuity. As but a single example, in the 1950s, American parents who assumed that their daughter would not be a soccer player at the age of 16 would have been correct. Yet, in 1990, a great many American girls play soccer.[6]

I know of no recordings equivalent to Macfarlane's from other cultures, but an interesting account of birthing among the Zinacanteco of South-central Mexico appears to show the same processes at work. In their summary of developmental research among the Zinacanteco, Greenfield, Brazelton, and Childs (1989) reported a man's account of his son's birth at which the son "was given three chilies to hold so that it would . . . know to buy chili when it grew up. It was given a billhood, a digging stick, an axe, and a [strip of] palm so that it would learn to weave palm" (p. 177). Baby

---

[6]In addition, as life-span developmental psychologists emphasize, unique historical events (a war, a depression) may provoke great discontinuity in development (Hetherington, Lerner, & Perlmutter, 1988).

girls are given an equivalent set of objects associated with adult female status. The future orientation of differential treatment of the babies is not only present in ritual, but coded in the Zinacantecan saying, "For in the newborn baby is the future of our world."

THE FUTURE IN THE PRESENT DURING EARLY CHILDHOOD AND ADULTHOOD

My next examples of the proleptic mechanisms of development illustrate how adults bring different futures into the present to shape children's experiences, depending on what kind of future they remember. Tobin, Wu, and Davidson (1989) conducted a comparative study of preschool socialization in three locales: Hawaii, Japan, and China. They recorded classroom interactions which they then showed to teachers and other audiences in all three countries to evoke their interpretations and basic cultural schemata relevant to the preschool child. For economy's sake, only the Japanese and American data will be discussed.

When Tobin and his colleagues videotaped a day in the life of a Japanese preschool, young Hiroki was acting up. He greeted the visitors by exposing his penis and waving it at them. He initiated fights, disrupted other children's games, and made obscene comments.

American preschool teachers who later observed the videotape disapproved of Hiroki's behavior, his teacher's handling of it, and many aspects of life in the Japanese classroom, in general. Starting first with the overall ambience of the classroom, Americans were scandalized by the fact that there were 30 preschoolers and only one teacher in the classroom. How could this be in an affluent country like Japan? They could not understand why Hiroki was not punished by being isolated.

Japanese observers had a very different reaction to the tape and a correspondingly different interpretation of Hiroki's behavior and the classroom at large. First, although teachers acknowledged that it would be very pleasant for *them* to have a smaller classroom, they believed it would be bad for the children, who "need to have the experience of being in a large group in order to learn to relate to lots of children in lots of kinds of situations" (p. 37). When asked about their ideal notion of class size, the Japanese teachers generally named 15 or more students per teacher in contrast with 4–8 students that represent American preschool teachers' ideal. When Japanese preschool teachers observed a tape of an American preschool, they worried about the children. "A class that size seems kind of sad and underpopulated," one remarked (p. 37). Another added, "I wonder how you teach a child to become a member of a group in a class that small" (p. 38).

Members of the two cultures also had very different interpretations of the probable reasons for Hiroki's behavior. One American speculated that Hiroki misbehaved because he was intellectually gifted and easily became bored. Not only did the Japanese reject this notion (on the grounds that speed is not the same as intelligence), but they offered a different interpretation. To them, such words as *smart* and *intelligent* are almost synonymous with *well-behaved* and *praiseworthy*, neither of which applied to Hiroki. They believed that Hiroki had a "dependency disorder." Because of the absence of a mother in the home, he did not know how to be properly dependent and, consequently, how to be sensitive to others and obedient. Isolating Hiroki, they reasoned, would not help. Rather, he needed to learn to get along in his group and develop the proper understanding in that context. Tobin and his colleagues commented, "Japanese teachers and Japanese society place [great value] on equality and the notion that children's success and failure and their potential to become successful versus failed adults has more to do with effort and character and thus with what can be learned and taught in school than with raw inborn ability" (p. 24).

The Japanese who watched the tape also disapproved of the promotion of individualism that they observed in tapes of an American classroom, believing that "a child's humanity is realized most fully not so much in his ability to be independent from the group as his ability to cooperate and feel part of the group" (p. 39). One Japanese school administrator added, "For my tastes there is something about the American approach [where children are asked to explain their feelings when they misbehave] that is a bit too heavy, too adultlike, too severe and controlled for young children" (p. 53).

There are many interesting implications to be drawn from these observations, only a tiny fraction of which I have touched on here. However, in the present context my purpose is to relate them to the situation such children will encounter as adults, in particular, the situation that Japanese boys will face should they pursue a career in the "American pastime" of baseball.

My source in this case is a fascinating account of the fate of American baseball players who play in the Japanese major leagues (Whiting, 1989). Despite their great skill, experience, and physical size, American ballplayers generally have a very difficult time in Japan. There are many reasons for their difficulties, but crucial is a completely different understanding of keys to success in this team sport, a difference that mirrors differences in preschool education in the two cultures to an amazing degree. The title of the book *You Gotta Have Wa* pinpoints one key difference. *Wa* is the Japanese word for group harmony and, according to Whiting, it is what "most dramatically differentiates Japanese baseball from the American game" (p. 70). American ballplayers maintain that individual initiative and innate ability are the key ingredients to success, whereas the Japanese emphasize that "the individual was nothing without others and that even the most talented people need constant direction" (p. 70). Linked to the emphasis on group harmony is an equivalent emphasis on *doryoku*, the ability to persevere in the face of adversity as the key to success; whereas Americans emphasized individual talent.

Whiting pointed out that the ideals of *wa* and *doryoku* are cornerstones of not only Japanese baseball, but Japanese business as well. He said, "*Wa* is the motto of large multinational corporations, like Hitachi, while Sumimoto, Toshiba, and other leading Japanese firms send junior executives on outdoor retreats, where they meditate and perform spirit-strengthening exercises, wearing only loin-clothes and headbands with *doryoku* emblazoned on them (p. 74).

Despite their acknowledged talent, American players who understand the sources of success, the cultivation of which can clearly be seen in their preschool education, are generally unable to submit to the Japanese way of doing things. In a remark which echoes poignantly on the Japanese disapproval of the American emphasis on verbalizing and valuing personal feelings over group harmony, one American ballplayer who had a long and acrimonious public dispute with his manager was led to ask in desperation, "Don't you think that's going too far? What about my feelings? I have my pride, you know." To which the manager replied, "I understand your feelings, however there are more important things(p. 93)"

Here again we see an example in which culture operating on young children exerts an effect that is conditioned not by present necessity, but by deep beliefs about "how things work" and how things will work in the life of the child later on. The constraints arising from notions of adult life may have relatively minor consequences in the present life of the child; it makes no earthshattering difference to infants if they are dressed in blue or pink or are growing up to be Japanese or American—yet, as Dollard pointed out, the cumulative effects of such differential patterns of interaction governed by images of the future are very clear but they are very clearly not easily accessed for purposes of self-reflection.

SOME CONCLUDING OBSERVATIONS

If space allowed, I would continue to discuss a number of different examples of the process of prolepsis that can profitably be addressed with the kind of cultural theory of mind that I am proposing. My colleagues and I collected many examples of classroom discourse which yield readily to a proleptic analysis (Newman, Griffin, & Cole, 1989). For example, we recorded interactions and examined them for evidence about the ways in which teachers attempt to teach children about mixing chemicals. The data were coded to record when the teacher offered help and a judgment about whether such help was needed or not. In a great many cases, this judgment was straightforward. Yet, in a significant number of cases the teacher offered help, and it was simply unclear if the child needed it or had evoked it at all. When asked about these uncodable occasions, the teacher said that she gave the added help because she knew that the children were going to need that particular skill in the next lesson. She wanted to make sure they understood so they would not get lost later. Teaching number facts and short division with remainders yields to the same analysis: Teachers are speaking in proleptic terms whose meanings are not to be found on the surface of their talk with children, but rather, hidden as deep presuppositions.

I have not, as yet, been able to rethink thoroughly the implications of the cases I analyzed here for Miller's notion of the teleology in a servo-mechanical rocket. In cases where there is a fixed goal, set ahead of time by cultural agency and "wired into" the device, the resulting system of interactions loses the ever-contingent nature of human thought in which not only distance from preconceived object to preconceived means is calculated, but the very existence of relevant parameters parsable as distance, object, means, and so on need to be established.[7]

The meaning/teleology constraining human interaction is nowhere adequately reified in scientific concepts and practices. Unable to procede further, I conclude with two literary fragments that capture particularly well some of the properties of culturally mediated mind that I have been talking about, but which I have not yet been able to model in my research. Each concerns the crucial backward-looking property of the cultural mode of thinking; each locates the future "behind the back" of humans; each strikes me as totally convincing with respect to the way in which it characterizes both the existential uncertainty of humans and our species' constant striving for unreachable perfect knowledge.

In one of his historical essays, Benjamin (1968) wrote about a poem purported to describe a painting by Paul Klee. The poem is attributed to Gerhard Scholem:

My wing is ready for flight;
I would like to turn back.
If I stayed timeless time
I would have little luck.

---

[7]I am treading clumsily here on territory that is covered more gracefully and authoritatively in Shutz (1962), James (1975), among others. Shutz, for example, wrote, "Meaning . . . is not a quality inherent in certain experiences emerging within our stream of consciousness but the result of an interpretation of a past experience looked at from the present. Now with a reflective attitude." (p. 210).

Benjamin wrote as follows:

A Klee painting "Angelus Novus" shows an angel looking as though he is about to move away from something he is fixedly contemplating. His eyes are staring, his mouth is open, his wings are spread. This is how one pictures the angel of history. His face is turned toward the past. Where we perceive a chain of events, he sees one single catastrophe which keeps piling wreckage upon wreckage and hurls it in front of his feet. The angel would like to stay, awaken the dead, and make whole what has been smashed. But a storm is blowing from Paradise; it has got caught in his wings with such violence that the angel can no longer close them. This storm irresistibly propels him into the future to which his back is turned, while the pile of debris before him grows skyward. This storm is what we call progress. (pp. 257–58)

From T.S. Eliot's, *The Four Quartets* (1959):

So here I am, in the middle way, having had twenty years—
Twenty years largely wasted, the years of *l'entre deux guerres*—
Trying to learn to use words, and every attempt
Is a wholly new start, and a different kind of failure
Because one has only learnt to get the better of words
For the thing one no longer has to say, or the way in which
One is no longer disposed to say it. And so each new venture
Is a new beginning, a raid on the inarticulate
With shabby equipment always deteriorating
In the general mess of imprecision of feeling,
Undisciplined squads of emotion. And what there is to conquer
By strength and submission, has already been discovered
Once or twice, or several times, by men whom one cannot hope
To emulate—but there is no competition—
There is only the fight to recover what has been lost
And found and lost again and again; and now under conditions
That seem unpropitious. But perhaps neither gain nor loss.
For us, there is only the trying. The rest is not our business. (pp. 21–22)

I was raised in a cultural setting that did not place much hope in the utility of religious world views, and a society which has come to distrust deeply the claims of savants to be able to tell the future. The future is not knowable in the telling, only in the remembering.

ACKNOWLEDGMENTS

The ideas expressed herein have been substantially enriched by the opportunity to discuss them informally with the following scholars who participate in the XLCHC study/discussion group: Phil Agre, Tom Benson, Antonio Bettencourt, William Blanton, Ellice Forman, Steve Draper, Jill Edwards, William Gardner, Joe Glick, Claude Goldenberg, Glenn Humphreys, Russell Hunt, Alfred Lang, David Middleton, Aksel Mortensen, Judit Moschkovich, Claire O'Malley, Pedro Portes, Tony Scott, Robert Serpell, Addison Stone, Roland Tharp, Jonathan Tudge, Emily Van Zee, Gordon Wells, and Jim Wertsch.

REFERENCES

Benjamin, W. (1968). *Illuminations*. New York:Harcourt, Brace & World.

Bernstein, N. A. (1967). *The coordination and regulation of movement*. Oxford: Pergamon.

Boring, E. (1963). *The physical dimensions of consciousness*. New York: Dover. (Original work published 1933)

Bruner, J. S. (1990). *Acts of meaning*. Cambridge, MA: Harvard University Press.

Burke, K. (1973). *The philosophy of symbolic form*. Berkeley: University of California Press. (Original work published 1941)

Cole, M. (1988). Cross-cultural research in the socio-historical tradition. *Human Development, 31*, 137–157.

Cole, M. (1990). Cultural psychology: A once and future discipline? In J. J. Berman (Ed.), *Nebraska Symposium on Motivation, 1989: Cross-cultural perspectives (Vol. 37, pp. 279–336). Lincoln: University of Nebraska Press*.

Cole, M. (1991). On cultural psychology: [Review of *Acts of meaning, Cultural psychology: Essays on comparative human development, Human behavior in global perspective: An introduction to cross-cultural psychology*]. *American Anthropologist, 93* (2), 435–439.

D'Andrade, R. (1986). Three scientific world views and the covering law model. In D. Fiske & R. Shweder (Eds), *Meta-theory in the social sciences (pp. 19–40)*. Chicago: University of Chicago Press.

Dollard, J. (1935). *Criteria for the study of life histories*. New Haven, CT: Yale University Press.

Edelman, G. (1989). *The remembered present: A biological theory of consciousness*. New York: Basic Books.

Eliot, T. S. (1959). *Four Quartets*. London: Faber & Faber.

Geertz, C. (1973). *The interpretation of cultures*. New York: Basic Books.

Giddens, A. (1984). *The constitution of society*. Cambridge: Cambridge University Press.

Gottlieb, L. (1973). *Behavioral embryology*. New York: Academic Press.

Greenfield, P. M., Brazelton, T. B., & Childs, C. P. (1989). From birth to maturity in Zinacantan: Ontogenesis in cultural context. In V. Bricker & G. Gossen (Eds.), *Ethnographic encounters in southern Mesoamerica: Celebratory essays in honor of Evon Z. Vogt. Albany: Institute of Mesoamerican Studies, State University of New York*.

Hetherington, M., Lerner, R., & Perlmutter, M. (1988). *Child development in lifespan development*. Hillsdale, NJ: Lawrence Erlbaum Associates.

Hinde, R. (1987). *Individuals, relationships, and culture*. Cambridge: Cambridge University Press.

Ilyenkov, E. V. (1977). The concept of the ideal. In *Philosophy in the USSR: Problems of dialetical materialism.*(pp. 71–99). Moscow: Progress.

Ingvar, D. H. (1985). Memory for the future. *Human Neurobiology, 4*, 127–136.

James, W. (1975). *Pragmatism*. Cambridge, MA: Harvard University Press.

Leontiev, A. N. (1930). Studies in the cultural development of the child, III. The development of voluntary attention in the child. *Journal of Genetic Psychology,37*, 52–81.

Luria, A. R. (1928). The problem of the cultural development of the child. *Journal of Genetic Psychology, 35*, 493–506.

Luria, A. R. (1970). *Traumatic aphasia: Its syndromes, psychology and treatment*. (D. Bowden, Trans.). The Hague: Mouton (Original work published 1948)

Luria, A. R. (1979). *The making of mind: The autobiography of A. R. Luria* (M. Cole & S. Cole, Eds.). Cambridge, MA: Harvard University Press.

Macfarlane, A. (1978). *The psychology of childbirth*. Cambridge, MA: Harvard University Press.

Miller, J. (1983). *States of mind*. New York: Pantheon.

Miller, G. A., Galanter, E., & Pribram, K. (1960). *Plans and the structure of behavior*. New York: Holt, Rinehart, & Winston.

Newman, D., Griffin, P., & Cole, M. (1989). *The construction zone: Working for cognitive change in school*. New York: Cambridge University Press.

Parker, K., & Gibson, K. (1990). *"Language" and intelligence in monkeys and apes*. New York: Cambridge University Press.

Richardson, S. A., & Guttmacher, A. F. (1967). *Childbirthing: Its social and psychological aspects*. Baltimore, MD: William & Wilkens.

Rogoff, B. (1989). *Apprenticeship in thinking*. Cambridge: Cambridge University Press.

Rommetveit, R. (1974). *On message structure: A framework for the study of language and communication*. London/New York: Wiley.

Rubin, J. Z., Provezano, F. J., & Luria, Z. (1974). The eye of the beholder: Parents' view on sex of newborns. *American Journal of Orthopsychiatry, 44*, 512–519.

Sahlins, M. (1976). *Culture and practical reason*. Chicago: University of Chicago Press.

Schutz, A. (1962). *The problem of social reality*. The Hague: Martinus Nijhoff.

Shweder, R. (1990). *Thinking through cultures*. Cambridge, MA: Harvard University Press.

Stone, C. A., & Wertsch, J. V. (1984). A social interactional analysis of learning disabilities. *Journal of Learning Disabilities, 17*, 194–199.

Tobin, J. J., Wu, D. Y. H., & Davidson, D. H. (1989). *Preschools in three cultures*. New Haven, CT: Yale University Press.

Valsiner, J. (1988). *Soviet developmental psychology*. Bloomington: Indiana University Press.

Vygotsky, L. S. (1929). The problem of the cultural development of the child, II. *Journal of Genetic Psychology, 36*, 414–434.

Vygotsky, L. S. (1987). Thinking and speech. In N. Minick (Trans.),*The collected works of L. S. Vygotsky: Vol. 1. Problems of general psychology* (pp. 39-358). New York: Plenum Press. (Original work published 1934)

Vygotsky, L. S. (1978). *Mind in society: The development of higher psychological processes* (M. Cole, V. John-Steiner, S. Scribner, & E. Souberman, Eds.). Cambridge, MA: Harvard University Press.

Wartofsky, M. (1979). *Models: Representation and scientific understanding*. Dordrecht: Reidel.

Wertsch, J. V. (1985). *Vygotsky and the social formation of mind*. Cambridge, MA: Harvard University Press.

Wittgenstein, L. (1972). *Philosophical investigations* (G. E. M. Anscombe, Trans.). Oxford: Basil Blackwell & Mort.

White, L. (1942). On the use of tools by primates. *Journal of Comparative Psychology, 34*, 369–374.

White, L. (1959). The concept of culture. *American Anthropologist, 61*, 227–251.

Whiting, R. (1989). *You've gotta have Wa*. New York: Macmillan.

Author Index

Subject Index